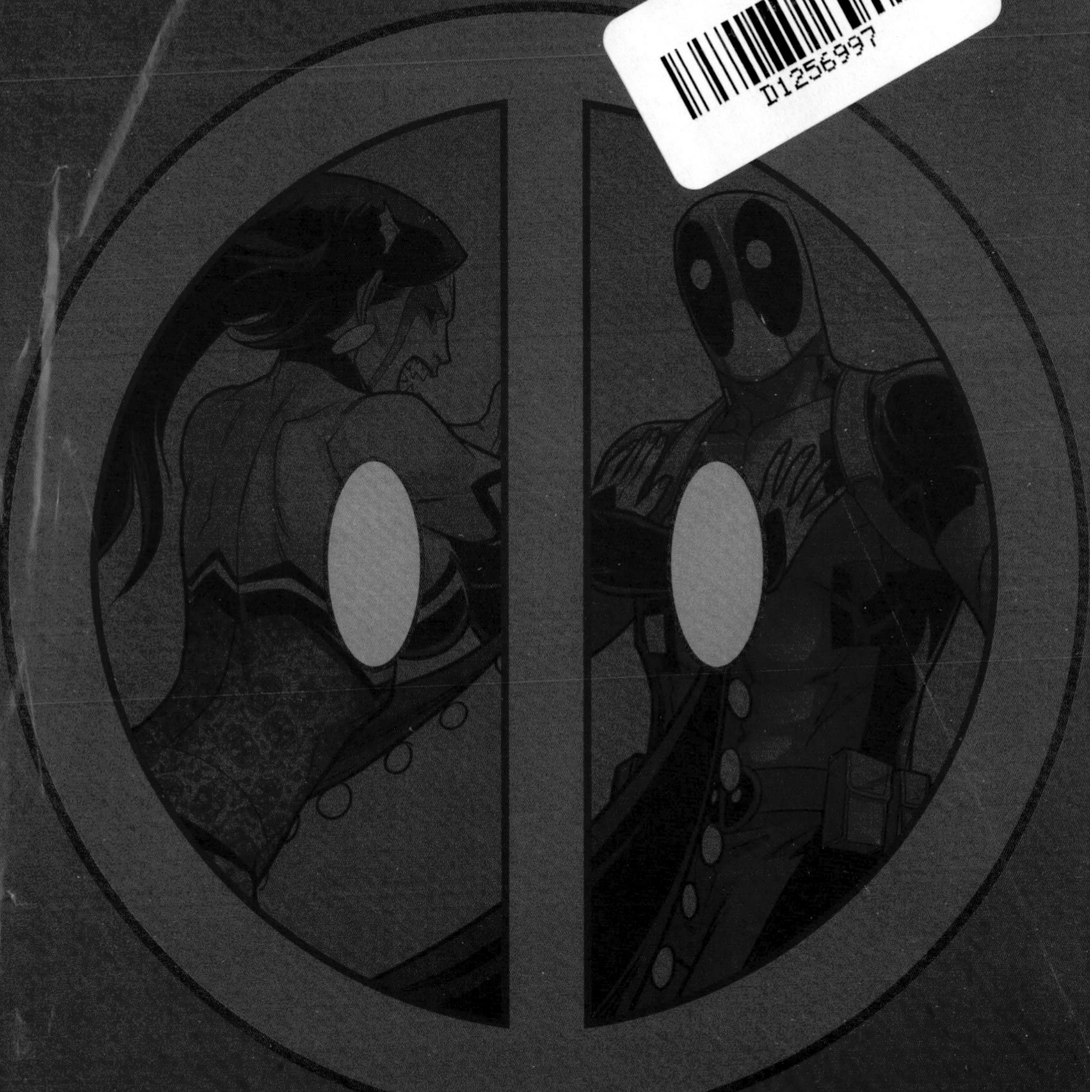

DEADPOOL

'TIL DEATH DO US...

DEADPOOL #28-29

GERRY DUGGAN
writer

SALVA ESPIN
artist

RUTH REDMOND
colorist

SPIDER-MAN/DEADPOOL #15-16

JOSHUA CORIN
writer

SCOTT KOBLISH
artist

NICK FILARDI
colorist

DEADPOOL & THE MERCS FOR MONEY #9-10

CHRISTOPHER HASTINGS
writer

SCOTT KOBLISH
artist

NICK FILARDI
colorist

VC's JOE SABINO
letterer

REILLY BROWN & JIM CHARALAMPIDIS
cover art

JORDAN D. WHITE, NICK LOWE & HEATHER ANTOS
editors

collection editor **JENNIFER GRÜNWALD**
assistant editor **CAITLIN O'CONNELL**
associate managing editor **KATERI WOODY**
editor, special projects **MARK D. BEAZLEY**
vp production & special projects **JEFF YOUNGQUIST**
svp print, sales & marketing **DAVID GABRIEL**
book designer **ADAM DEL RE**

editor in chief **AXEL ALONSO**
chief creative officer **JOE QUESADA**
president **DAN BUCKLEY**
executive producer **ALAN FINE**

DEADPOOL created by
ROB LIEFELD & FABIAN NICIEZA

DEADPOOL: WORLD'S GREATEST VOL. 8 — 'TIL DEATH DO US.... Contains material originally published in magazine form as DEADPOOL #28-29, SPIDER-MAN/DEADPOOL #15-16 and DEADPOOL & THE MERCS FOR MONEY #9-10. First printing 2017. ISBN# 978-1-302-90543-9. Published by MARVEL WORLDWIDE, INC., a subsidiary of MARVEL ENTERTAINMENT, LLC. OFFICE OF PUBLICATION: 135 West 50th Street, New York, NY 10020. Copyright © 2017 MARVEL. No similarity between any of the names, characters, persons, and/or institutions in this magazine with those of any living or dead person or institution is intended, and any such similarity which may exist is purely coincidental. Printed in Canada. DAN BUCKLEY, President, Marvel Entertainment; JOE QUESADA, Chief Creative Officer; TOM BREVOORT, SVP of Publishing; DAVID BOGART, SVP of Business Affairs & Operations, Publishing & Partnership; C.B. CEBULSKI, VP of Brand Management & Development, Asia; DAVID GABRIEL, SVP of Sales & Marketing, Publishing; JEFF YOUNGQUIST, VP of Production & Special Projects; DAN CARR, Executive Director of Publishing Technology; ALEX MORALES, Director of Publishing Operations; SUSAN CRESPI, Production Manager; STAN LEE, Chairman Emeritus. For information regarding advertising in Marvel Comics or on Marvel.com, please contact Vit DeBellis, Integrated Sales Manager, at vdebellis@marvel.com. For Marvel subscription inquiries, please call 888-511-5480. Manufactured between 6/30/2017 and 8/1/2017 by SOLISCO PRINTERS, SCOTT, QC, CANADA.

10 9 8 7 6 5 4 3 2 1

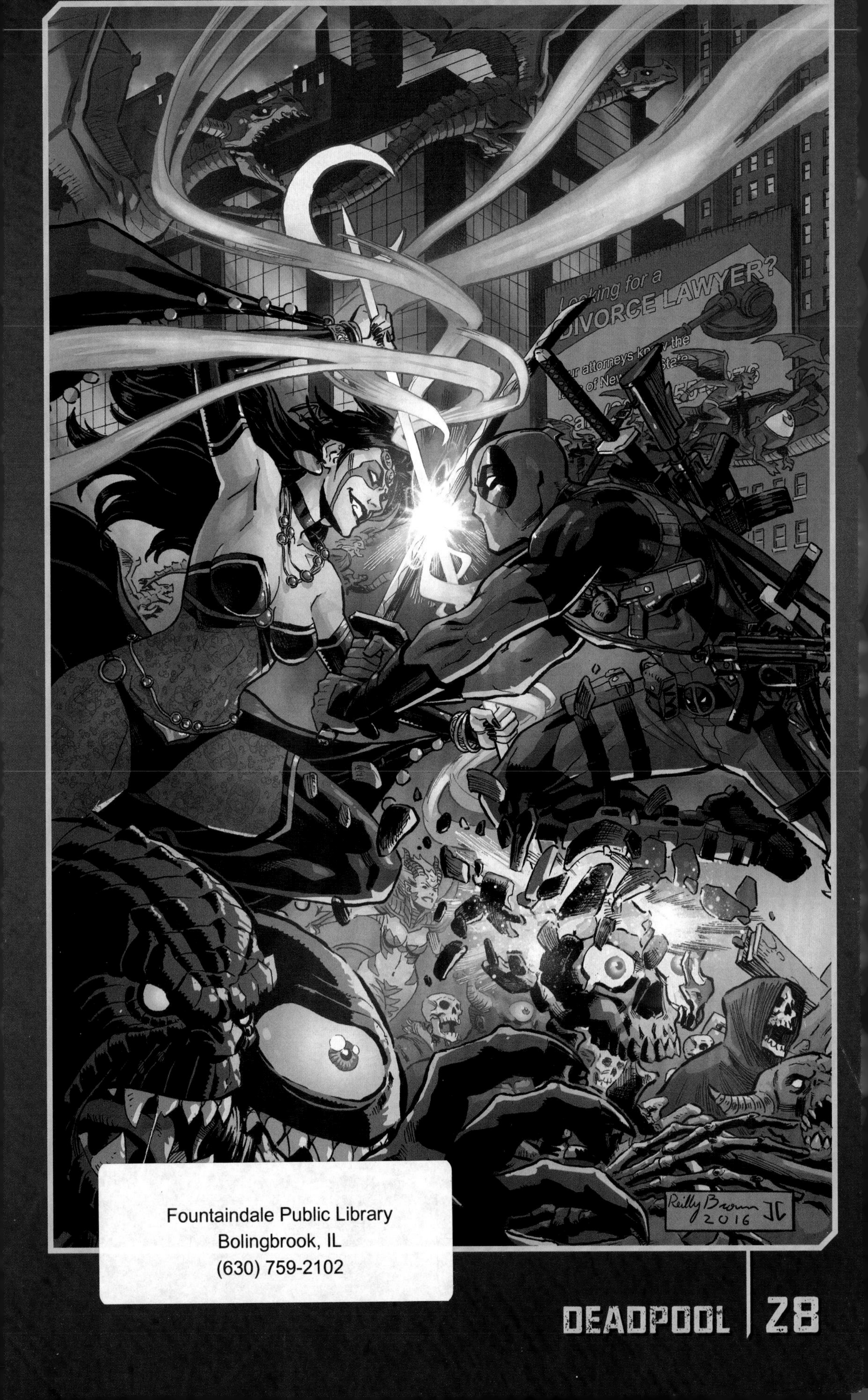
DIVORCE LAWYER?
Reilly Brown 2016 JC

Avenger...Assassin...Superstar...Smelly person...Possibly the world's most skilled mercenary, definitely the world's most annoying, Wade Wilson was chosen for a top-secret government program that gave him a healing factor allowing him to heal from any wound. Somehow, despite making his money as a gun for hire, Wade has become one of the most beloved "heroes" in the world. Call him the Merc with the Mouth...call him the Regeneratin' Degenerate...call him...

DEADPOOL

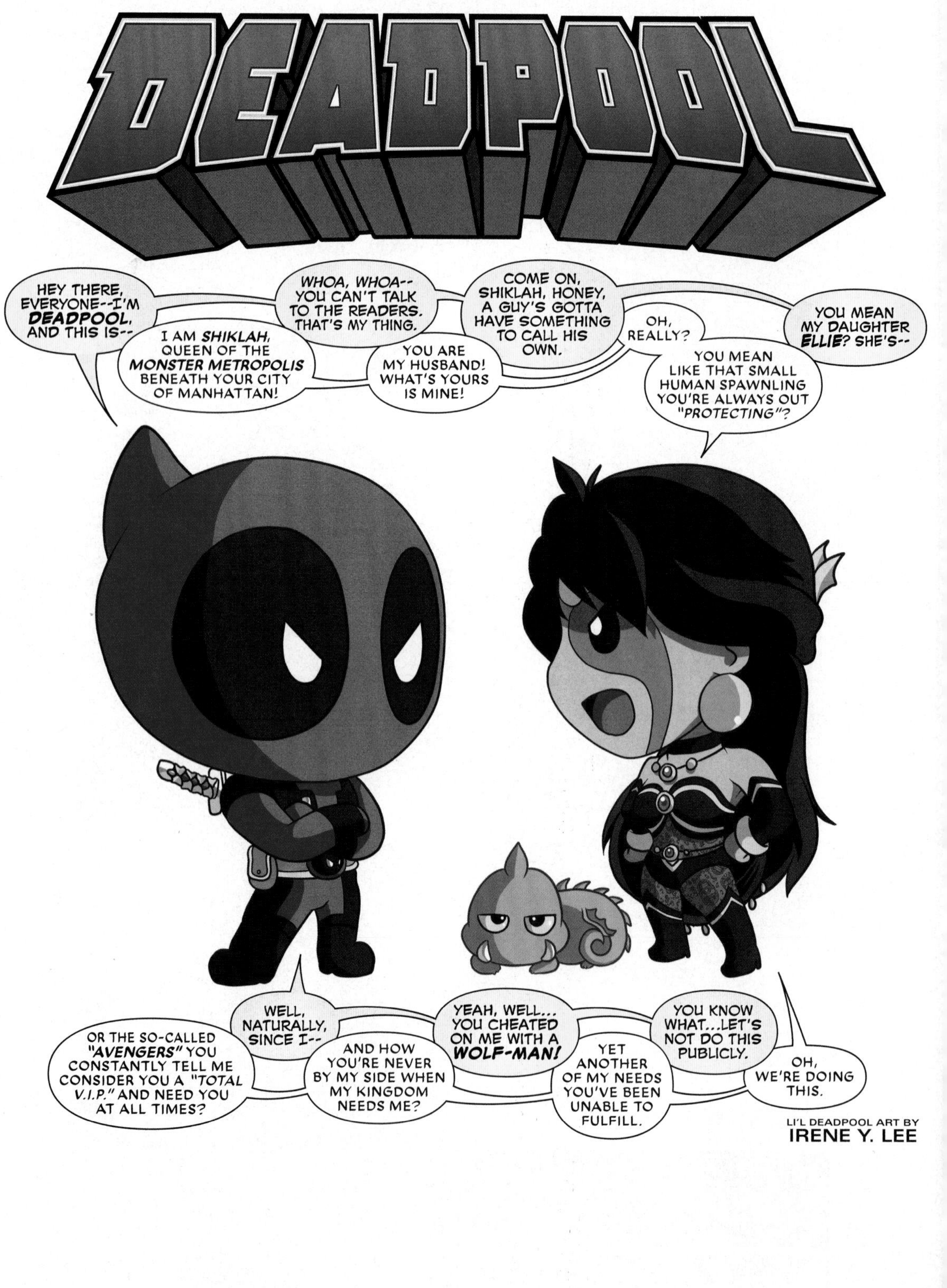
HEY THERE, EVERYONE--I'M *DEADPOOL*, AND THIS IS--
I AM *SHIKLAH*, QUEEN OF THE *MONSTER METROPOLIS* BENEATH YOUR CITY OF MANHATTAN!
WHOA, WHOA--YOU CAN'T TALK TO THE READERS. THAT'S MY THING.
YOU ARE MY HUSBAND! WHAT'S YOURS IS MINE!
COME ON, SHIKLAH, HONEY, A GUY'S GOTTA HAVE SOMETHING TO CALL HIS OWN.
OH, REALLY?
YOU MEAN LIKE THAT SMALL HUMAN SPAWNLING YOU'RE ALWAYS OUT "*PROTECTING*"?
YOU MEAN MY DAUGHTER *ELLIE*? SHE'S--
OR THE SO-CALLED "*AVENGERS*" YOU CONSTANTLY TELL ME CONSIDER YOU A "*TOTAL V.I.P.*" AND NEED YOU AT ALL TIMES?
WELL, NATURALLY, SINCE I--
AND HOW YOU'RE NEVER BY MY SIDE WHEN MY KINGDOM NEEDS ME?
YEAH, WELL... YOU CHEATED ON ME WITH A *WOLF-MAN!*
YET ANOTHER OF MY NEEDS YOU'VE BEEN UNABLE TO FULFILL.
YOU KNOW WHAT...LET'S NOT DO THIS PUBLICLY.
OH, WE'RE DOING THIS.

LI'L DEADPOOL ART BY
IRENE Y. LEE

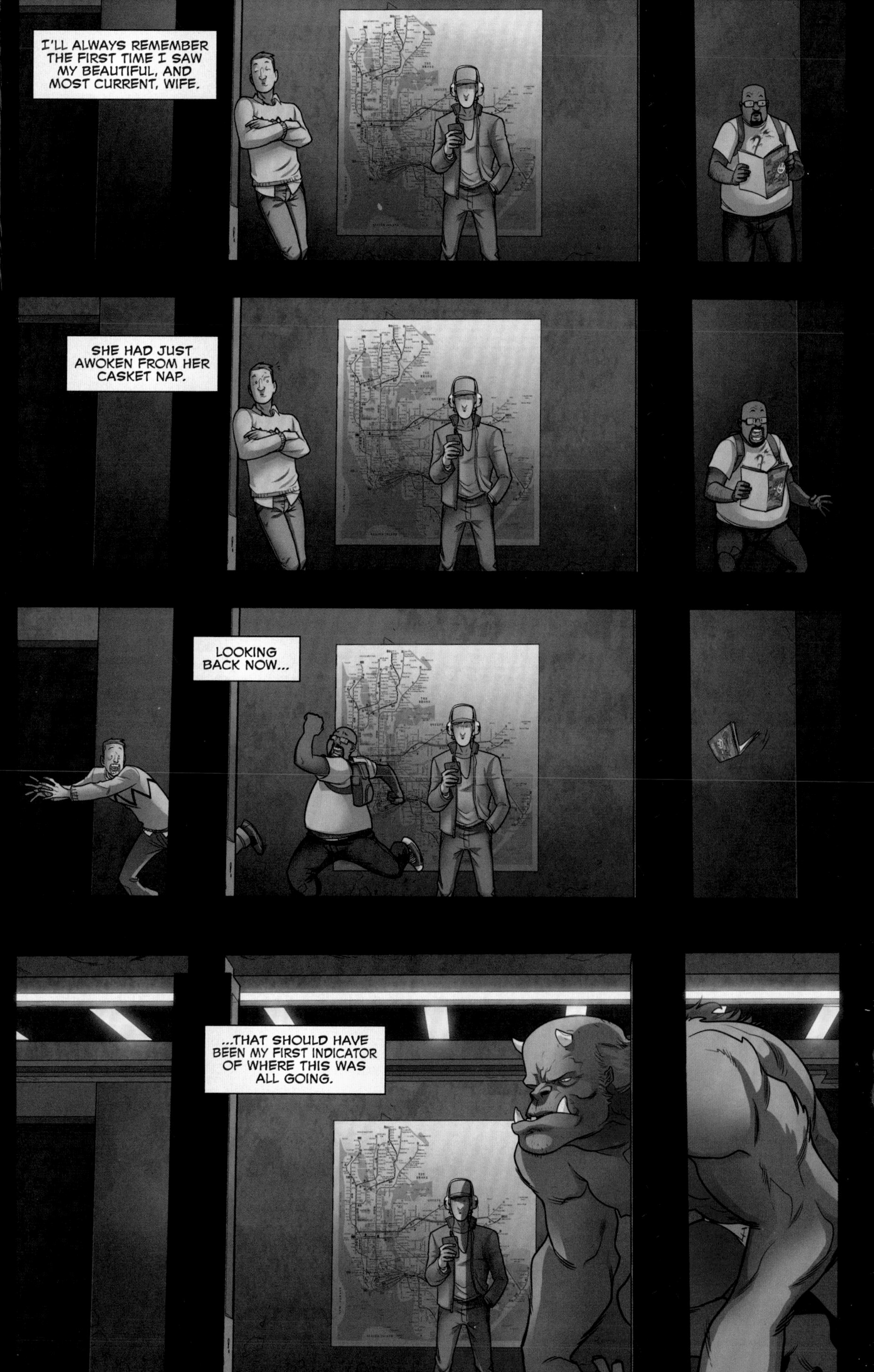
I'LL ALWAYS REMEMBER THE FIRST TIME I SAW MY BEAUTIFUL, AND MOST CURRENT, WIFE.
SHE HAD JUST AWOKEN FROM HER CASKET NAP.
LOOKING BACK NOW...
...THAT SHOULD HAVE BEEN MY FIRST INDICATOR OF WHERE THIS WAS ALL GOING.

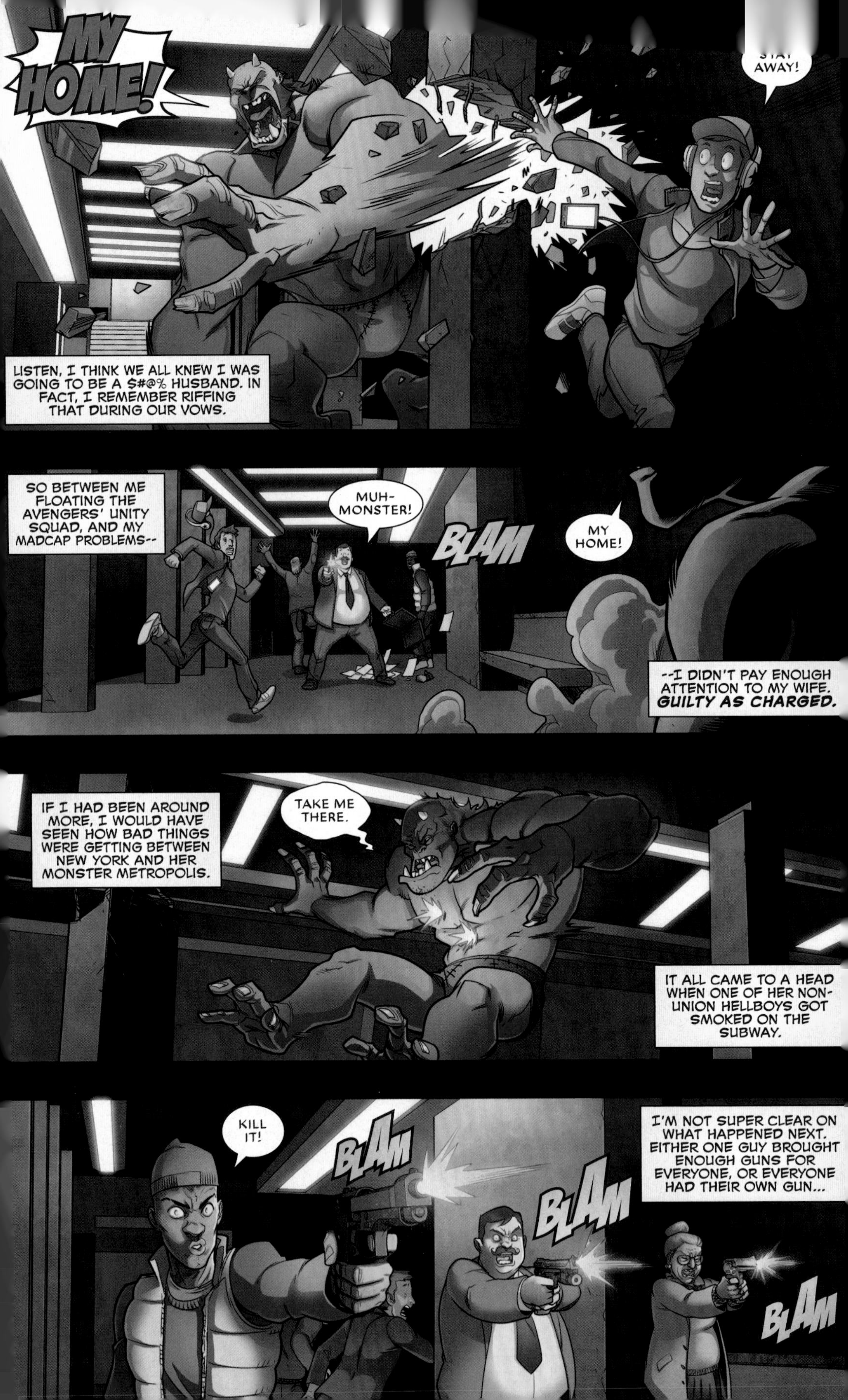
MY HOME!
STAY AWAY!
LISTEN, I THINK WE ALL KNEW I WAS GOING TO BE A $#@% HUSBAND. IN FACT, I REMEMBER RIFFING THAT DURING OUR VOWS.
SO BETWEEN ME FLOATING THE AVENGERS' UNITY SQUAD, AND MY MADCAP PROBLEMS--
MUH-MONSTER!
BLAM
MY HOME!
--I DIDN'T PAY ENOUGH ATTENTION TO MY WIFE. GUILTY AS CHARGED.
IF I HAD BEEN AROUND MORE, I WOULD HAVE SEEN HOW BAD THINGS WERE GETTING BETWEEN NEW YORK AND HER MONSTER METROPOLIS.
TAKE ME THERE.
IT ALL CAME TO A HEAD WHEN ONE OF HER NON-UNION HELLBOYS GOT SMOKED ON THE SUBWAY.
KILL IT!
BLAM
I'M NOT SUPER CLEAR ON WHAT HAPPENED NEXT. EITHER ONE GUY BROUGHT ENOUGH GUNS FOR EVERYONE, OR EVERYONE HAD THEIR OWN GUN...
BLAM
BLAM

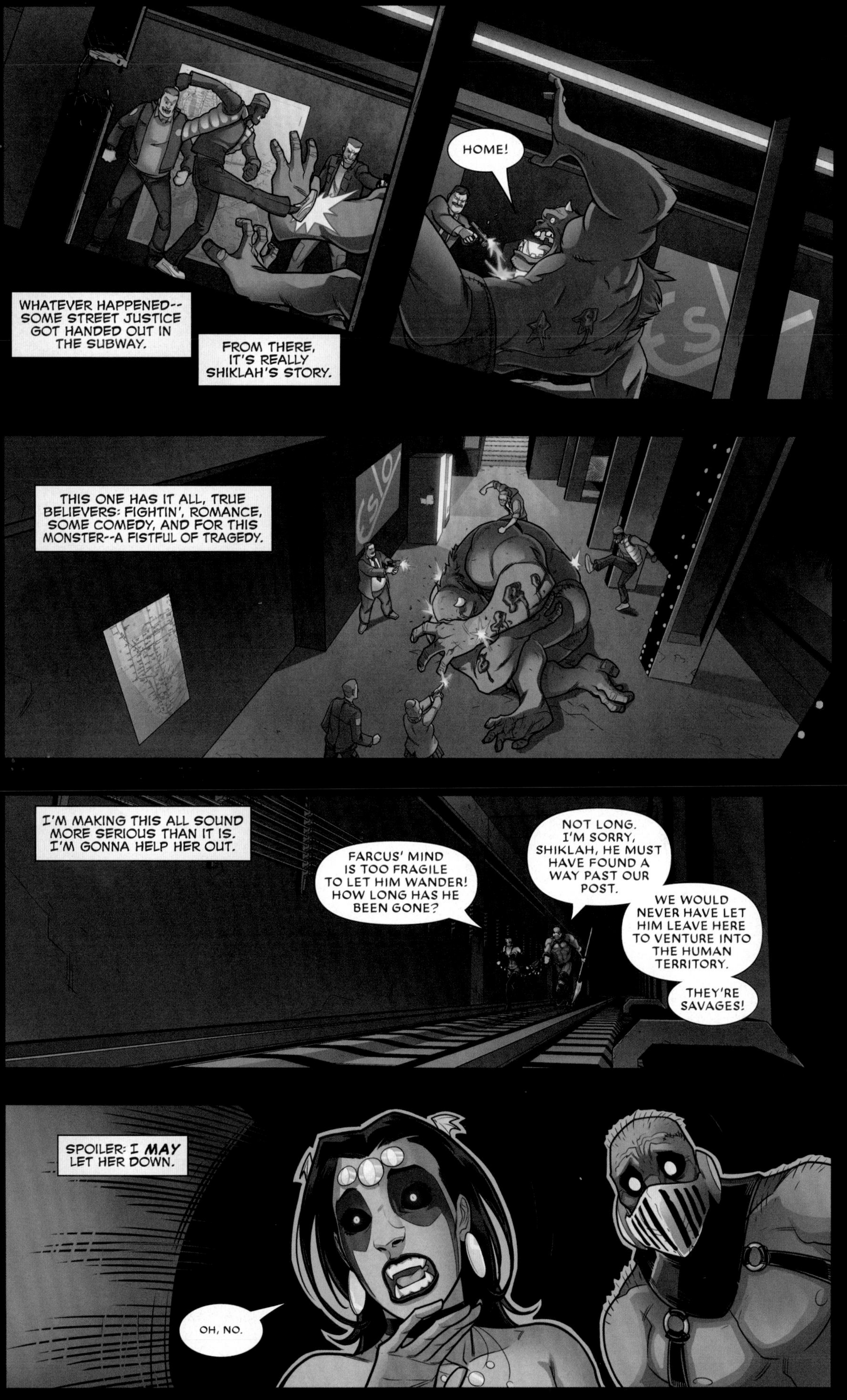

HOME!
WHATEVER HAPPENED-- SOME STREET JUSTICE GOT HANDED OUT IN THE SUBWAY.
FROM THERE, IT'S REALLY SHIKLAH'S STORY.
THIS ONE HAS IT ALL, TRUE BELIEVERS: FIGHTIN', ROMANCE, SOME COMEDY, AND FOR THIS MONSTER--A FISTFUL OF TRAGEDY.
I'M MAKING THIS ALL SOUND MORE SERIOUS THAN IT IS. I'M GONNA HELP HER OUT.
FARCUS' MIND IS TOO FRAGILE TO LET HIM WANDER! HOW LONG HAS HE BEEN GONE?
NOT LONG. I'M SORRY, SHIKLAH, HE MUST HAVE FOUND A WAY PAST OUR POST.
WE WOULD NEVER HAVE LET HIM LEAVE HERE TO VENTURE INTO THE HUMAN TERRITORY.
THEY'RE SAVAGES!
SPOILER: I MAY LET HER DOWN.
OH, NO.

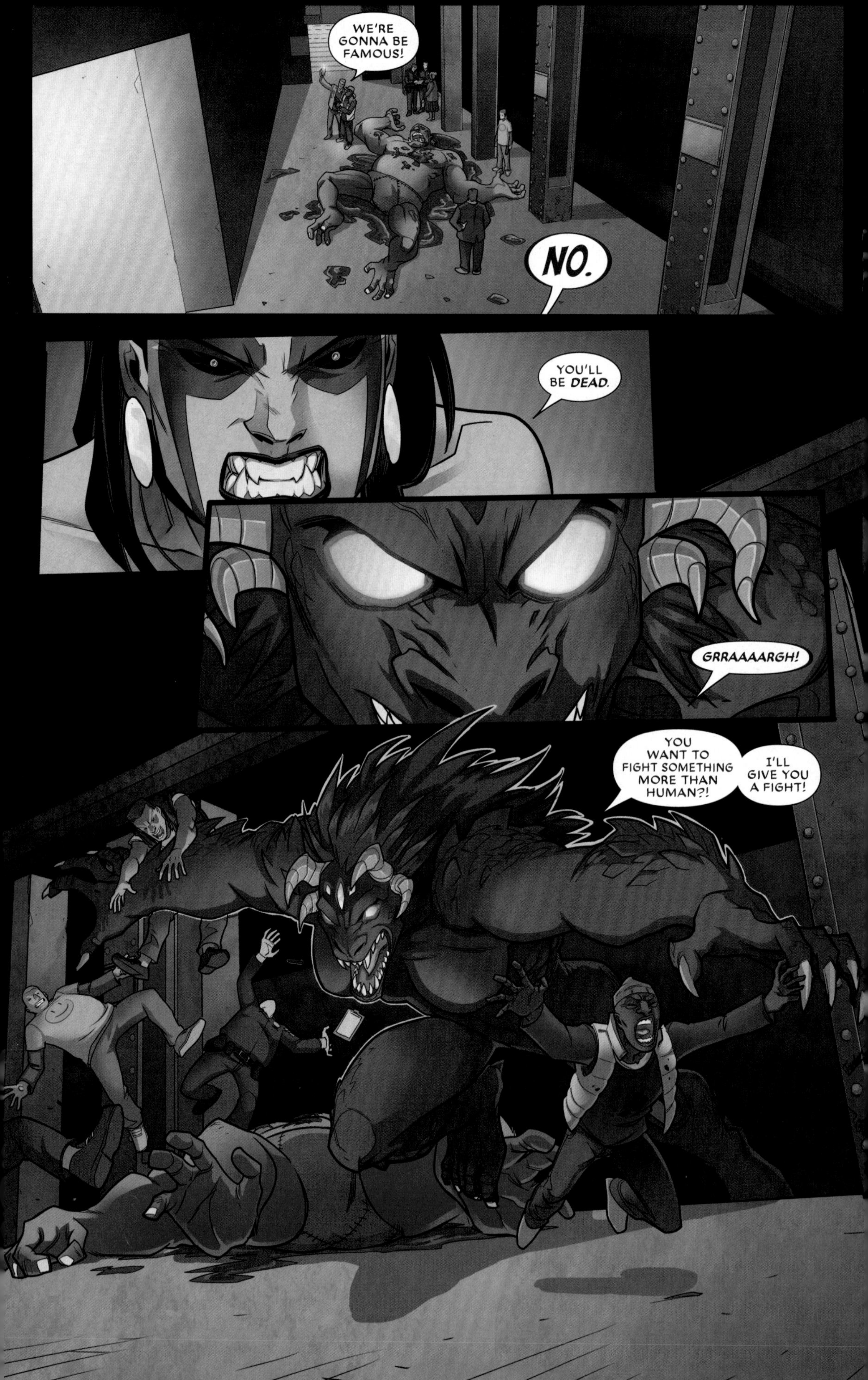

WE'RE GONNA BE FAMOUS!
NO.
YOU'LL BE DEAD.
GRRAAAARGH!
YOU WANT TO FIGHT SOMETHING MORE THAN HUMAN?!
I'LL GIVE YOU A FIGHT!

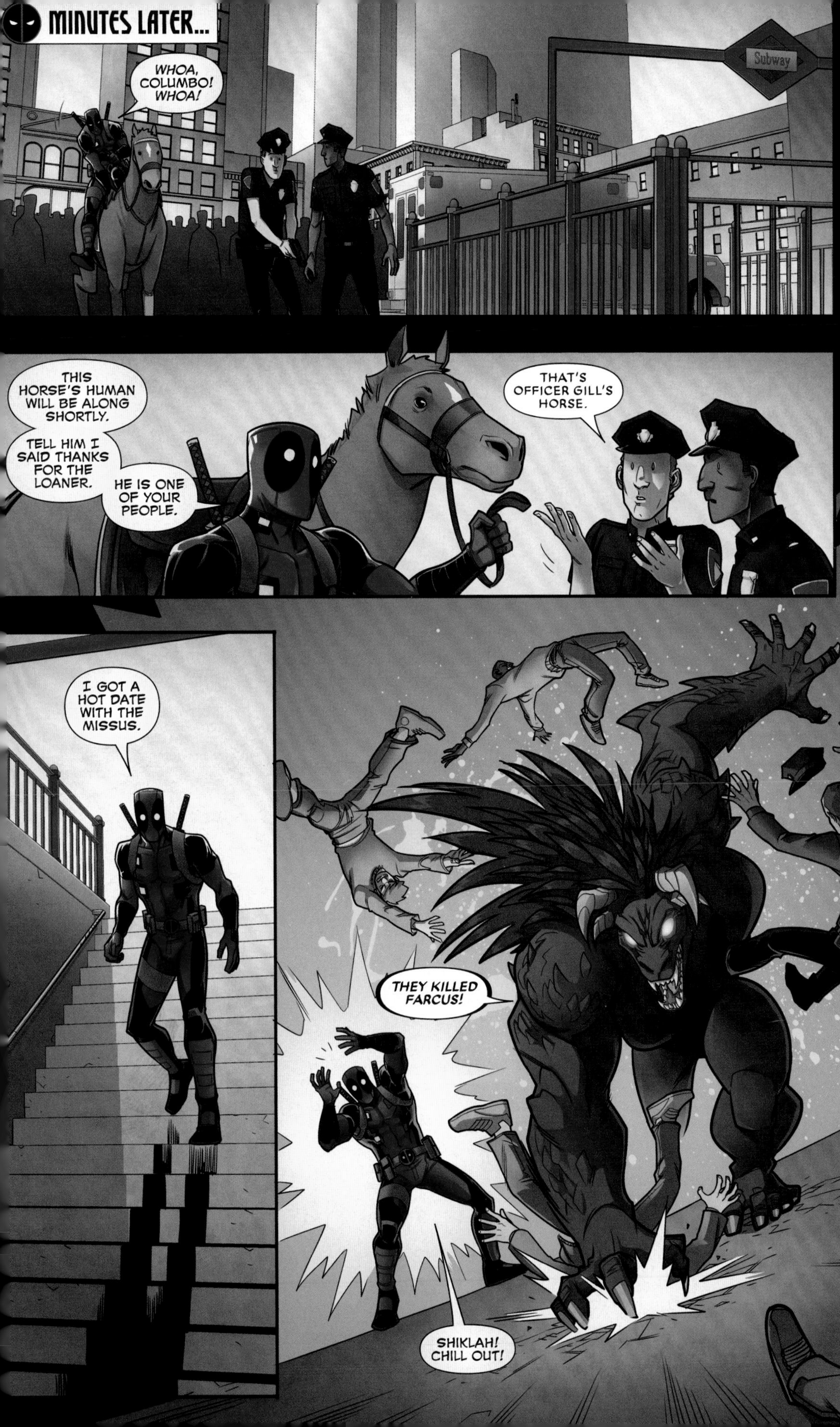
MINUTES LATER...
WHOA, COLUMBO! WHOA!
Subway
THIS HORSE'S HUMAN WILL BE ALONG SHORTLY.
TELL HIM I SAID THANKS FOR THE LOANER.
HE IS ONE OF YOUR PEOPLE.
THAT'S OFFICER GILL'S HORSE.
I GOT A HOT DATE WITH THE MISSUS.
THEY KILLED FARCUS!
SHIKLAH! CHILL OUT!

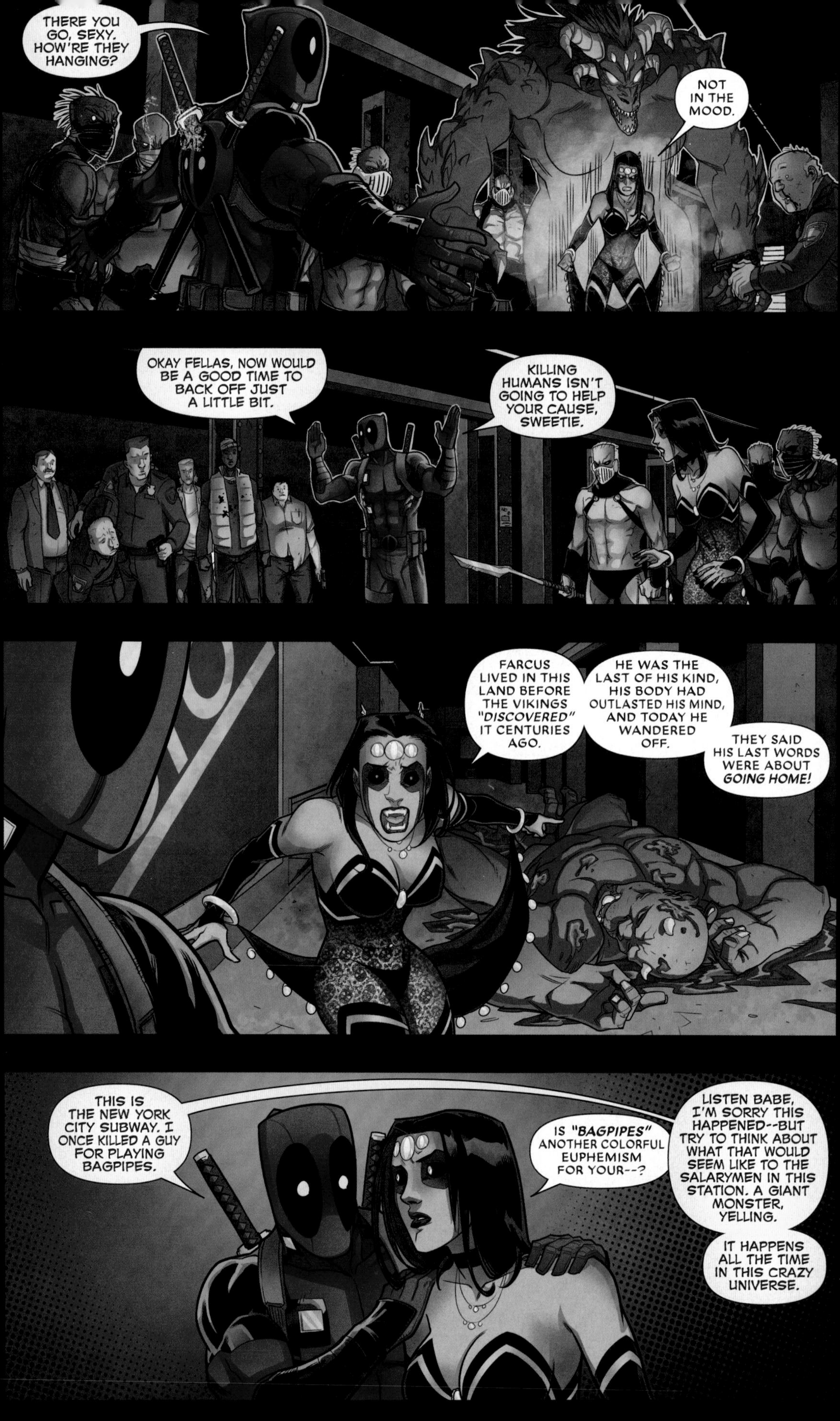
THERE YOU GO, SEXY. HOW'RE THEY HANGING?
NOT IN THE MOOD.
OKAY FELLAS, NOW WOULD BE A GOOD TIME TO BACK OFF JUST A LITTLE BIT.
KILLING HUMANS ISN'T GOING TO HELP YOUR CAUSE, SWEETIE.
FARCUS LIVED IN THIS LAND BEFORE THE VIKINGS "DISCOVERED" IT CENTURIES AGO.
HE WAS THE LAST OF HIS KIND, HIS BODY HAD OUTLASTED HIS MIND, AND TODAY HE WANDERED OFF.
THEY SAID HIS LAST WORDS WERE ABOUT GOING HOME!
THIS IS THE NEW YORK CITY SUBWAY. I ONCE KILLED A GUY FOR PLAYING BAGPIPES.
IS "BAGPIPES" ANOTHER COLORFUL EUPHEMISM FOR YOUR--?
LISTEN BABE, I'M SORRY THIS HAPPENED--BUT TRY TO THINK ABOUT WHAT THAT WOULD SEEM LIKE TO THE SALARYMEN IN THIS STATION. A GIANT MONSTER, YELLING.
IT HAPPENS ALL THE TIME IN THIS CRAZY UNIVERSE.

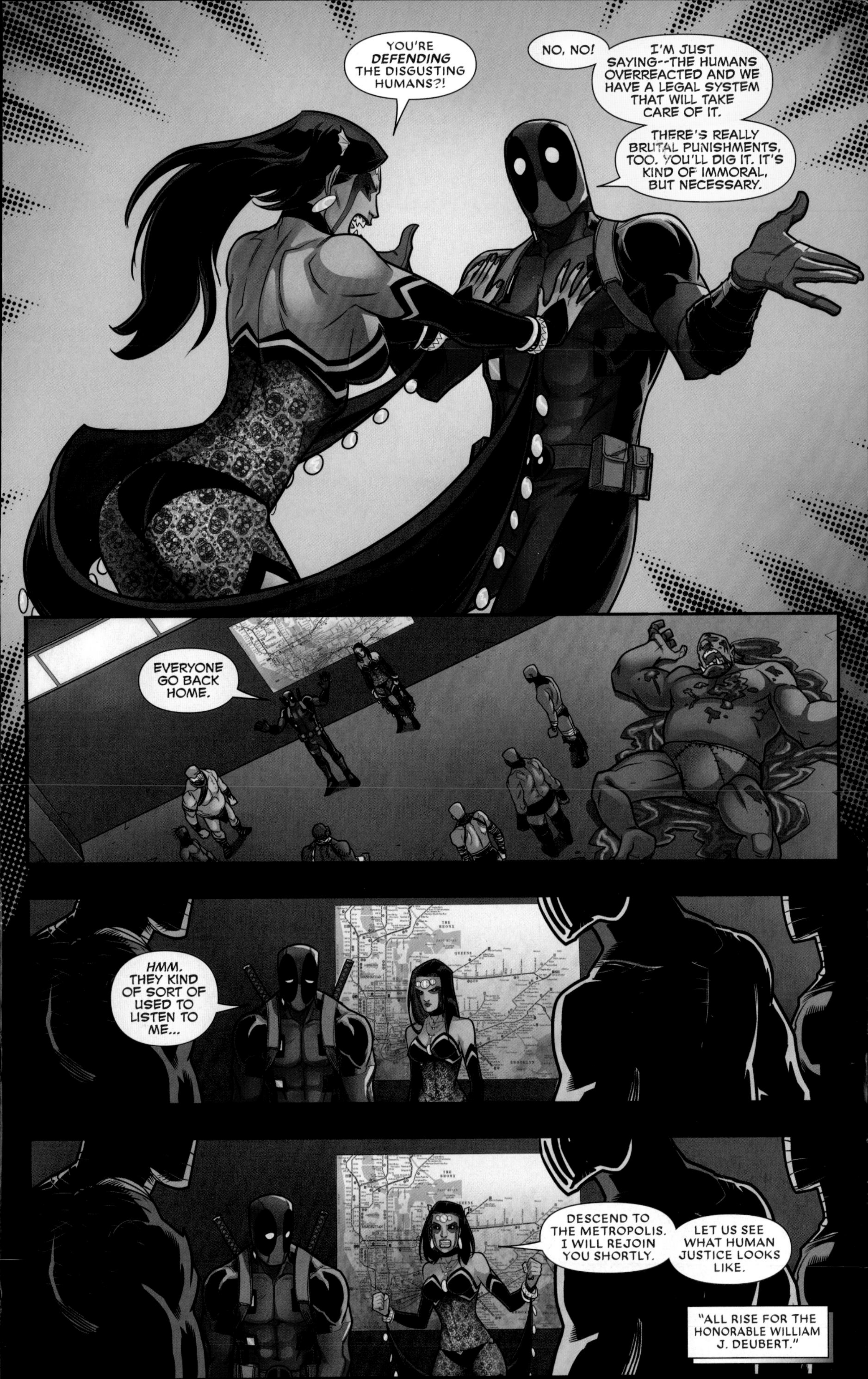
YOU'RE DEFENDING THE DISGUSTING HUMANS?!
NO, NO!
I'M JUST SAYING--THE HUMANS OVERREACTED AND WE HAVE A LEGAL SYSTEM THAT WILL TAKE CARE OF IT.
THERE'S REALLY BRUTAL PUNISHMENTS, TOO. YOU'LL DIG IT. IT'S KIND OF IMMORAL, BUT NECESSARY.
EVERYONE GO BACK HOME.
HMM. THEY KIND OF SORT OF USED TO LISTEN TO ME...
DESCEND TO THE METROPOLIS. I WILL REJOIN YOU SHORTLY.
LET US SEE WHAT HUMAN JUSTICE LOOKS LIKE.
"ALL RISE FOR THE HONORABLE WILLIAM J. DEUBERT."

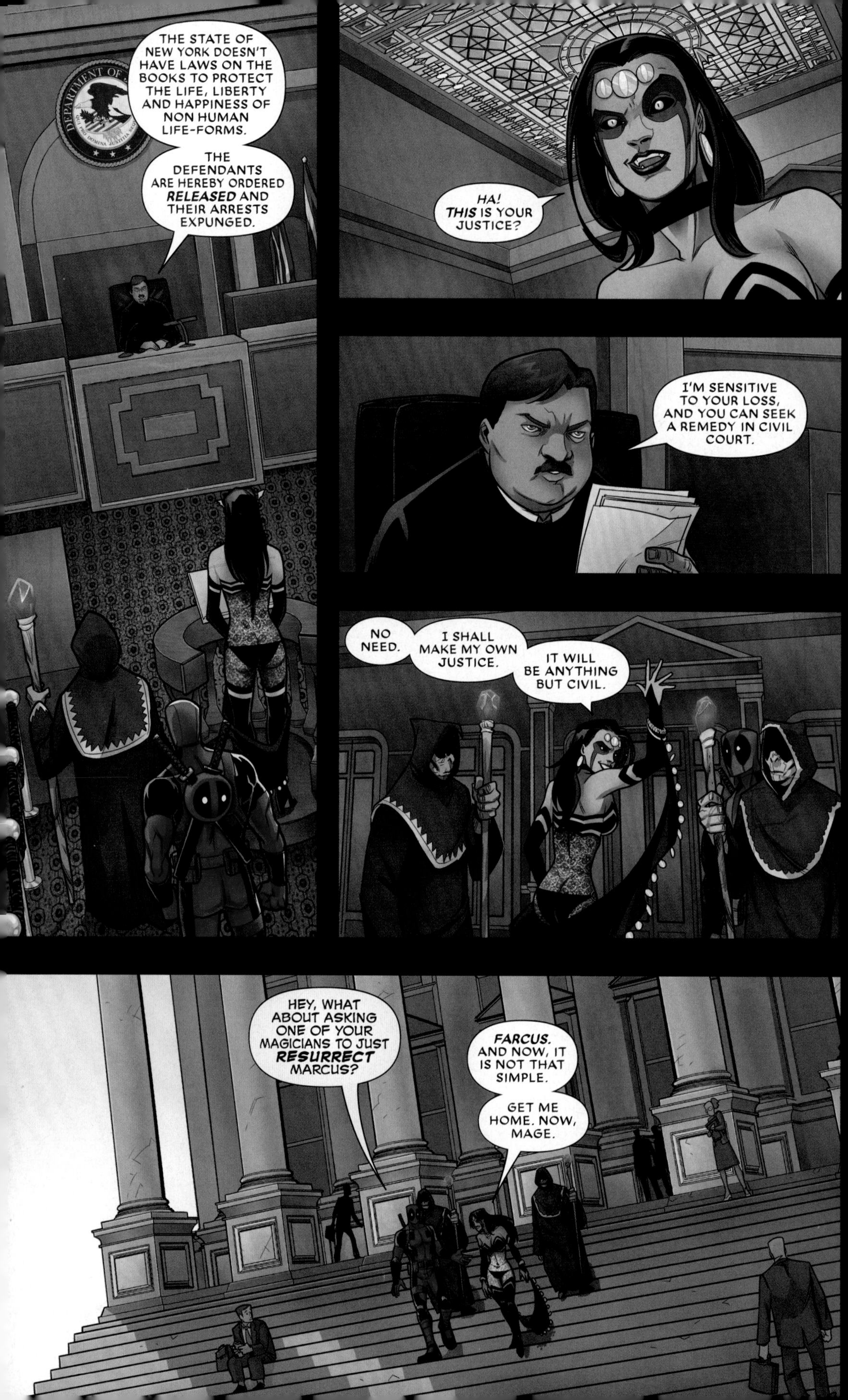
THE STATE OF NEW YORK DOESN'T HAVE LAWS ON THE BOOKS TO PROTECT THE LIFE, LIBERTY AND HAPPINESS OF NON HUMAN LIFE-FORMS.
THE DEFENDANTS ARE HEREBY ORDERED RELEASED AND THEIR ARRESTS EXPUNGED.
HA! THIS IS YOUR JUSTICE?
I'M SENSITIVE TO YOUR LOSS, AND YOU CAN SEEK A REMEDY IN CIVIL COURT.
NO NEED.
I SHALL MAKE MY OWN JUSTICE.
IT WILL BE ANYTHING BUT CIVIL.
HEY, WHAT ABOUT ASKING ONE OF YOUR MAGICIANS TO JUST RESURRECT MARCUS?
FARCUS. AND NOW, IT IS NOT THAT SIMPLE.
GET ME HOME. NOW, MAGE.

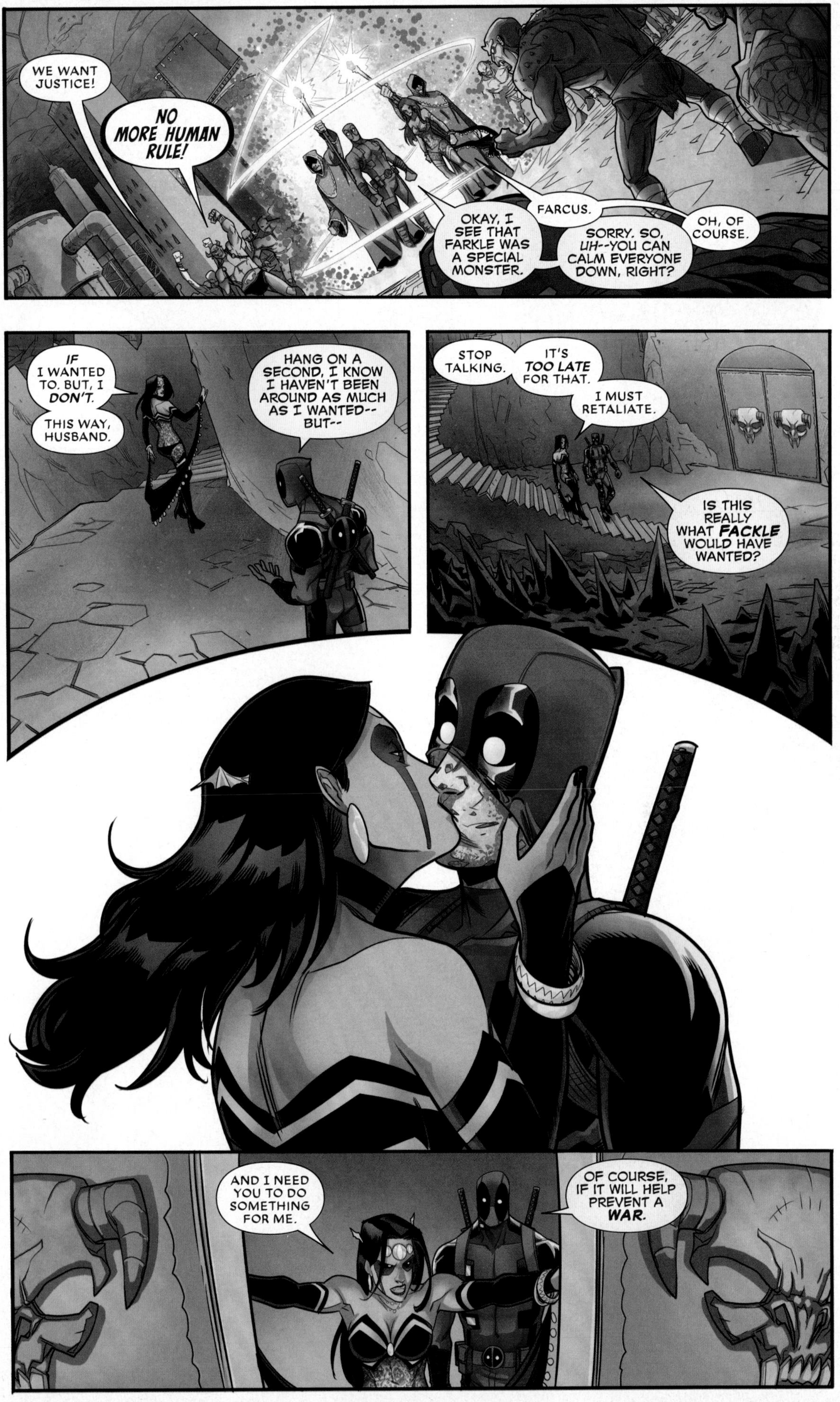
WE WANT JUSTICE!
NO MORE HUMAN RULE!
OKAY, I SEE THAT FARKLE WAS A SPECIAL MONSTER.
FARCUS.
SORRY. SO, UH--YOU CAN CALM EVERYONE DOWN, RIGHT?
OH, OF COURSE.
IF I WANTED TO. BUT, I DON'T.
THIS WAY, HUSBAND.
HANG ON A SECOND, I KNOW I HAVEN'T BEEN AROUND AS MUCH AS I WANTED-- BUT--
STOP TALKING.
IT'S TOO LATE FOR THAT.
I MUST RETALIATE.
IS THIS REALLY WHAT FACKLE WOULD HAVE WANTED?
AND I NEED YOU TO DO SOMETHING FOR ME.
OF COURSE, IF IT WILL HELP PREVENT A WAR.

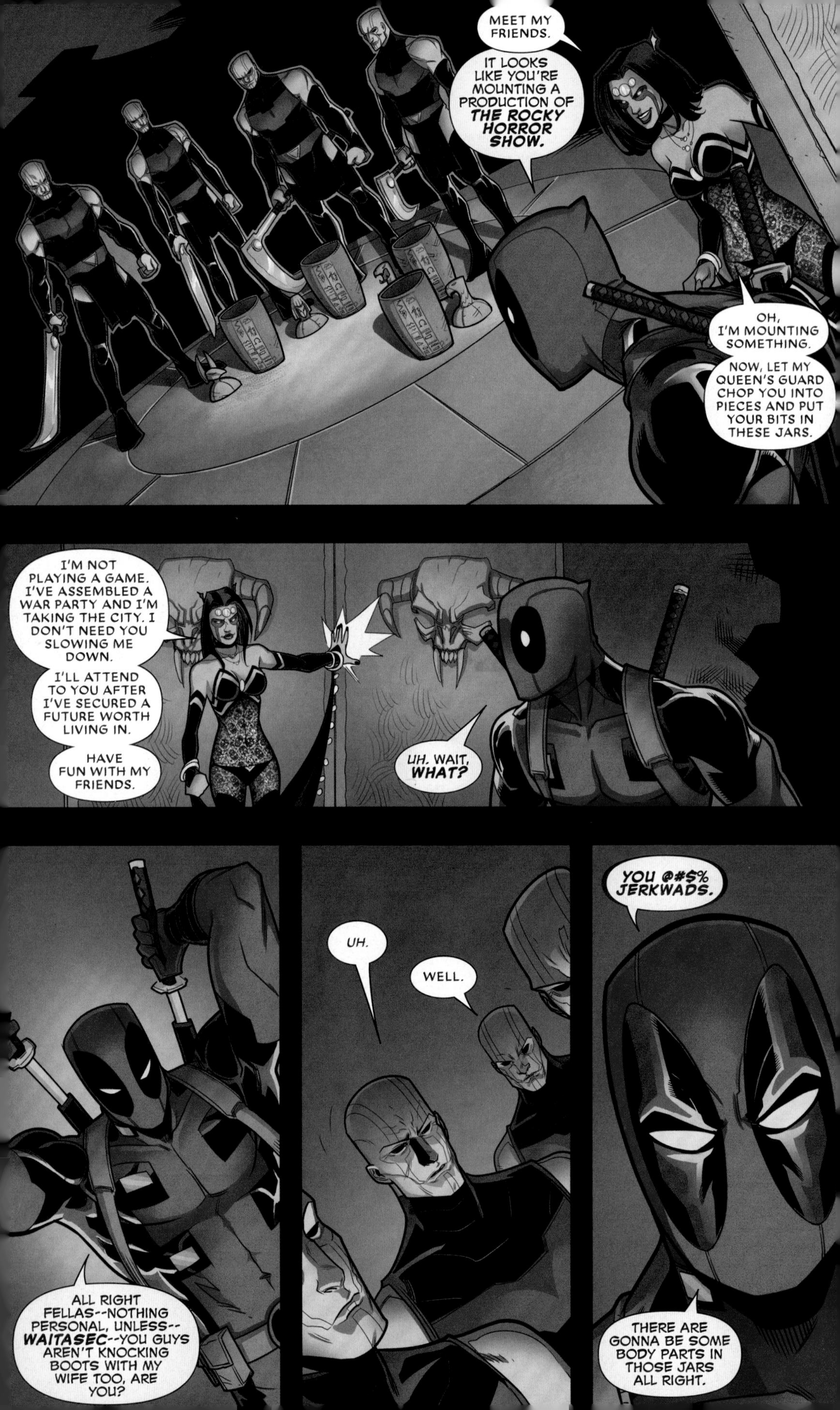
MEET MY FRIENDS.
IT LOOKS LIKE YOU'RE MOUNTING A PRODUCTION OF ***THE ROCKY HORROR SHOW.***
OH, I'M MOUNTING SOMETHING.
NOW, LET MY QUEEN'S GUARD CHOP YOU INTO PIECES AND PUT YOUR BITS IN THESE JARS.
I'M NOT PLAYING A GAME. I'VE ASSEMBLED A WAR PARTY AND I'M TAKING THE CITY. I DON'T NEED YOU SLOWING ME DOWN.
I'LL ATTEND TO YOU AFTER I'VE SECURED A FUTURE WORTH LIVING IN.
HAVE FUN WITH MY FRIENDS.
UH, WAIT, ***WHAT?***
ALL RIGHT FELLAS--NOTHING PERSONAL, UNLESS-- ***WAITASEC***--YOU GUYS AREN'T KNOCKING BOOTS WITH MY WIFE TOO, ARE YOU?
UH.
WELL.
YOU @#$% JERKWADS.
THERE ARE GONNA BE SOME BODY PARTS IN THOSE JARS ALL RIGHT.

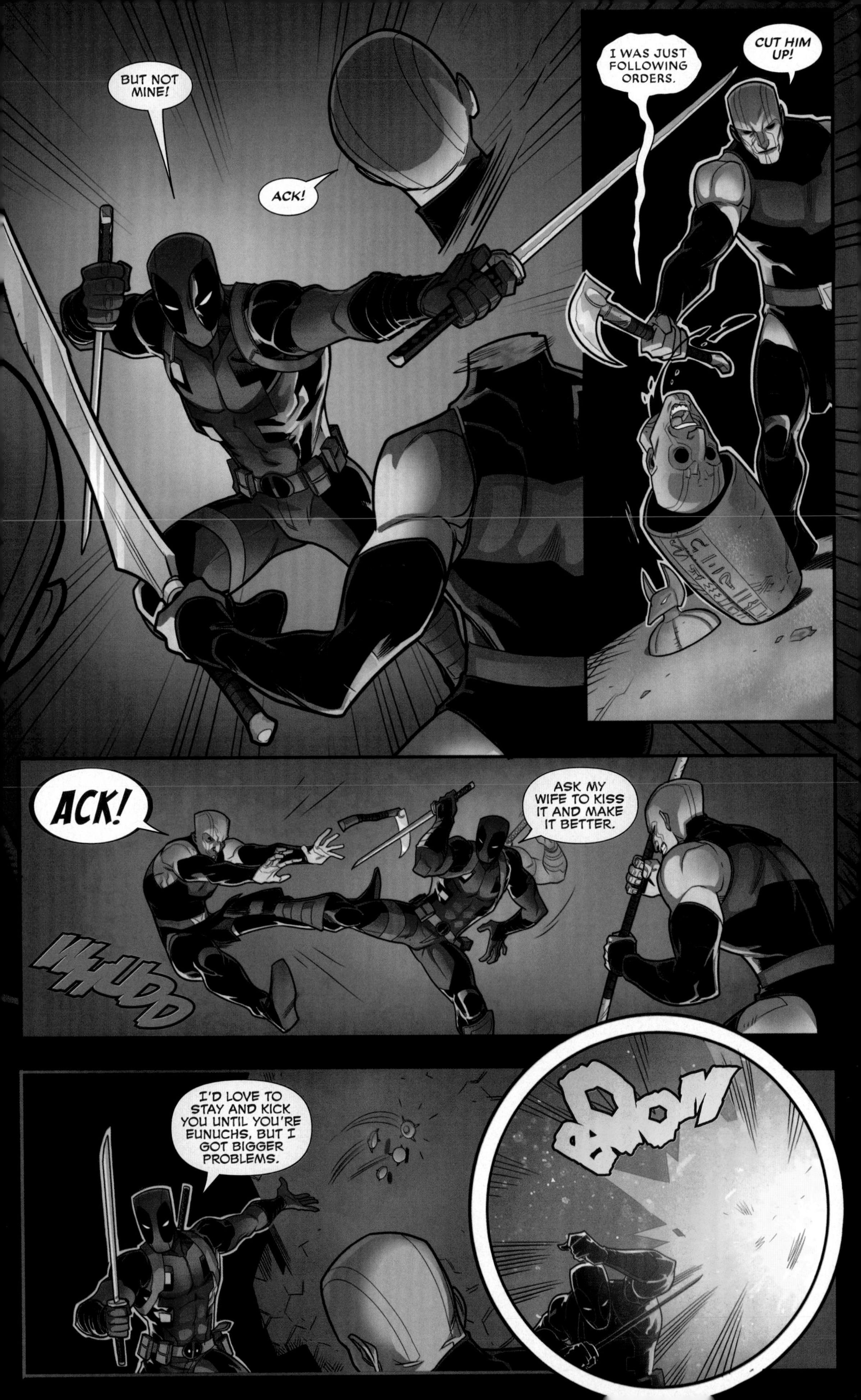
BUT NOT MINE!
ACK!
I WAS JUST FOLLOWING ORDERS.
CUT HIM UP!
ACK!
ASK MY WIFE TO KISS IT AND MAKE IT BETTER.
WHUDD
I'D LOVE TO STAY AND KICK YOU UNTIL YOU'RE EUNUCHS, BUT I GOT BIGGER PROBLEMS.
BOOM

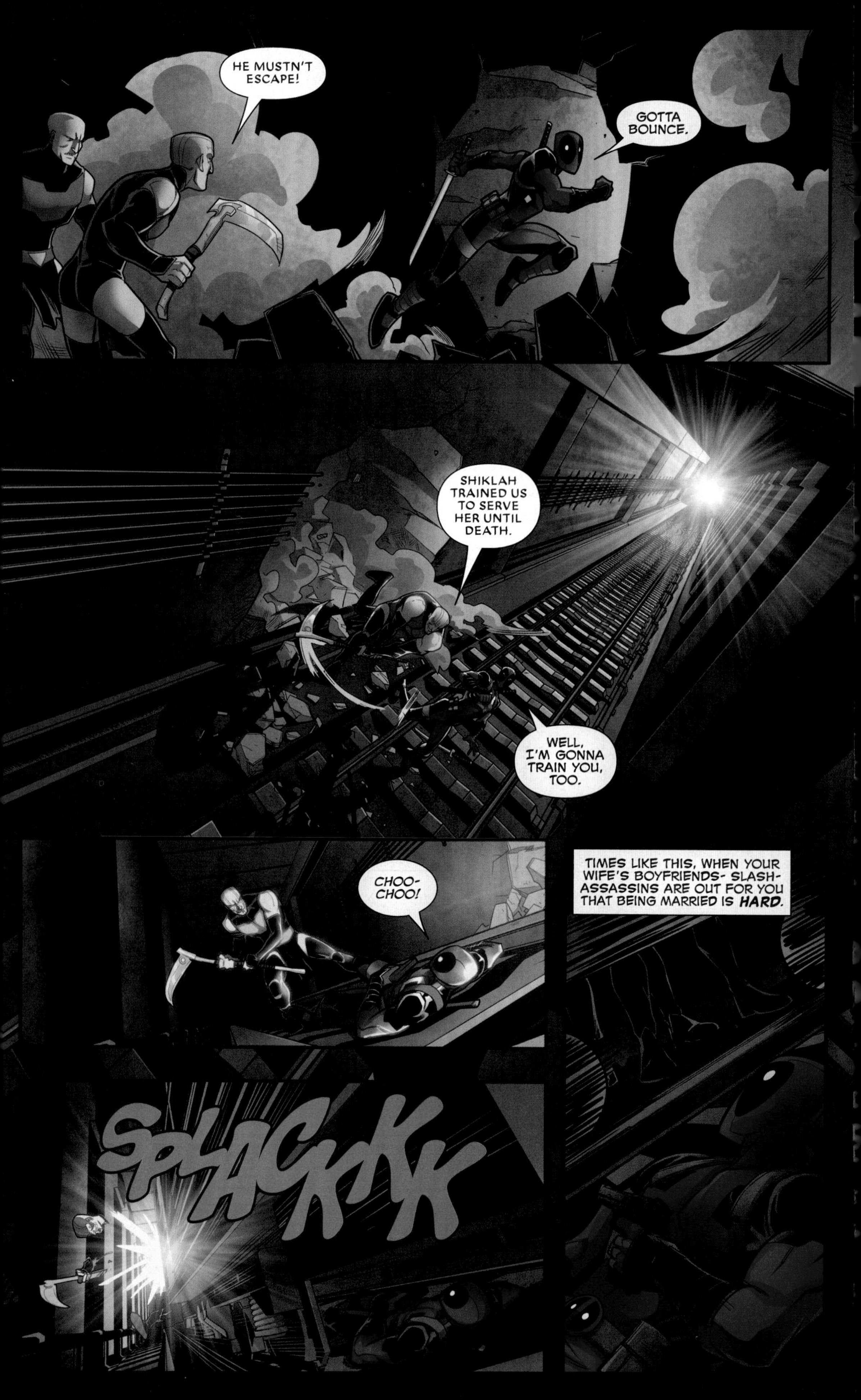
HE MUSTN'T ESCAPE!
GOTTA BOUNCE.
SHIKLAH TRAINED US TO SERVE HER UNTIL DEATH.
WELL, I'M GONNA TRAIN YOU, TOO.
CHOO-CHOO!
TIMES LIKE THIS, WHEN YOUR WIFE'S BOYFRIENDS- SLASH-ASSASSINS ARE OUT FOR YOU THAT BEING MARRIED IS HARD.
SPLACKKK

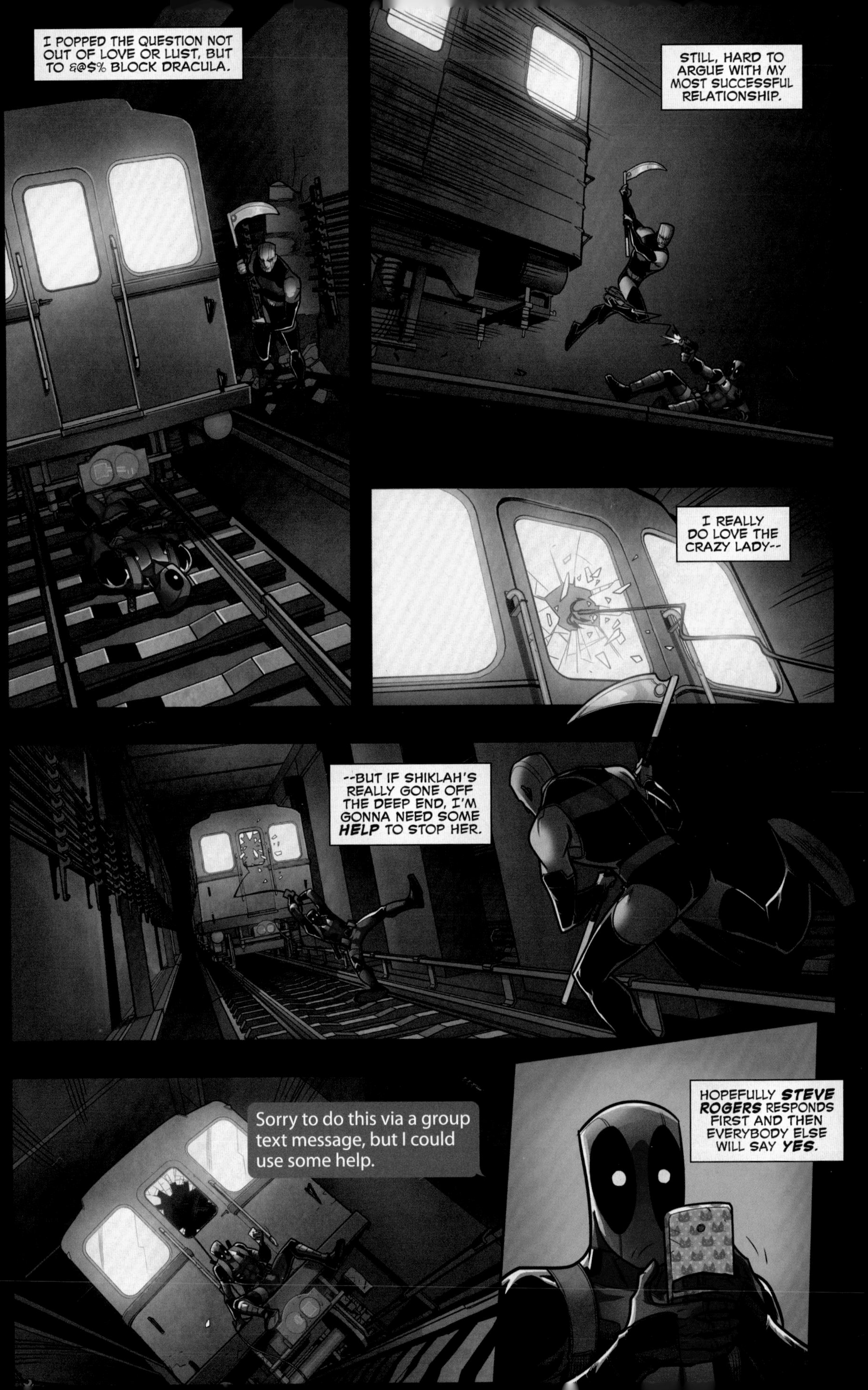
I POPPED THE QUESTION NOT OUT OF LOVE OR LUST, BUT TO &@$% BLOCK DRACULA.
STILL, HARD TO ARGUE WITH MY MOST SUCCESSFUL RELATIONSHIP.
I REALLY DO LOVE THE CRAZY LADY--
--BUT IF SHIKLAH'S REALLY GONE OFF THE DEEP END, I'M GONNA NEED SOME HELP TO STOP HER.
Sorry to do this via a group text message, but I could use some help.
HOPEFULLY STEVE ROGERS RESPONDS FIRST AND THEN EVERYBODY ELSE WILL SAY YES.

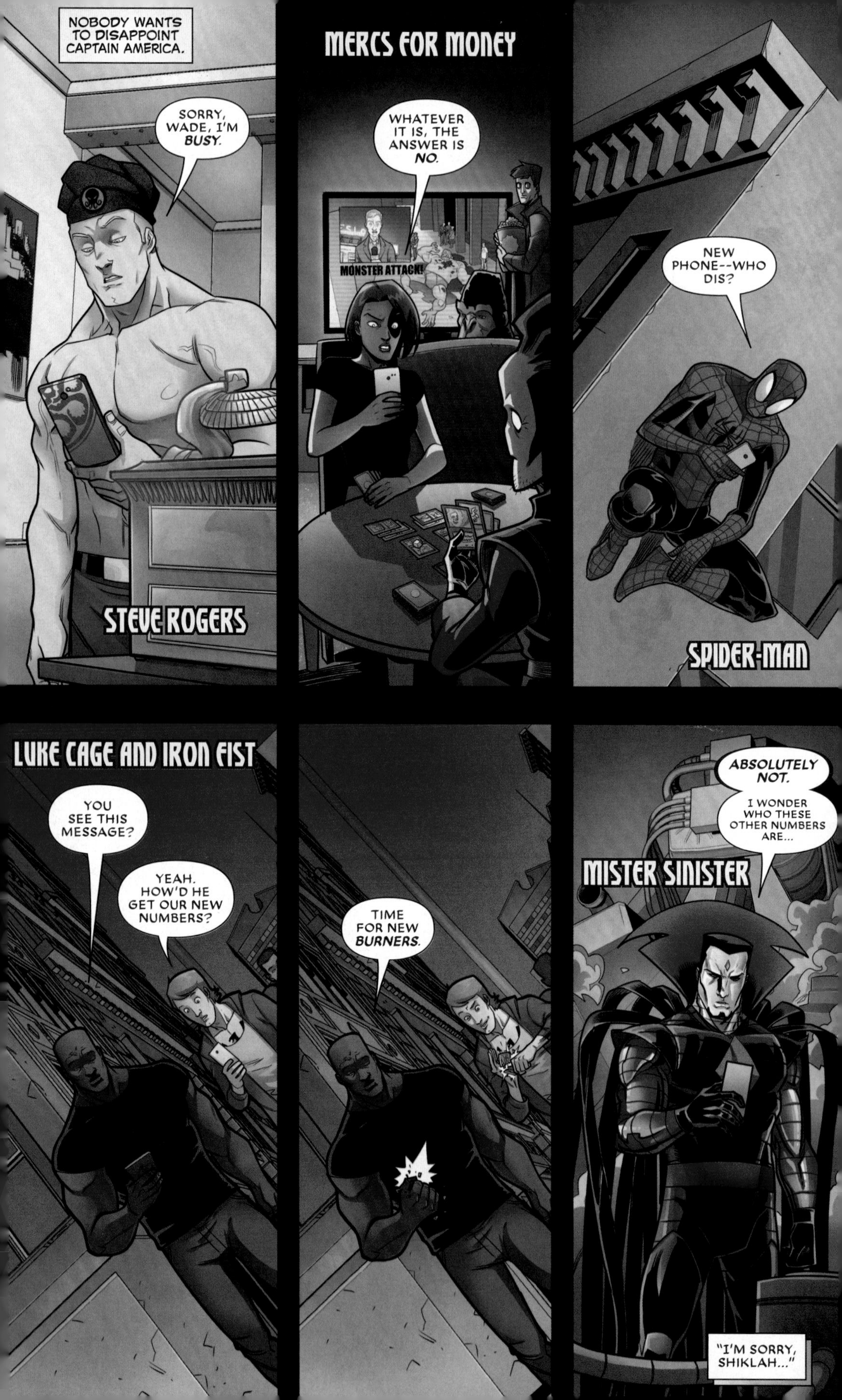
NOBODY WANTS TO DISAPPOINT CAPTAIN AMERICA.
SORRY, WADE, I'M BUSY.
STEVE ROGERS
MERCS FOR MONEY
WHATEVER IT IS, THE ANSWER IS NO.
MONSTER ATTACK!
NEW PHONE--WHO DIS?
SPIDER-MAN
LUKE CAGE AND IRON FIST
YOU SEE THIS MESSAGE?
YEAH. HOW'D HE GET OUR NEW NUMBERS?
TIME FOR NEW BURNERS.
ABSOLUTELY NOT.
I WONDER WHO THESE OTHER NUMBERS ARE...
MISTER SINISTER
"I'M SORRY, SHIKLAH..."

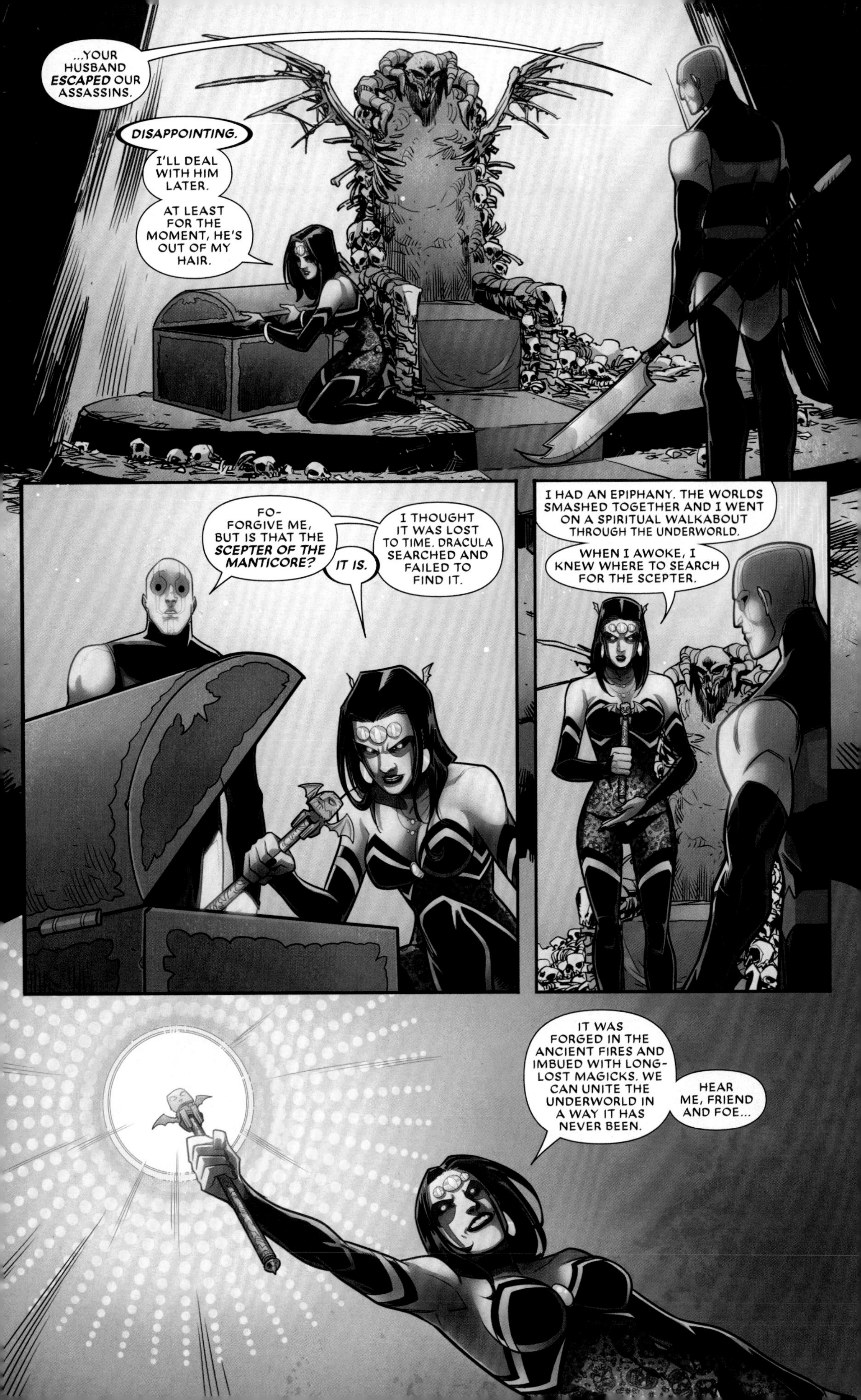
...YOUR HUSBAND *ESCAPED* OUR ASSASSINS.
DISAPPOINTING.
I'LL DEAL WITH HIM LATER.
AT LEAST FOR THE MOMENT, HE'S OUT OF MY HAIR.
FO- FORGIVE ME, BUT IS THAT THE *SCEPTER OF THE MANTICORE?*
IT IS.
I THOUGHT IT WAS LOST TO TIME. DRACULA SEARCHED AND FAILED TO FIND IT.
I HAD AN EPIPHANY. THE WORLDS SMASHED TOGETHER AND I WENT ON A SPIRITUAL WALKABOUT THROUGH THE UNDERWORLD.
WHEN I AWOKE, I KNEW WHERE TO SEARCH FOR THE SCEPTER.
IT WAS FORGED IN THE ANCIENT FIRES AND IMBUED WITH LONG-LOST MAGICKS. WE CAN UNITE THE UNDERWORLD IN A WAY IT HAS NEVER BEEN.
HEAR ME, FRIEND AND FOE...

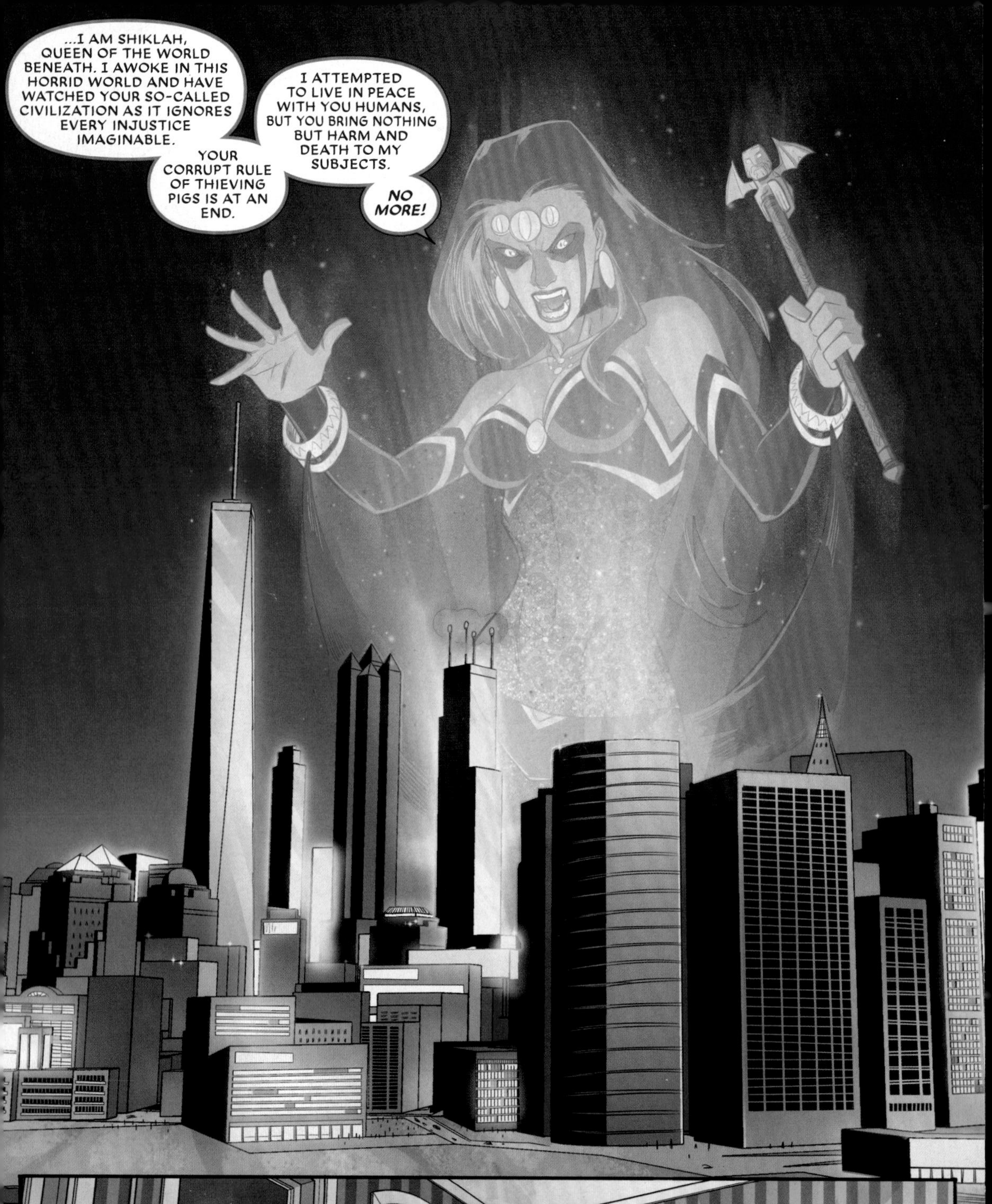
...I AM SHIKLAH, QUEEN OF THE WORLD BENEATH. I AWOKE IN THIS HORRID WORLD AND HAVE WATCHED YOUR SO-CALLED CIVILIZATION AS IT IGNORES EVERY INJUSTICE IMAGINABLE.
YOUR CORRUPT RULE OF THIEVING PIGS IS AT AN END.
I ATTEMPTED TO LIVE IN PEACE WITH YOU HUMANS, BUT YOU BRING NOTHING BUT HARM AND DEATH TO MY SUBJECTS.
NO MORE!

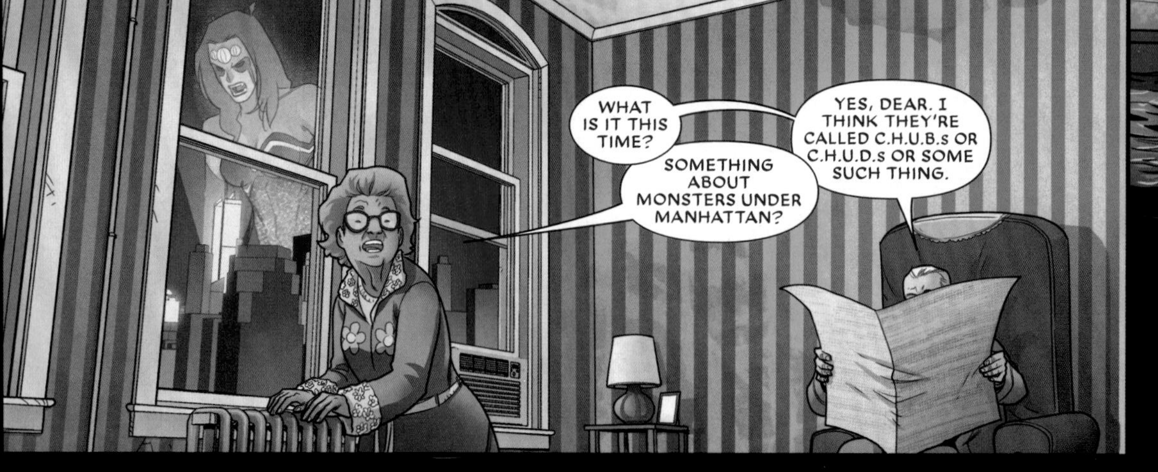
WHAT IS IT THIS TIME?
SOMETHING ABOUT MONSTERS UNDER MANHATTAN?
YES, DEAR. I THINK THEY'RE CALLED C.H.U.B.s OR C.H.U.D.s OR SOME SUCH THING.

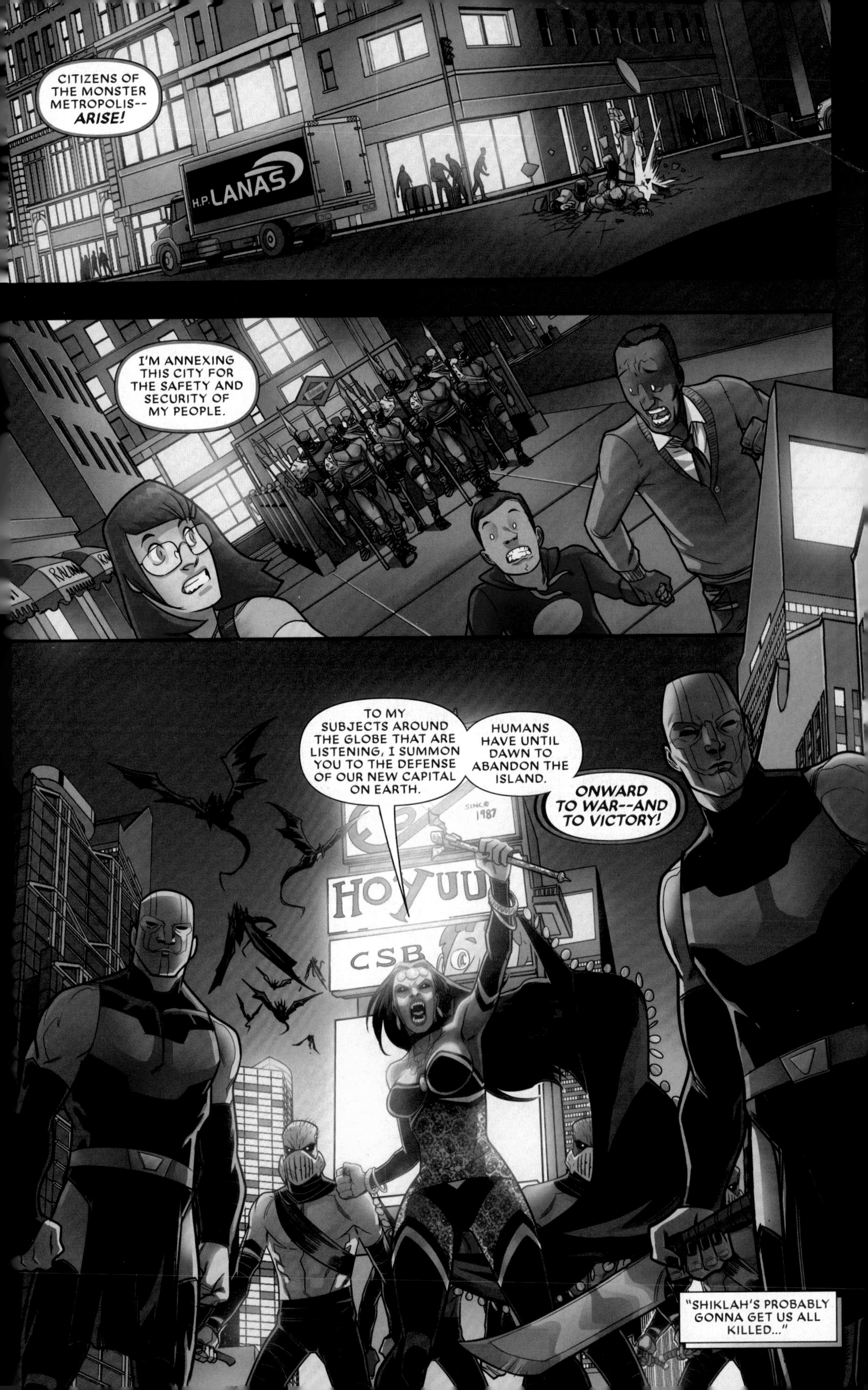
CITIZENS OF THE MONSTER METROPOLIS-- ARISE!
H.P. LANAS
I'M ANNEXING THIS CITY FOR THE SAFETY AND SECURITY OF MY PEOPLE.
TO MY SUBJECTS AROUND THE GLOBE THAT ARE LISTENING, I SUMMON YOU TO THE DEFENSE OF OUR NEW CAPITAL ON EARTH.
HUMANS HAVE UNTIL DAWN TO ABANDON THE ISLAND.
ONWARD TO WAR--AND TO VICTORY!
SINCE 1987
HOYUU
CSB
"SHIKLAH'S PROBABLY GONNA GET US ALL KILLED..."

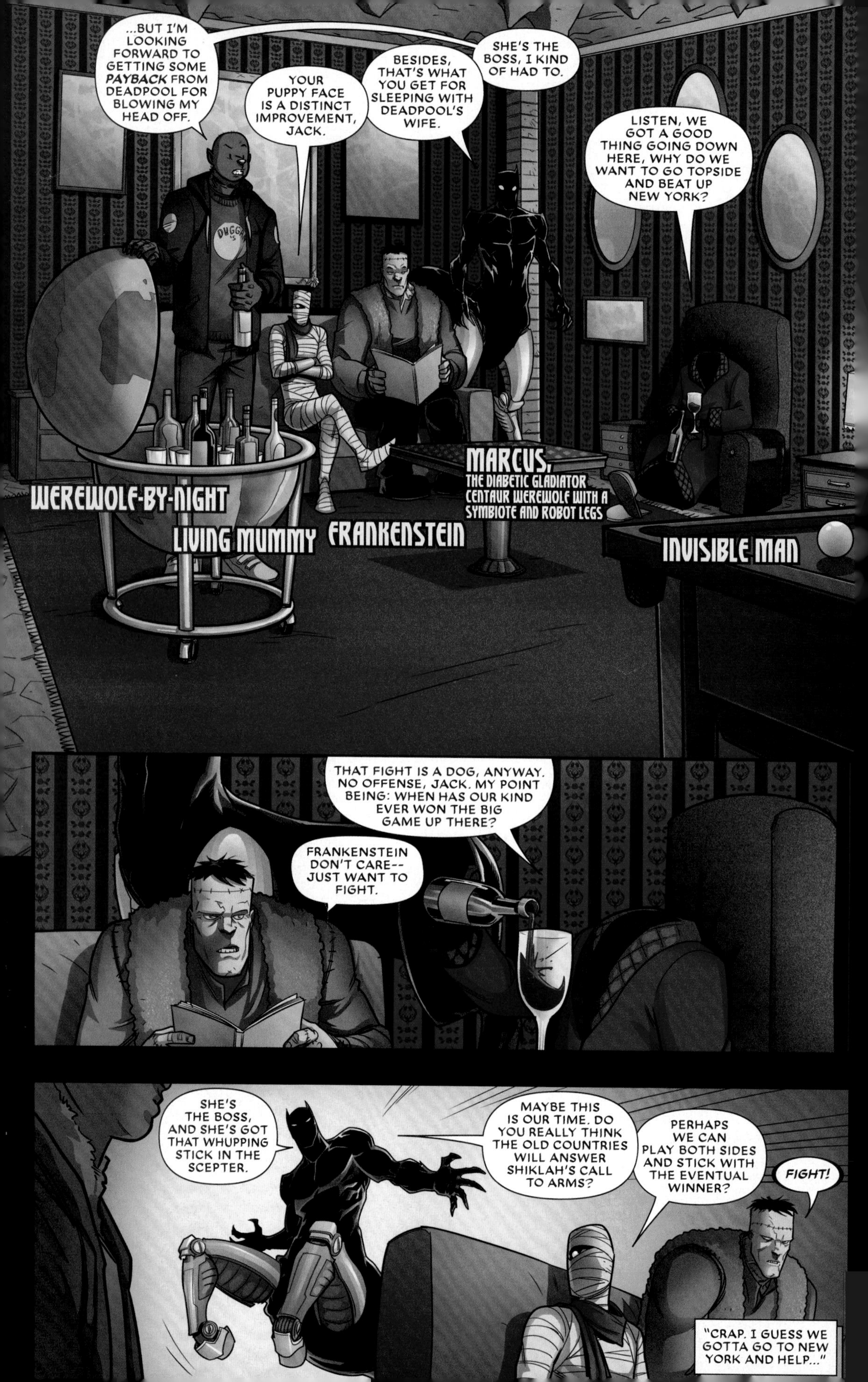

...BUT I'M LOOKING FORWARD TO GETTING SOME PAYBACK FROM DEADPOOL FOR BLOWING MY HEAD OFF.
YOUR PUPPY FACE IS A DISTINCT IMPROVEMENT, JACK.
BESIDES, THAT'S WHAT YOU GET FOR SLEEPING WITH DEADPOOL'S WIFE.
SHE'S THE BOSS, I KIND OF HAD TO.
LISTEN, WE GOT A GOOD THING GOING DOWN HERE, WHY DO WE WANT TO GO TOPSIDE AND BEAT UP NEW YORK?
WEREWOLF-BY-NIGHT
LIVING MUMMY
FRANKENSTEIN
MARCUS, THE DIABETIC GLADIATOR CENTAUR WEREWOLF WITH A SYMBIOTE AND ROBOT LEGS
INVISIBLE MAN
THAT FIGHT IS A DOG, ANYWAY. NO OFFENSE, JACK. MY POINT BEING: WHEN HAS OUR KIND EVER WON THE BIG GAME UP THERE?
FRANKENSTEIN DON'T CARE-- JUST WANT TO FIGHT.
SHE'S THE BOSS, AND SHE'S GOT THAT WHUPPING STICK IN THE SCEPTER.
MAYBE THIS IS OUR TIME. DO YOU REALLY THINK THE OLD COUNTRIES WILL ANSWER SHIKLAH'S CALL TO ARMS?
PERHAPS WE CAN PLAY BOTH SIDES AND STICK WITH THE EVENTUAL WINNER?
FIGHT!
"CRAP. I GUESS WE GOTTA GO TO NEW YORK AND HELP..."

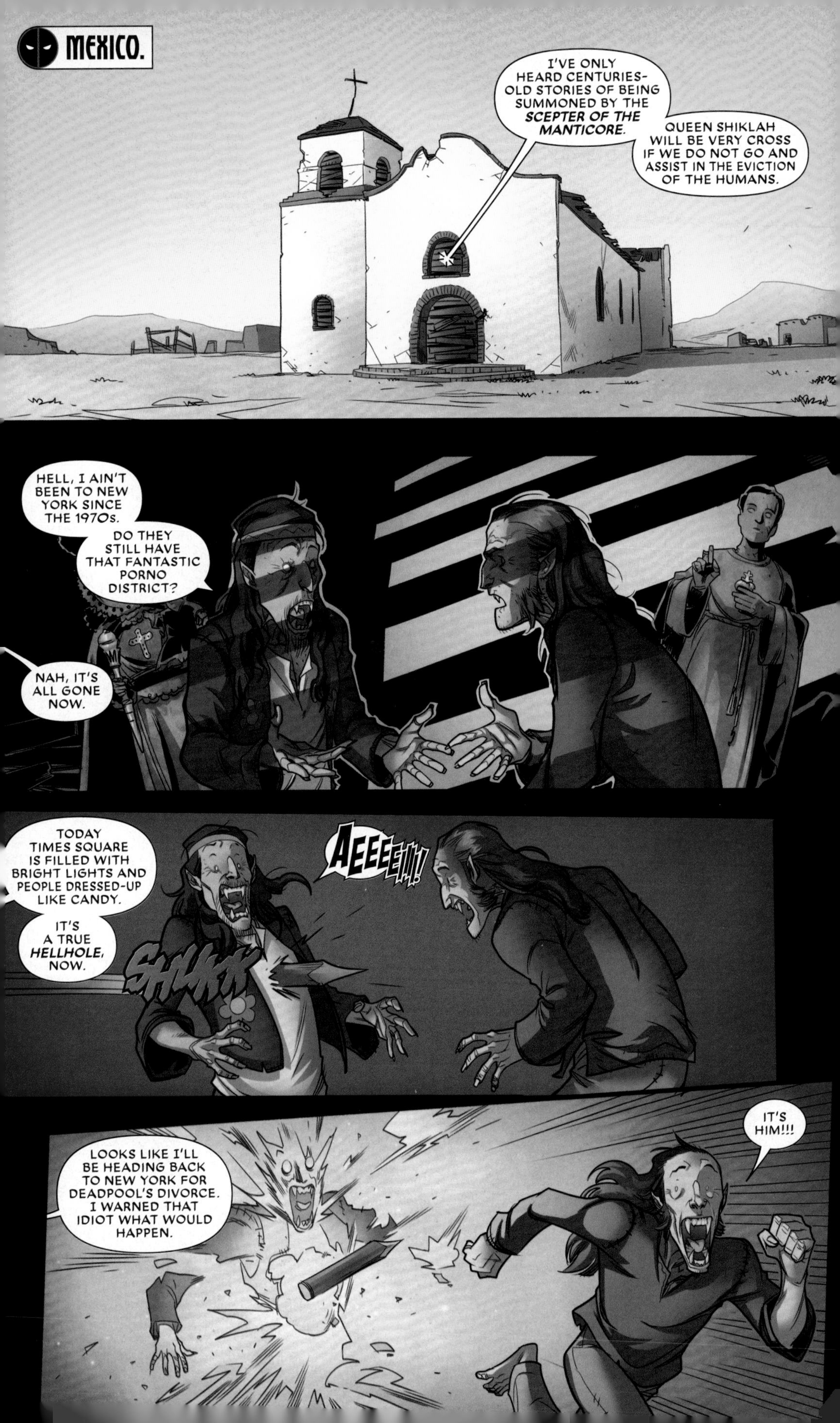
MEXICO.
I'VE ONLY HEARD CENTURIES-OLD STORIES OF BEING SUMMONED BY THE *SCEPTER OF THE MANTICORE*.
QUEEN SHIKLAH WILL BE VERY CROSS IF WE DO NOT GO AND ASSIST IN THE EVICTION OF THE HUMANS.
HELL, I AIN'T BEEN TO NEW YORK SINCE THE 1970s.
DO THEY STILL HAVE THAT FANTASTIC PORNO DISTRICT?
NAH, IT'S ALL GONE NOW.
TODAY TIMES SQUARE IS FILLED WITH BRIGHT LIGHTS AND PEOPLE DRESSED-UP LIKE CANDY.
IT'S A TRUE *HELLHOLE*, NOW.
AEEEEIII!
SHUKK
IT'S HIM!!!
LOOKS LIKE I'LL BE HEADING BACK TO NEW YORK FOR DEADPOOL'S DIVORCE. I WARNED THAT IDIOT WHAT WOULD HAPPEN.

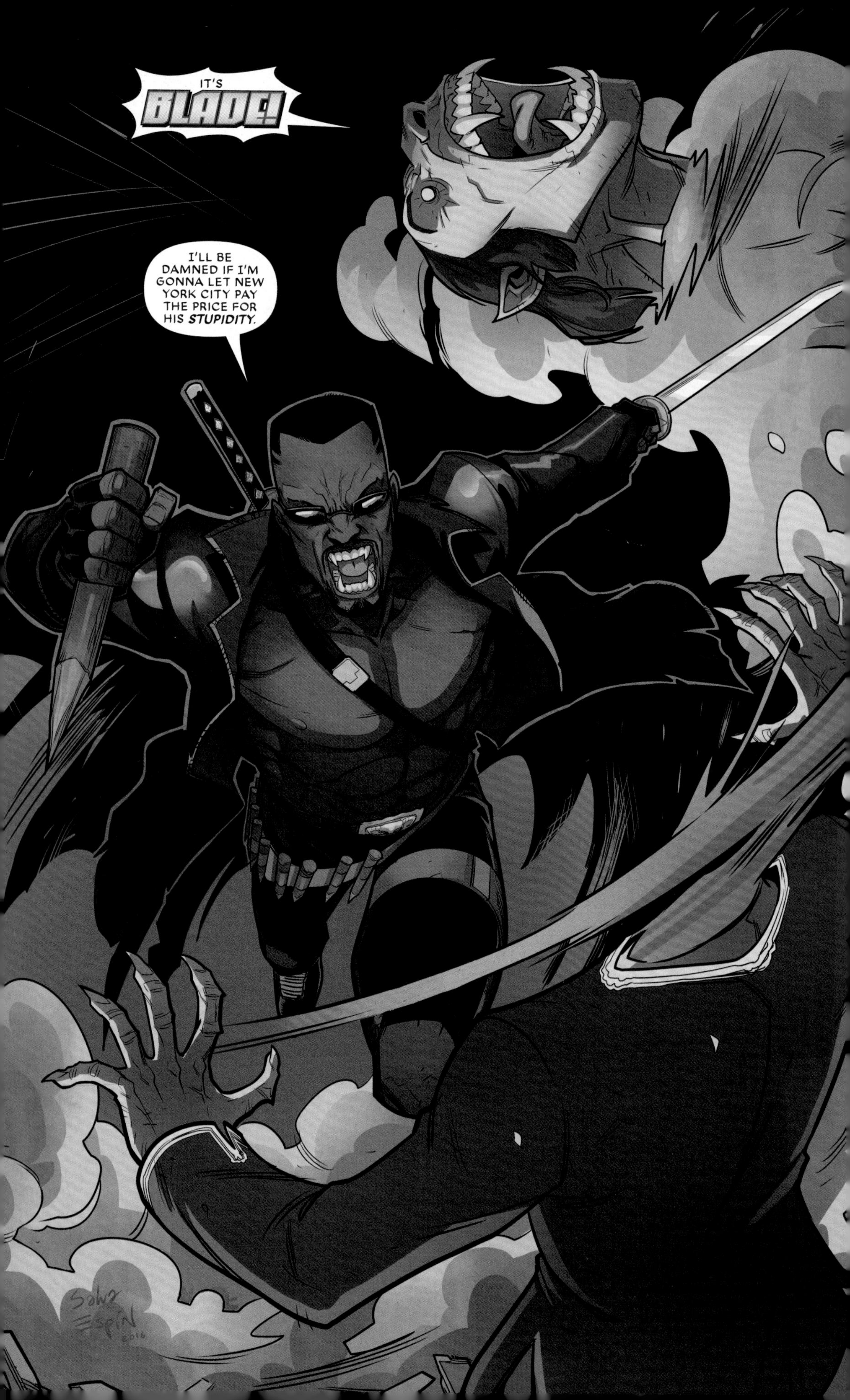
IT'S BLADE!
I'LL BE DAMNED IF I'M GONNA LET NEW YORK CITY PAY THE PRICE FOR HIS *STUPIDITY*.
Salva Espín 2016

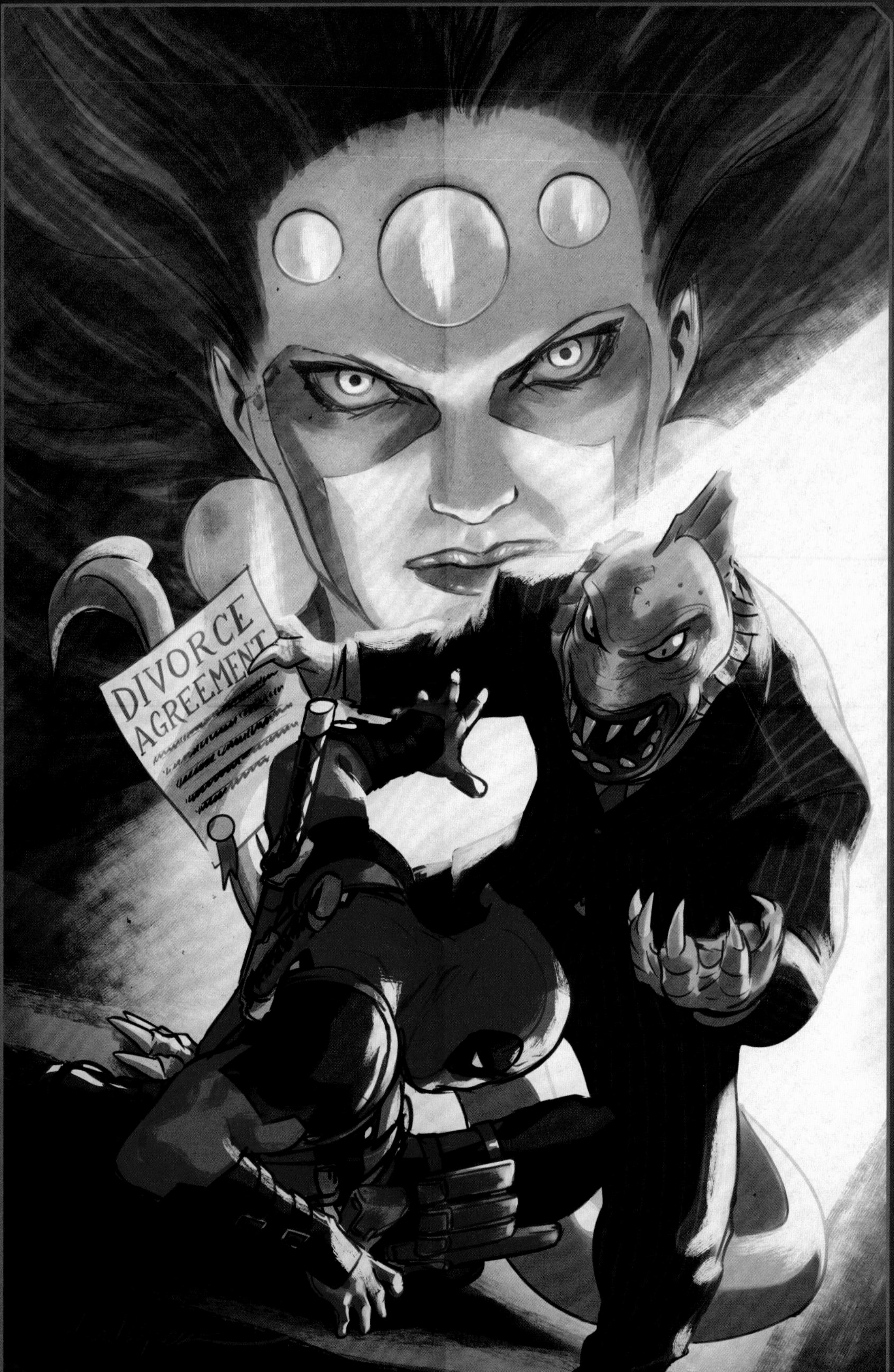
DIVORCE AGREEMENT

Deadpool #28 variant by DAVID LOPEZ

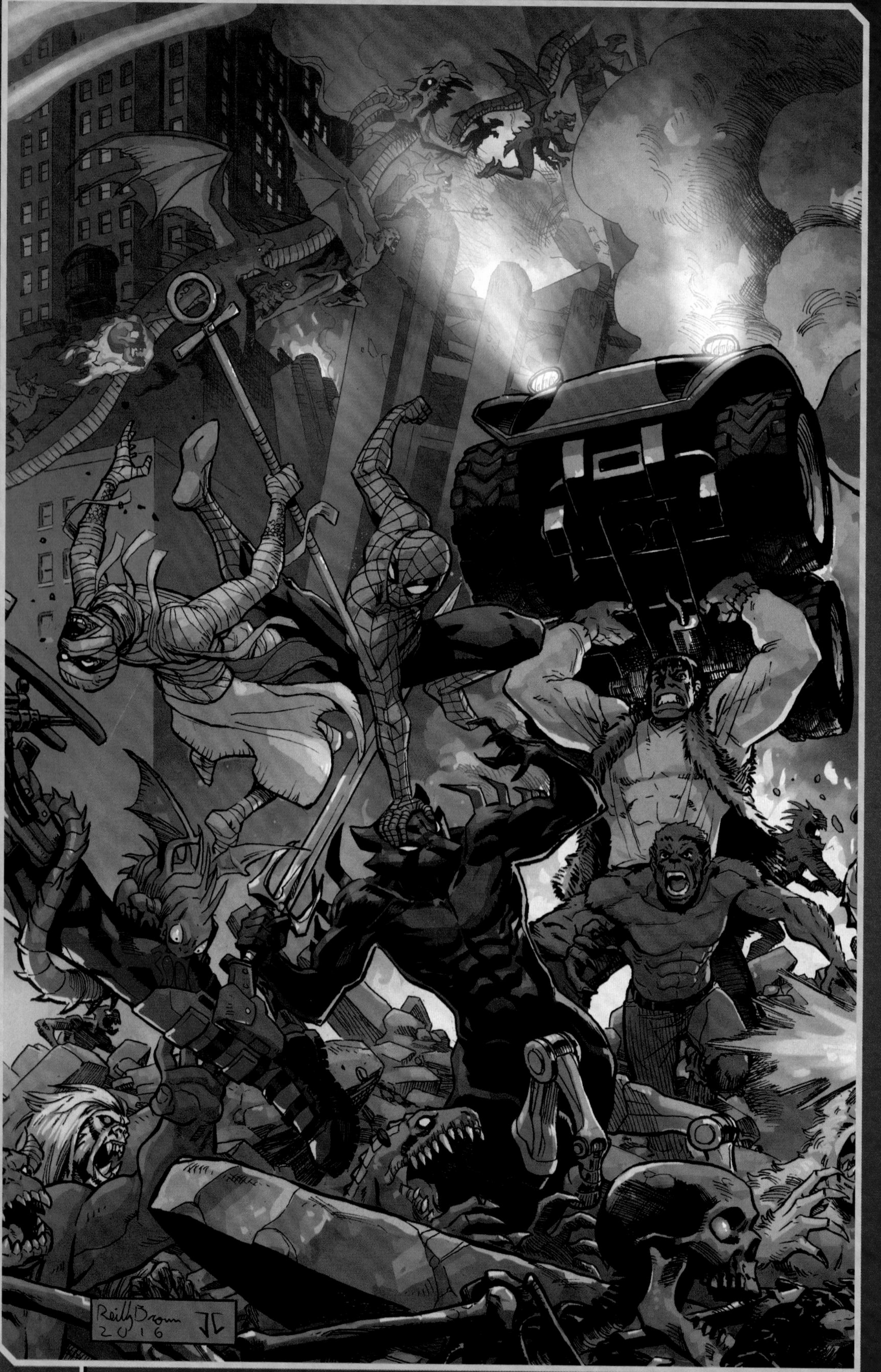
Reilly Brown
2016 JC

15 | SPIDER-MAN/DEADPOOL

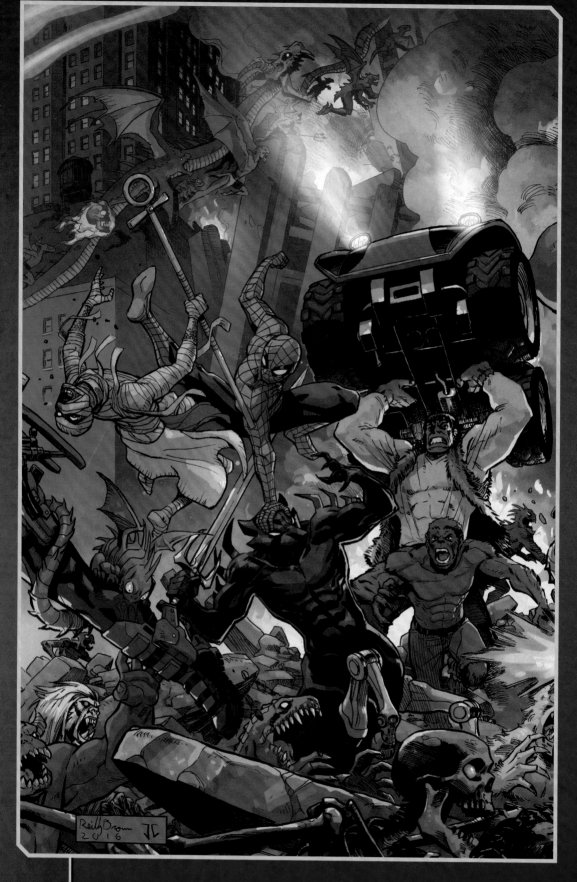

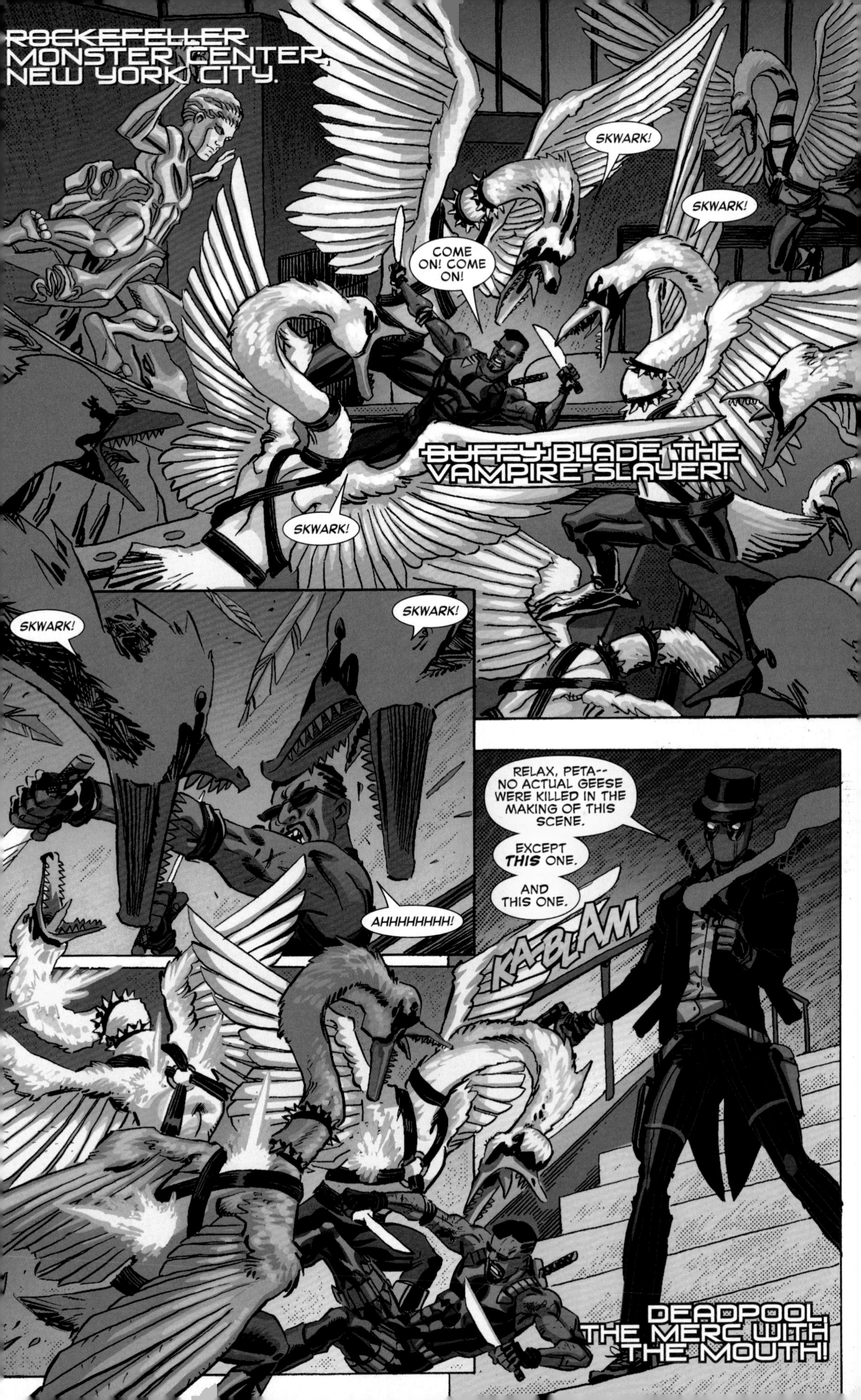

ROCKEFELLER MONSTER CENTER, NEW YORK CITY.
SKWARK!
SKWARK!
COME ON! COME ON!
~~BUFFY~~ BLADE THE VAMPIRE SLAYER!
SKWARK!
SKWARK!
SKWARK!
AHHHHHHHH!
RELAX, PETA--NO ACTUAL GEESE WERE KILLED IN THE MAKING OF THIS SCENE.
EXCEPT **THIS** ONE.
AND THIS ONE.
KA-BLAM
DEADPOOL, THE MERC WITH THE MOUTH!

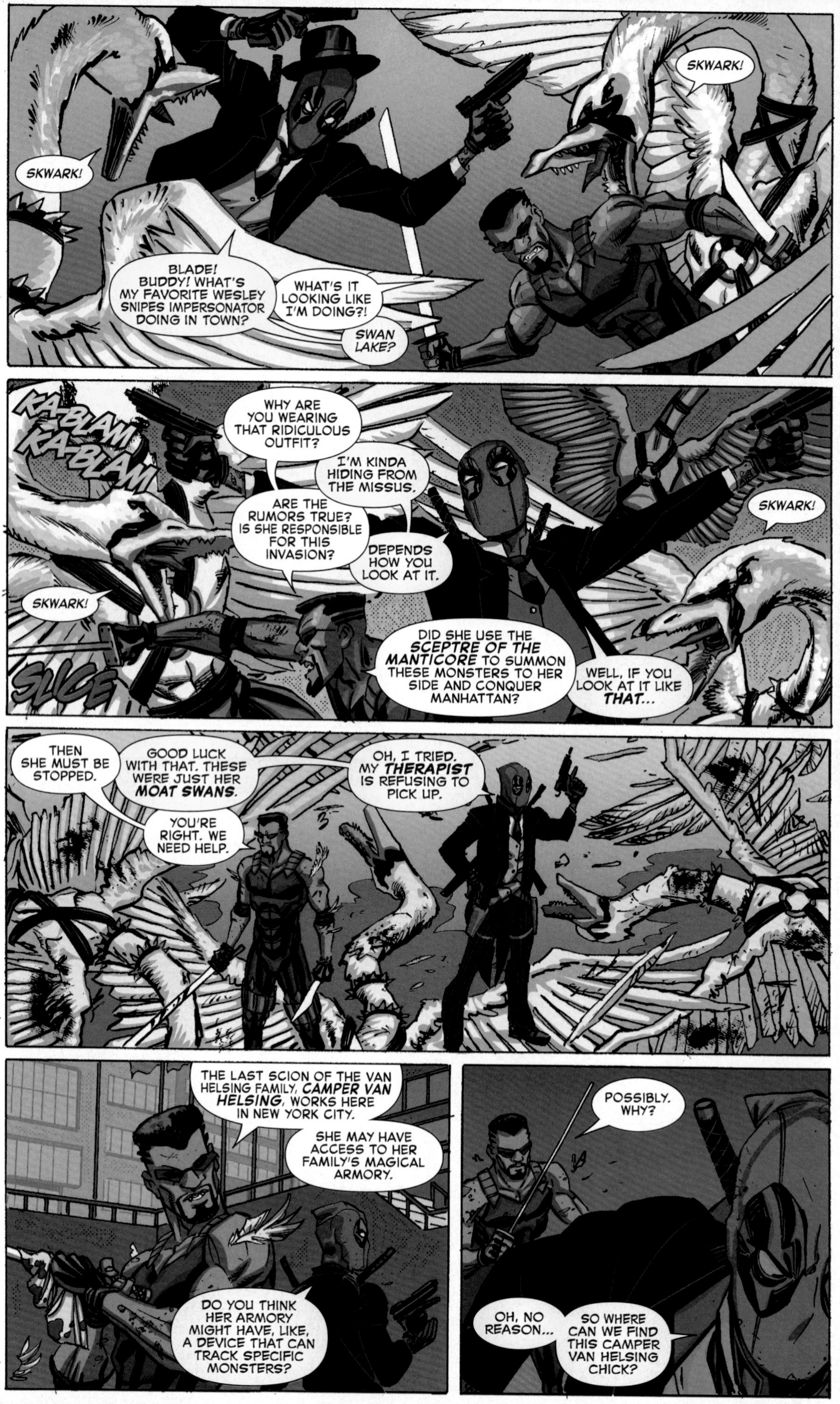
SKWARK!
SKWARK!
BLADE! BUDDY! WHAT'S MY FAVORITE WESLEY SNIPES IMPERSONATOR DOING IN TOWN?
WHAT'S IT LOOKING LIKE I'M DOING?!
SWAN LAKE?
KA-BLAM KA-BLAM
WHY ARE YOU WEARING THAT RIDICULOUS OUTFIT?
I'M KINDA HIDING FROM THE MISSUS.
SKWARK!
ARE THE RUMORS TRUE? IS SHE RESPONSIBLE FOR THIS INVASION?
DEPENDS HOW YOU LOOK AT IT.
SKWARK!
DID SHE USE THE SCEPTRE OF THE MANTICORE TO SUMMON THESE MONSTERS TO HER SIDE AND CONQUER MANHATTAN?
WELL, IF YOU LOOK AT IT LIKE THAT...
SLICE
THEN SHE MUST BE STOPPED.
GOOD LUCK WITH THAT. THESE WERE JUST HER MOAT SWANS.
OH, I TRIED. MY THERAPIST IS REFUSING TO PICK UP.
YOU'RE RIGHT. WE NEED HELP.
THE LAST SCION OF THE VAN HELSING FAMILY, CAMPER VAN HELSING, WORKS HERE IN NEW YORK CITY.
SHE MAY HAVE ACCESS TO HER FAMILY'S MAGICAL ARMORY.
DO YOU THINK HER ARMORY MIGHT HAVE, LIKE, A DEVICE THAT CAN TRACK SPECIFIC MONSTERS?
POSSIBLY. WHY?
OH, NO REASON...
SO WHERE CAN WE FIND THIS CAMPER VAN HELSING CHICK?

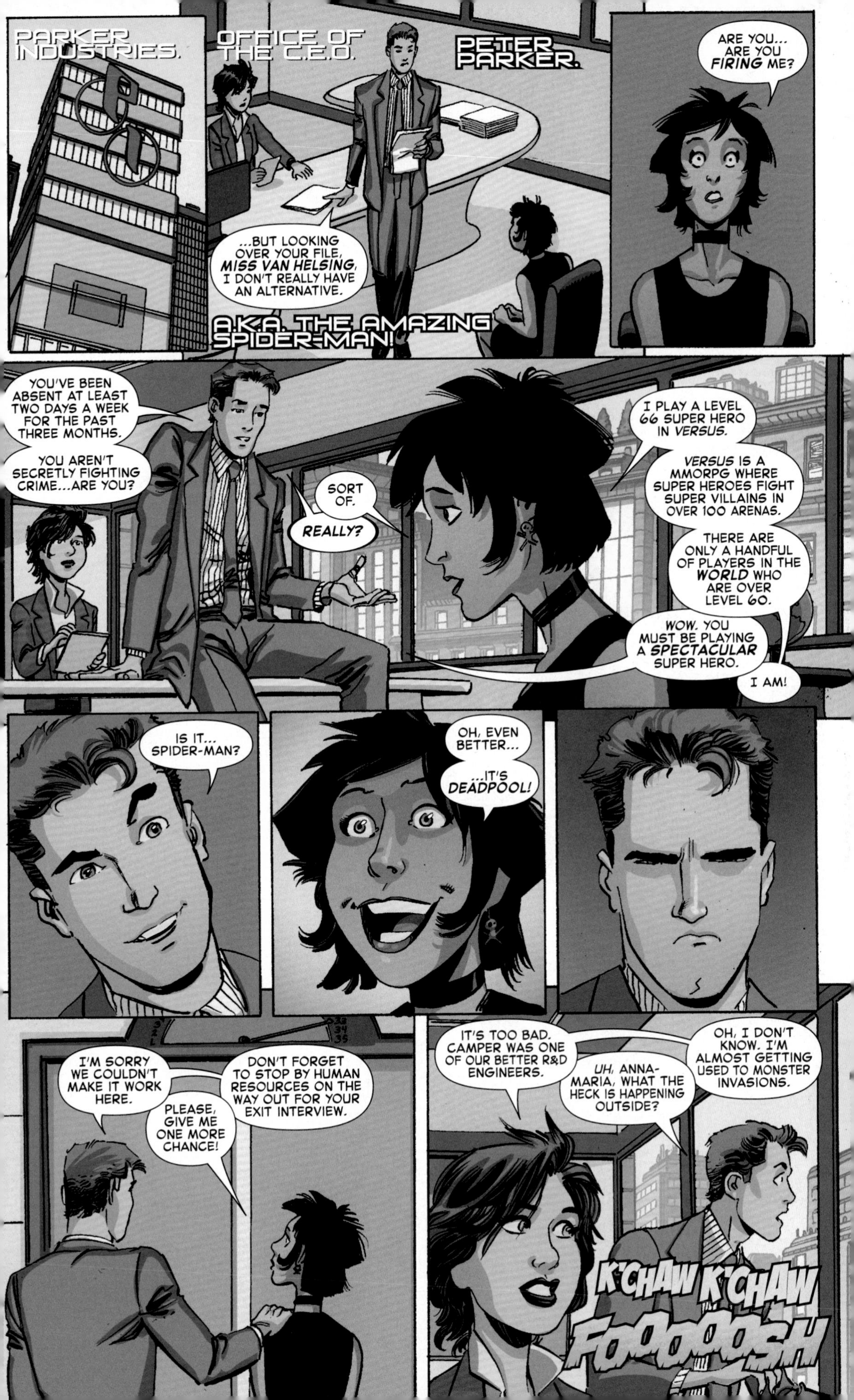
PARKER INDUSTRIES.
OFFICE OF THE C.E.O.
PETER PARKER.
...BUT LOOKING OVER YOUR FILE, MISS VAN HELSING, I DON'T REALLY HAVE AN ALTERNATIVE.
A.K.A. THE AMAZING SPIDER-MAN!
ARE YOU... ARE YOU FIRING ME?
YOU'VE BEEN ABSENT AT LEAST TWO DAYS A WEEK FOR THE PAST THREE MONTHS.
YOU AREN'T SECRETLY FIGHTING CRIME...ARE YOU?
SORT OF.
REALLY?
I PLAY A LEVEL 66 SUPER HERO IN VERSUS.
VERSUS IS A MMORPG WHERE SUPER HEROES FIGHT SUPER VILLAINS IN OVER 100 ARENAS.
THERE ARE ONLY A HANDFUL OF PLAYERS IN THE WORLD WHO ARE OVER LEVEL 60.
WOW. YOU MUST BE PLAYING A SPECTACULAR SUPER HERO.
I AM!
IS IT... SPIDER-MAN?
OH, EVEN BETTER...
...IT'S DEADPOOL!
I'M SORRY WE COULDN'T MAKE IT WORK HERE.
DON'T FORGET TO STOP BY HUMAN RESOURCES ON THE WAY OUT FOR YOUR EXIT INTERVIEW.
PLEASE, GIVE ME ONE MORE CHANCE!
IT'S TOO BAD. CAMPER WAS ONE OF OUR BETTER R&D ENGINEERS.
OH, I DON'T KNOW. I'M ALMOST GETTING USED TO MONSTER INVASIONS.
UH, ANNA-MARIA, WHAT THE HECK IS HAPPENING OUTSIDE?
K'CHAW K'CHAW
FOOOOOSH

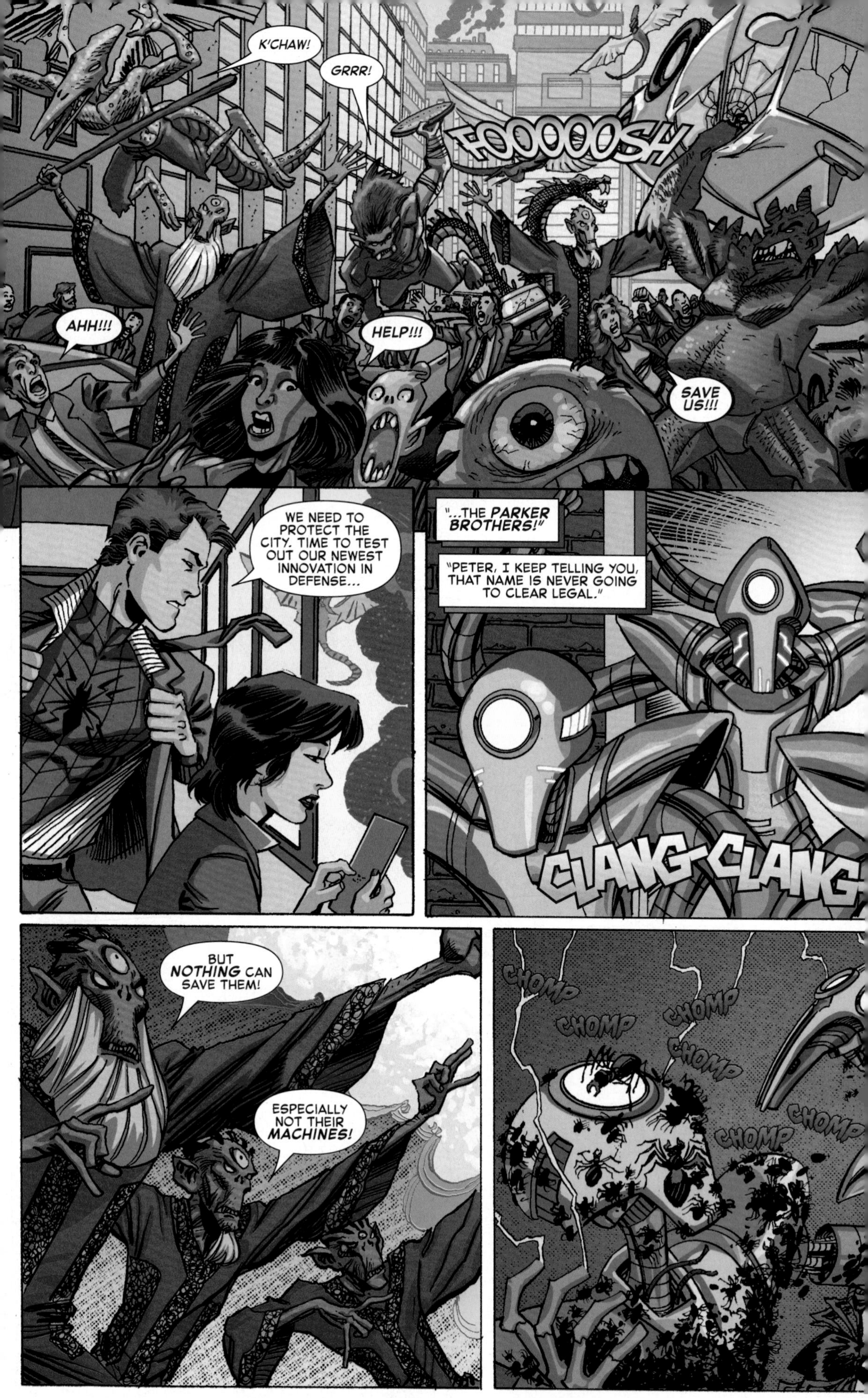
K'CHAW!
GRRR!
FOOOOOSH
AHH!!!
HELP!!!
SAVE US!!!
WE NEED TO PROTECT THE CITY. TIME TO TEST OUT OUR NEWEST INNOVATION IN DEFENSE...
"...THE PARKER BROTHERS!"
"PETER, I KEEP TELLING YOU, THAT NAME IS NEVER GOING TO CLEAR LEGAL."
CLANG-CLANG
BUT NOTHING CAN SAVE THEM!
ESPECIALLY NOT THEIR MACHINES!
CHOMP
CHOMP
CHOMP
CHOMP
CHOMP
CHOMP

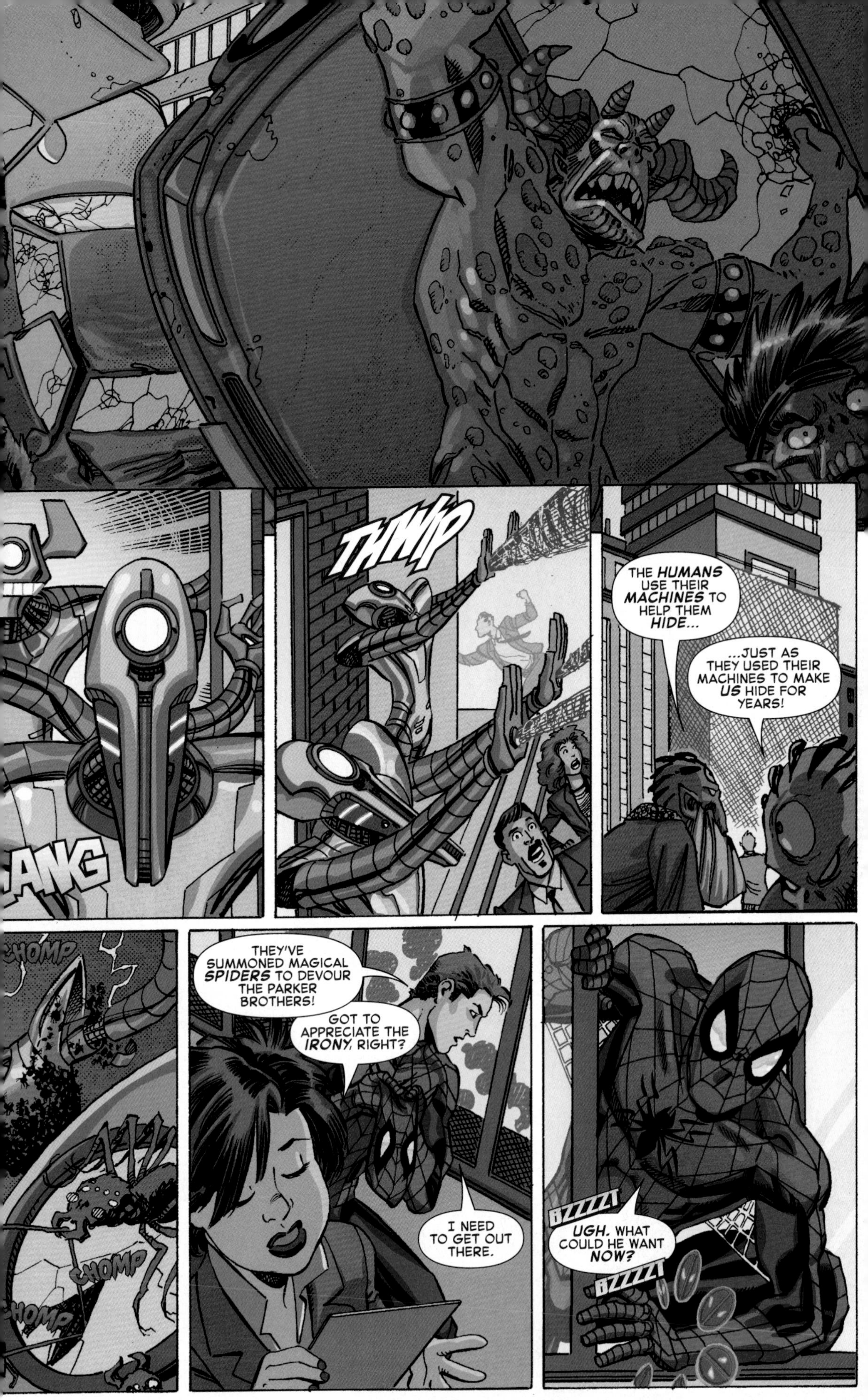

THWIP
ANG
THE HUMANS USE THEIR MACHINES TO HELP THEM HIDE...
...JUST AS THEY USED THEIR MACHINES TO MAKE US HIDE FOR YEARS!
CHOMP
CHOMP
CHOMP
THEY'VE SUMMONED MAGICAL SPIDERS TO DEVOUR THE PARKER BROTHERS!
GOT TO APPRECIATE THE IRONY, RIGHT?
I NEED TO GET OUT THERE.
BZZZZT
UGH. WHAT COULD HE WANT NOW?
BZZZZT

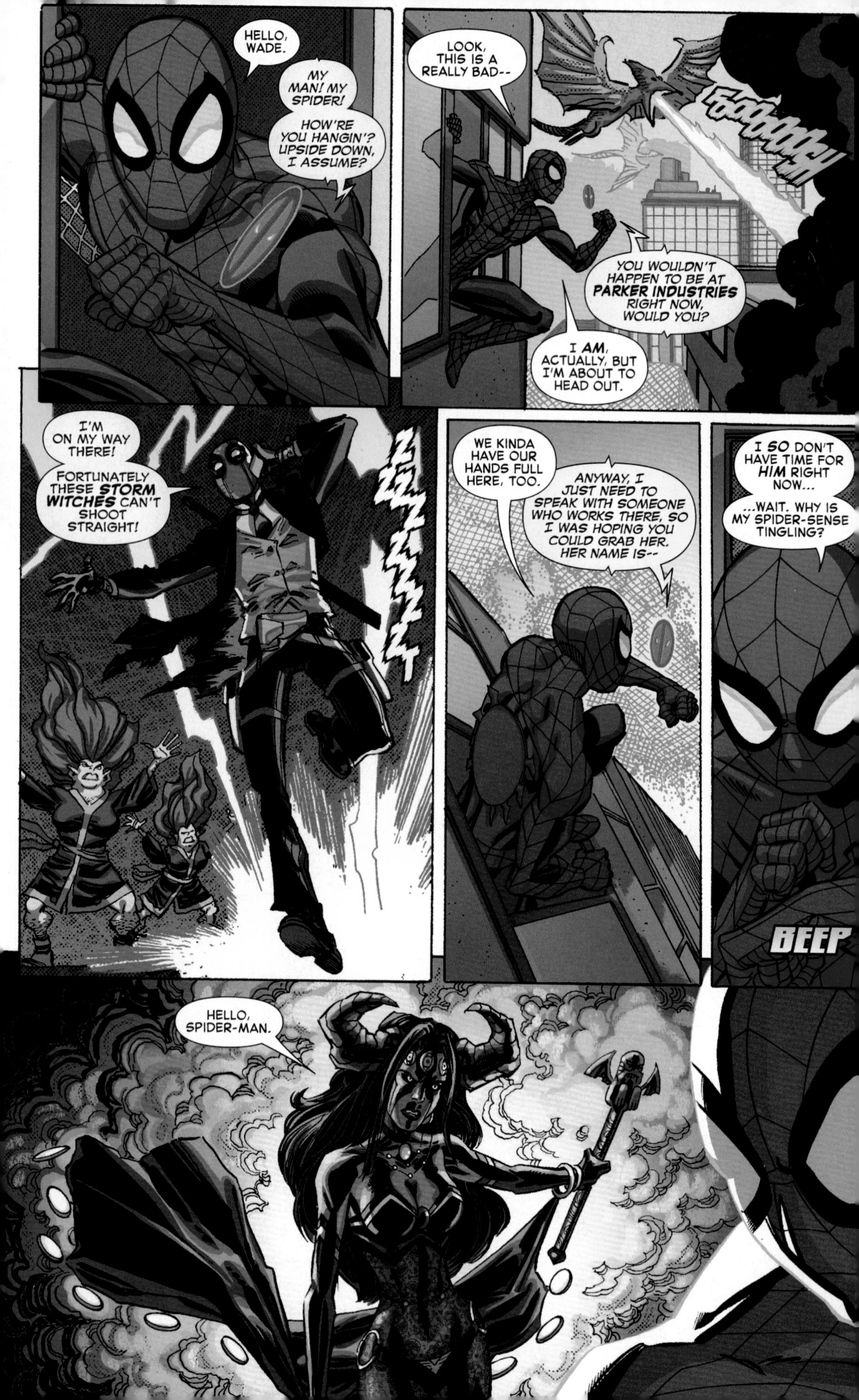

HELLO, WADE.
MY MAN! MY SPIDER!
HOW'RE YOU HANGIN'? UPSIDE DOWN, I ASSUME?
LOOK, THIS IS A REALLY BAD--
FOOOOOOOSH
YOU WOULDN'T HAPPEN TO BE AT PARKER INDUSTRIES RIGHT NOW, WOULD YOU?
I AM, ACTUALLY, BUT I'M ABOUT TO HEAD OUT.
I'M ON MY WAY THERE!
FORTUNATELY THESE STORM WITCHES CAN'T SHOOT STRAIGHT!
WE KINDA HAVE OUR HANDS FULL HERE, TOO.
ANYWAY, I JUST NEED TO SPEAK WITH SOMEONE WHO WORKS THERE, SO I WAS HOPING YOU COULD GRAB HER. HER NAME IS--
I SO DON'T HAVE TIME FOR HIM RIGHT NOW...
...WAIT. WHY IS MY SPIDER-SENSE TINGLING?
BEEP
HELLO, SPIDER-MAN.

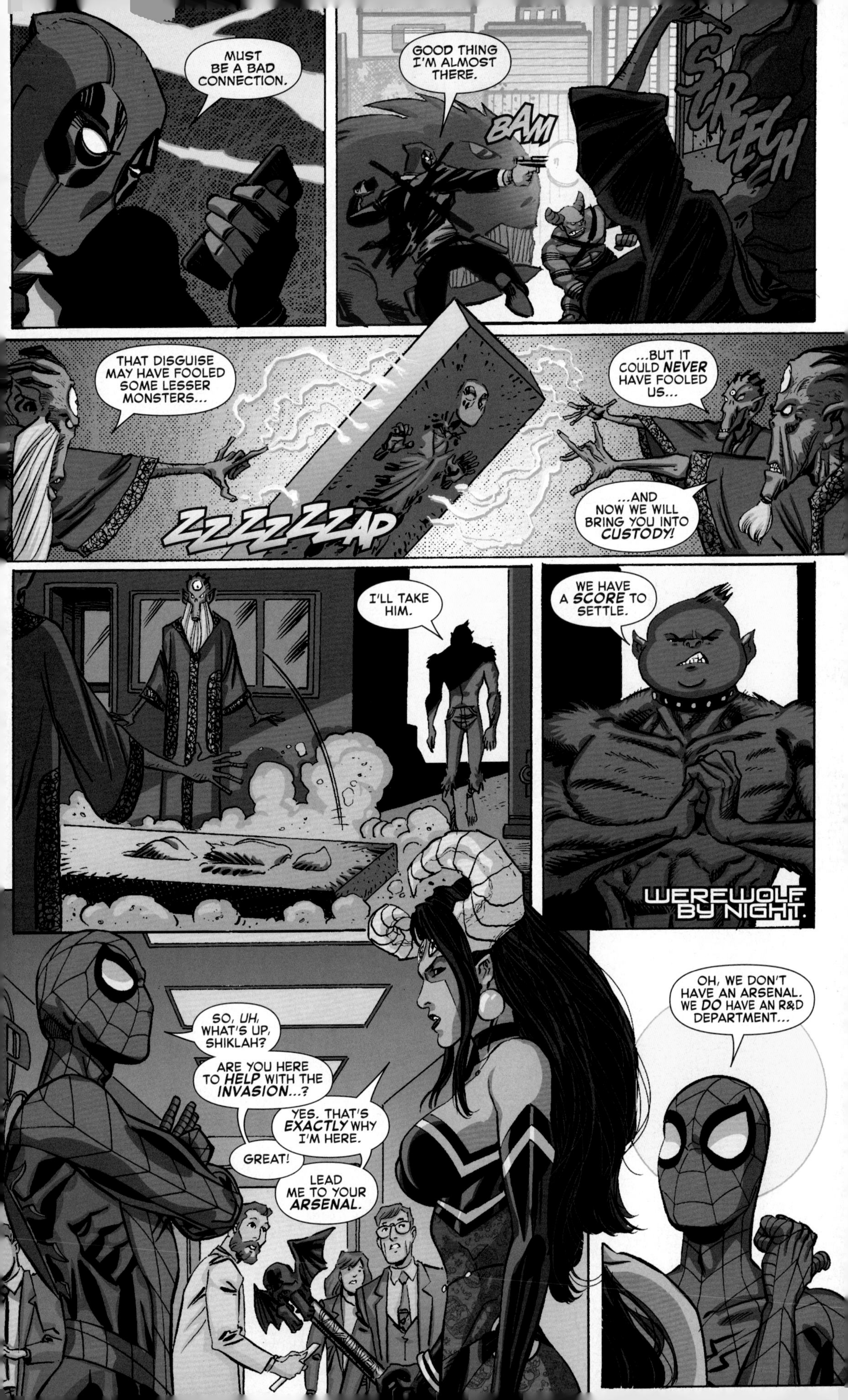
MUST BE A BAD CONNECTION.
GOOD THING I'M ALMOST THERE.
BAM
SCREECH
THAT DISGUISE MAY HAVE FOOLED SOME LESSER MONSTERS...
...BUT IT COULD NEVER HAVE FOOLED US...
...AND NOW WE WILL BRING YOU INTO CUSTODY!
ZZZZZZZAP
I'LL TAKE HIM.
WE HAVE A SCORE TO SETTLE.
WEREWOLF BY NIGHT.
SO, UH, WHAT'S UP, SHIKLAH?
ARE YOU HERE TO HELP WITH THE INVASION...?
YES. THAT'S EXACTLY WHY I'M HERE.
GREAT!
LEAD ME TO YOUR ARSENAL.
OH, WE DON'T HAVE AN ARSENAL. WE DO HAVE AN R&D DEPARTMENT...

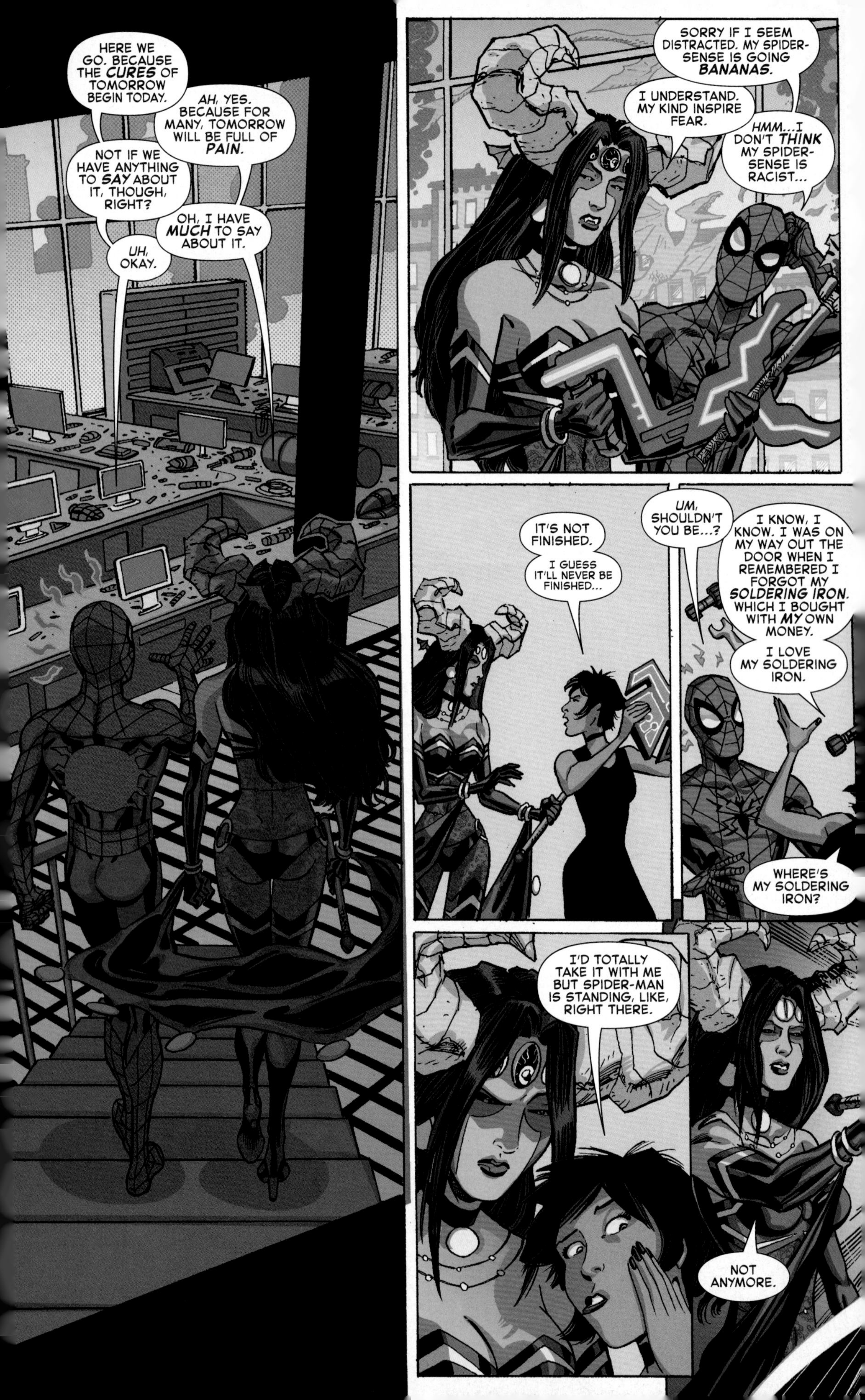
HERE WE GO. BECAUSE THE *CURES* OF TOMORROW BEGIN TODAY.
AH, YES. BECAUSE FOR MANY, TOMORROW WILL BE FULL OF ***PAIN.***
NOT IF WE HAVE ANYTHING TO ***SAY*** ABOUT IT, THOUGH, RIGHT?
OH, I HAVE ***MUCH*** TO SAY ABOUT IT.
UH, OKAY.
SORRY IF I SEEM DISTRACTED. MY SPIDER-SENSE IS GOING ***BANANAS.***
I UNDERSTAND. MY KIND INSPIRE FEAR.
*HMM...*I DON'T ***THINK*** MY SPIDER-SENSE IS RACIST...
IT'S NOT FINISHED.
I GUESS IT'LL NEVER BE FINISHED...
UM, SHOULDN'T YOU BE...?
I KNOW, I KNOW. I WAS ON MY WAY OUT THE DOOR WHEN I REMEMBERED I FORGOT MY ***SOLDERING IRON.*** WHICH I BOUGHT WITH ***MY*** OWN MONEY.
I LOVE MY SOLDERING IRON.
WHERE'S MY SOLDERING IRON?
I'D TOTALLY TAKE IT WITH ME BUT SPIDER-MAN IS STANDING, LIKE, RIGHT THERE.
NOT ANYMORE.

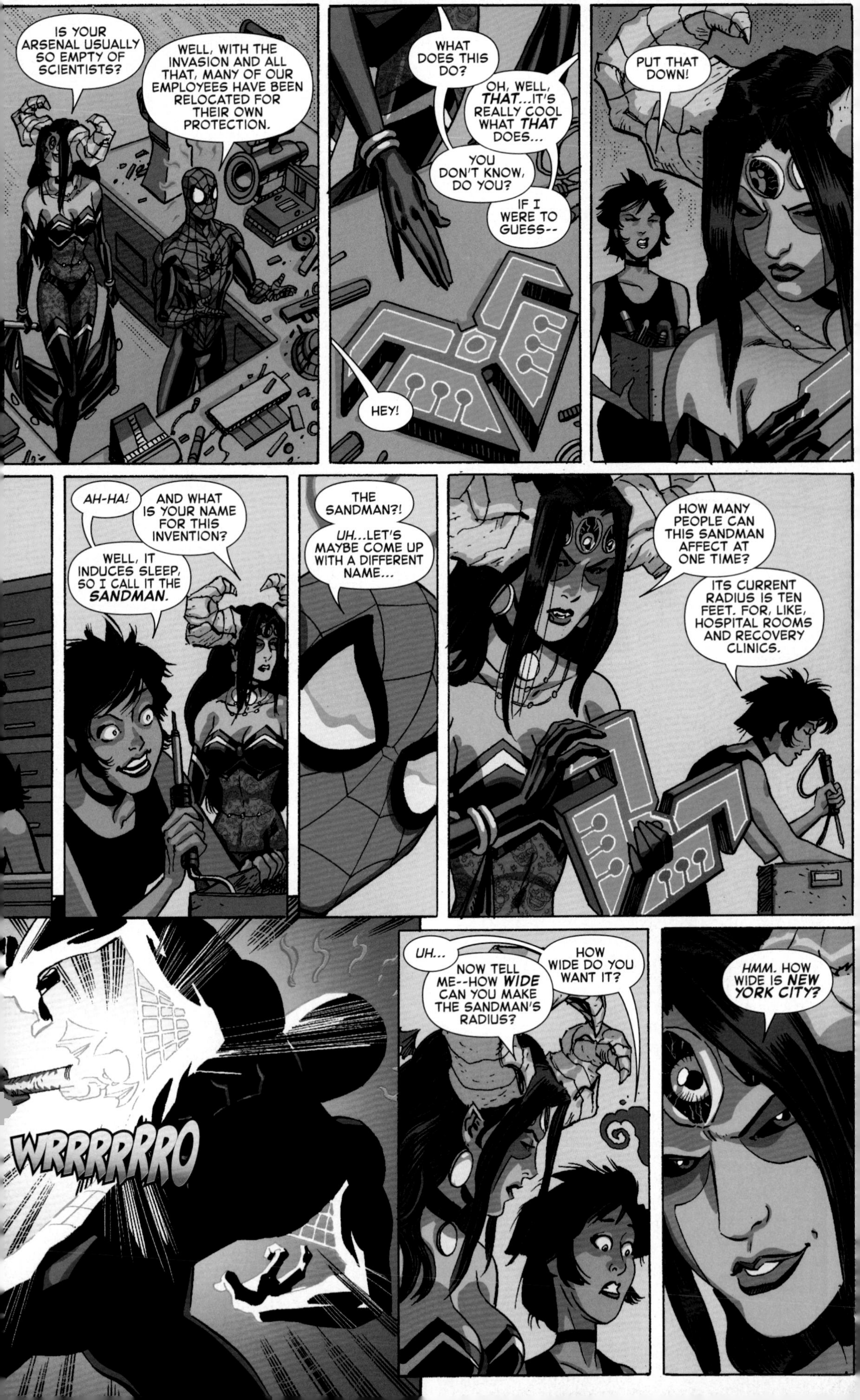
IS YOUR ARSENAL USUALLY SO EMPTY OF SCIENTISTS?
WELL, WITH THE INVASION AND ALL THAT, MANY OF OUR EMPLOYEES HAVE BEEN RELOCATED FOR THEIR OWN PROTECTION.
WHAT DOES THIS DO?
OH, WELL, *THAT*...IT'S REALLY COOL WHAT *THAT* DOES...
YOU DON'T KNOW, DO YOU?
IF I WERE TO GUESS--
HEY!
PUT THAT DOWN!
AH-HA!
AND WHAT IS YOUR NAME FOR THIS INVENTION?
WELL, IT INDUCES SLEEP, SO I CALL IT THE ***SANDMAN.***
THE SANDMAN?!
UH...LET'S MAYBE COME UP WITH A DIFFERENT NAME...
HOW MANY PEOPLE CAN THIS SANDMAN AFFECT AT ONE TIME?
ITS CURRENT RADIUS IS TEN FEET. FOR, LIKE, HOSPITAL ROOMS AND RECOVERY CLINICS.
WRRRRRRO
UH...
NOW TELL ME--HOW *WIDE* CAN YOU MAKE THE SANDMAN'S RADIUS?
HOW WIDE DO YOU WANT IT?
HMM. HOW WIDE IS ***NEW YORK CITY?***

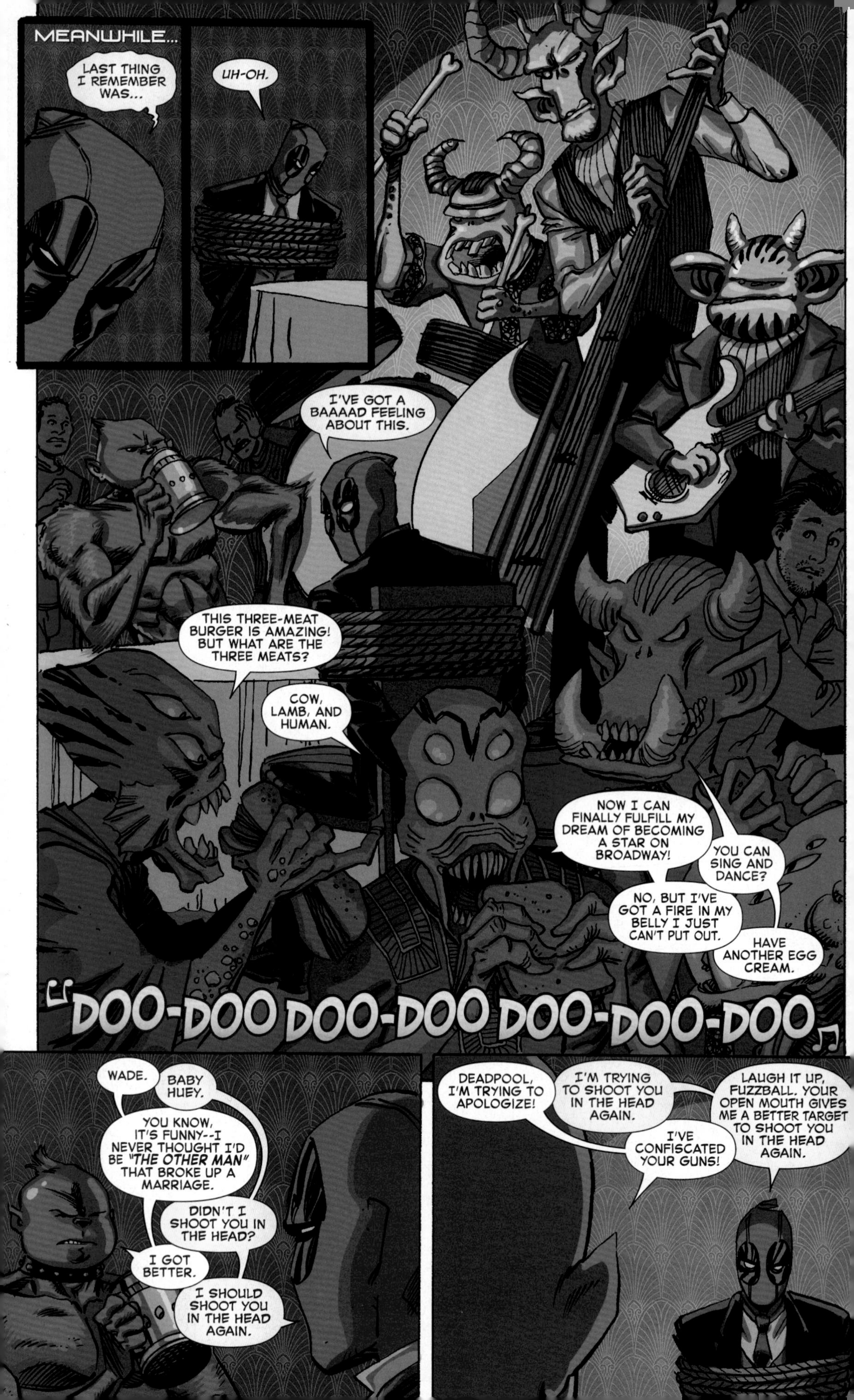
MEANWHILE...
LAST THING I REMEMBER WAS...
UH-OH.
I'VE GOT A BAAAAD FEELING ABOUT THIS.
THIS THREE-MEAT BURGER IS AMAZING! BUT WHAT ARE THE THREE MEATS?
COW, LAMB, AND HUMAN.
NOW I CAN FINALLY FULFILL MY DREAM OF BECOMING A STAR ON BROADWAY!
YOU CAN SING AND DANCE?
NO, BUT I'VE GOT A FIRE IN MY BELLY I JUST CAN'T PUT OUT.
HAVE ANOTHER EGG CREAM.
DOO-DOO DOO-DOO DOO-DOO-DOO
WADE.
BABY HUEY.
YOU KNOW, IT'S FUNNY--I NEVER THOUGHT I'D BE "THE OTHER MAN" THAT BROKE UP A MARRIAGE.
DIDN'T I SHOOT YOU IN THE HEAD?
I GOT BETTER.
I SHOULD SHOOT YOU IN THE HEAD AGAIN.
DEADPOOL, I'M TRYING TO APOLOGIZE!
I'M TRYING TO SHOOT YOU IN THE HEAD AGAIN.
I'VE CONFISCATED YOUR GUNS!
LAUGH IT UP, FUZZBALL. YOUR OPEN MOUTH GIVES ME A BETTER TARGET TO SHOOT YOU IN THE HEAD AGAIN.

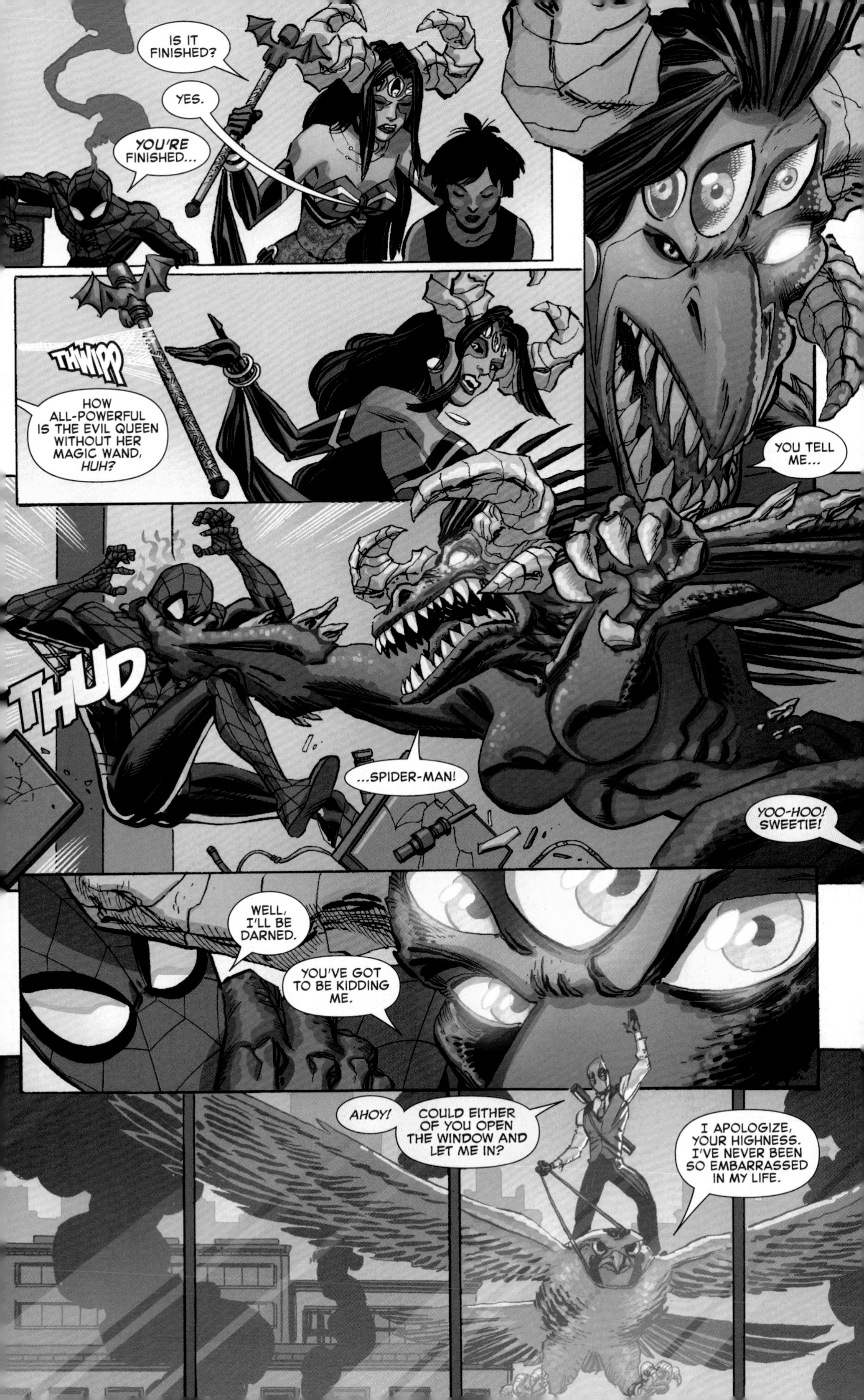
IS IT FINISHED?
YES.
YOU'RE FINISHED...
THWIPP
HOW ALL-POWERFUL IS THE EVIL QUEEN WITHOUT HER MAGIC WAND, HUH?
YOU TELL ME...
THUD
...SPIDER-MAN!
YOO-HOO! SWEETIE!
WELL, I'LL BE DARNED.
YOU'VE GOT TO BE KIDDING ME.
AHOY!
COULD EITHER OF YOU OPEN THE WINDOW AND LET ME IN?
I APOLOGIZE, YOUR HIGHNESS. I'VE NEVER BEEN SO EMBARRASSED IN MY LIFE.

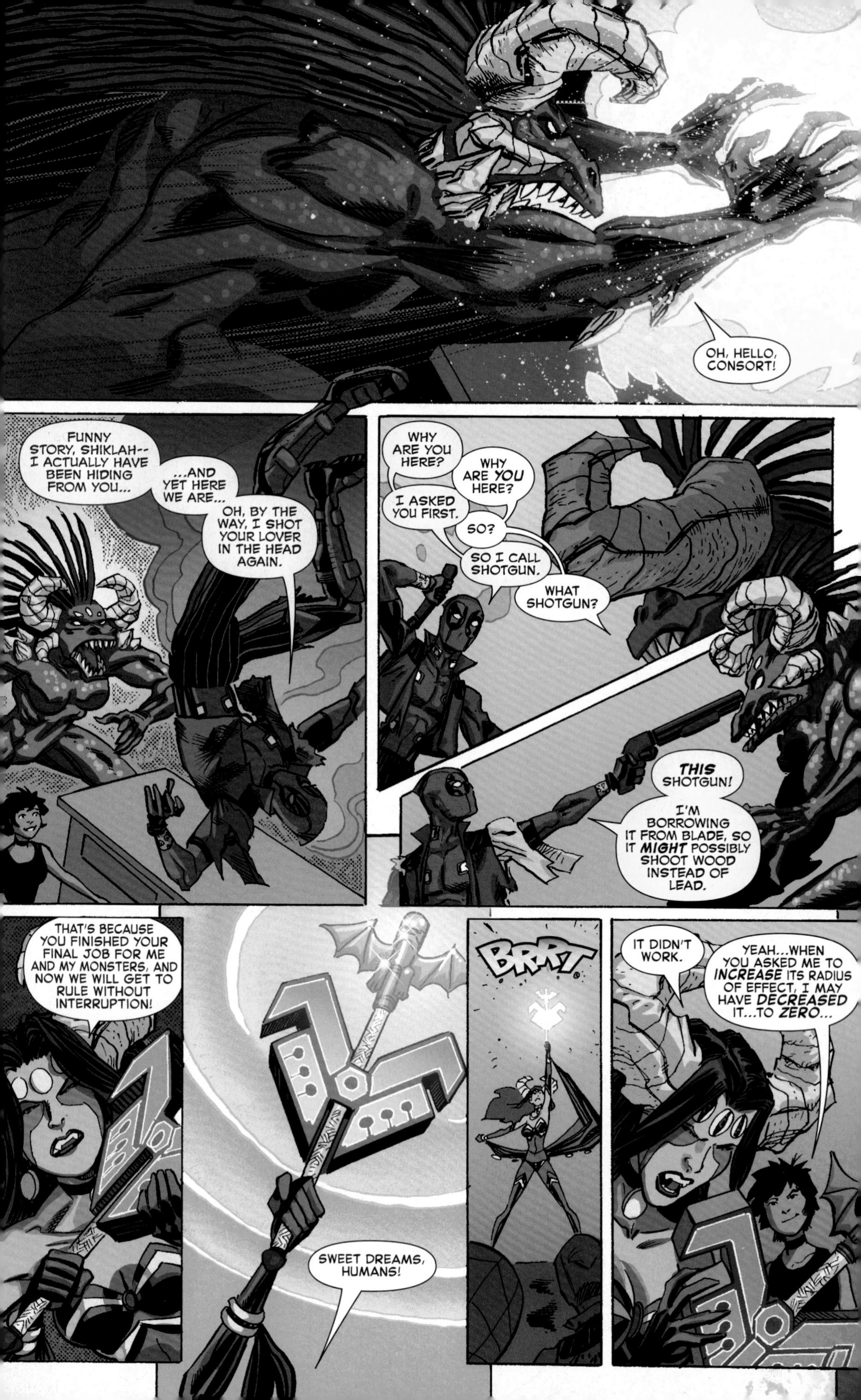
OH, HELLO, CONSORT!
FUNNY STORY, SHIKLAH-- I ACTUALLY HAVE BEEN HIDING FROM YOU...
...AND YET HERE WE ARE...
OH, BY THE WAY, I SHOT YOUR LOVER IN THE HEAD AGAIN.
WHY ARE YOU HERE?
WHY ARE YOU HERE?
I ASKED YOU FIRST.
SO?
SO I CALL SHOTGUN.
WHAT SHOTGUN?
THIS SHOTGUN!
I'M BORROWING IT FROM BLADE, SO IT MIGHT POSSIBLY SHOOT WOOD INSTEAD OF LEAD.
THAT'S BECAUSE YOU FINISHED YOUR FINAL JOB FOR ME AND MY MONSTERS, AND NOW WE WILL GET TO RULE WITHOUT INTERRUPTION!
SWEET DREAMS, HUMANS!
BRRRT
IT DIDN'T WORK.
YEAH...WHEN YOU ASKED ME TO INCREASE ITS RADIUS OF EFFECT, I MAY HAVE DECREASED IT...TO ZERO...

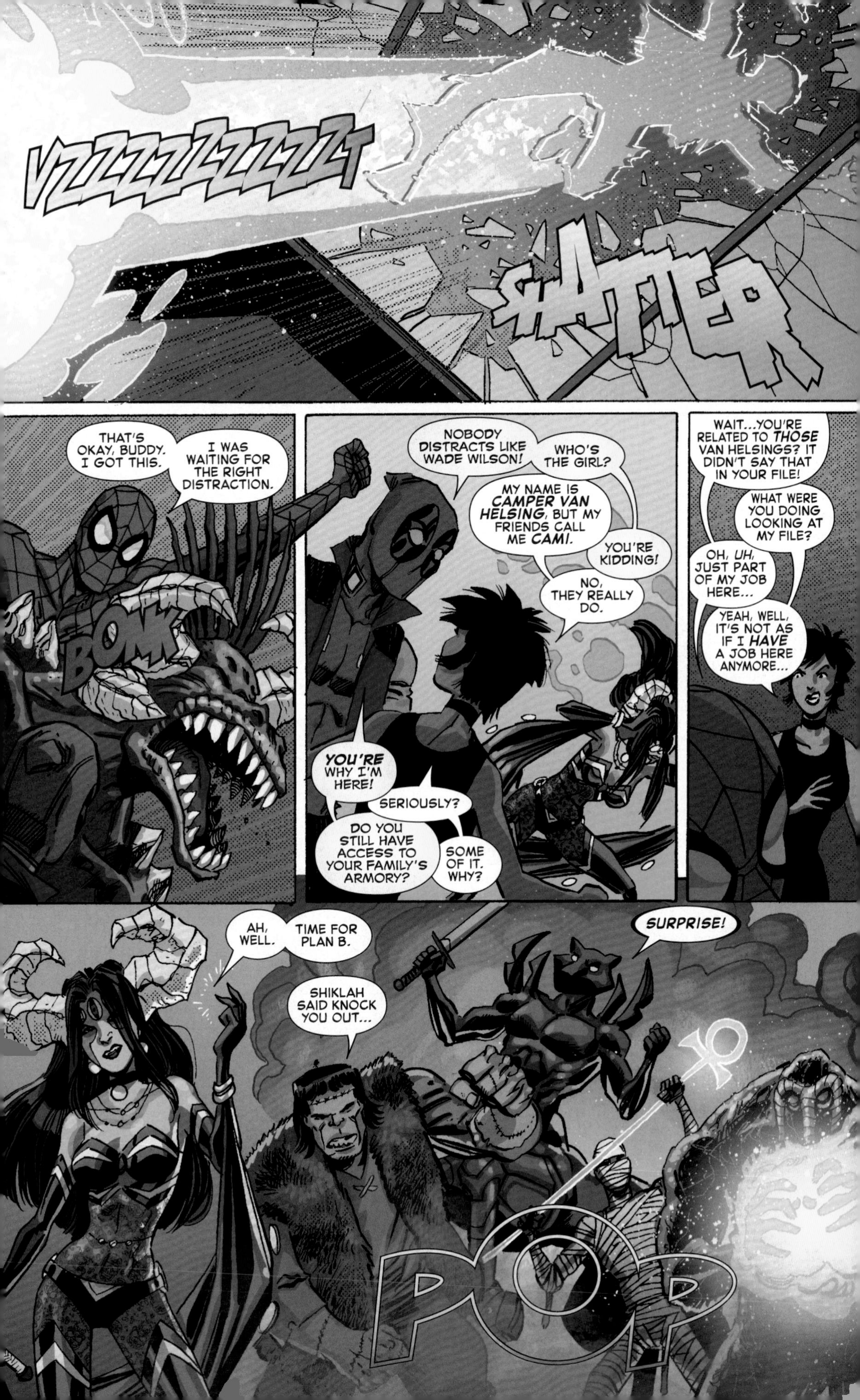
VZZZZZZZZZZZT
SHATTER
THAT'S OKAY, BUDDY. I GOT THIS.
I WAS WAITING FOR THE RIGHT DISTRACTION.
BOM
NOBODY DISTRACTS LIKE WADE WILSON!
WHO'S THE GIRL?
MY NAME IS CAMPER VAN HELSING, BUT MY FRIENDS CALL ME CAMI.
YOU'RE KIDDING!
NO, THEY REALLY DO.
YOU'RE WHY I'M HERE!
SERIOUSLY?
DO YOU STILL HAVE ACCESS TO YOUR FAMILY'S ARMORY?
SOME OF IT. WHY?
WAIT...YOU'RE RELATED TO THOSE VAN HELSINGS? IT DIDN'T SAY THAT IN YOUR FILE!
WHAT WERE YOU DOING LOOKING AT MY FILE?
OH, UH, JUST PART OF MY JOB HERE...
YEAH, WELL, IT'S NOT AS IF I HAVE A JOB HERE ANYMORE...
AH, WELL.
TIME FOR PLAN B.
SURPRISE!
SHIKLAH SAID KNOCK YOU OUT...
POP

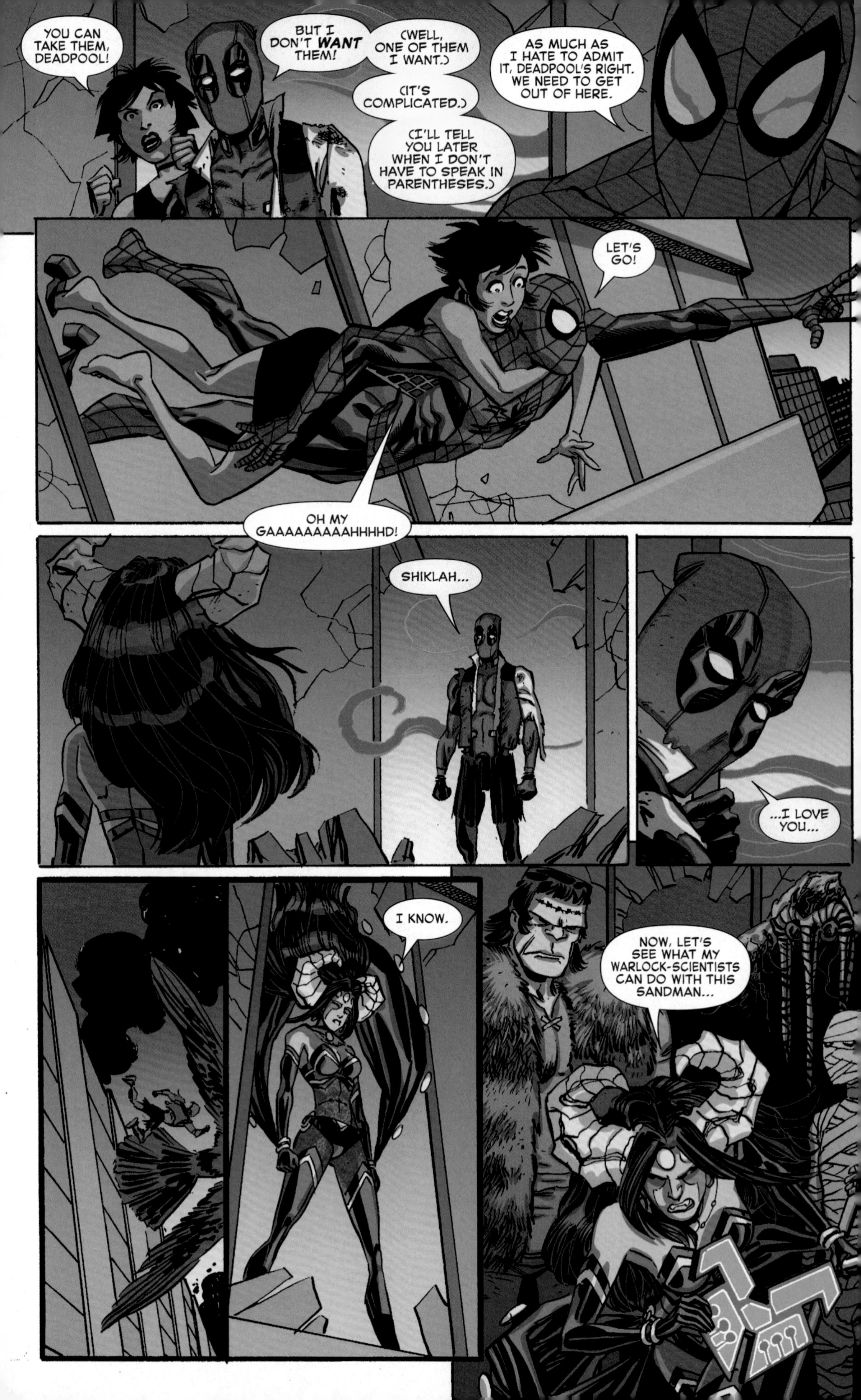
YOU CAN TAKE THEM, DEADPOOL!
BUT I DON'T *WANT* THEM!
(WELL, ONE OF THEM I WANT.)
(IT'S COMPLICATED.)
(I'LL TELL YOU LATER WHEN I DON'T HAVE TO SPEAK IN PARENTHESES.)
AS MUCH AS I HATE TO ADMIT IT, DEADPOOL'S RIGHT. WE NEED TO GET OUT OF HERE.
LET'S GO!
OH MY GAAAAAAAAAHHHHD!
SHIKLAH...
...I LOVE YOU...
I KNOW.
NOW, LET'S SEE WHAT MY WARLOCK-SCIENTISTS CAN DO WITH THIS SANDMAN...

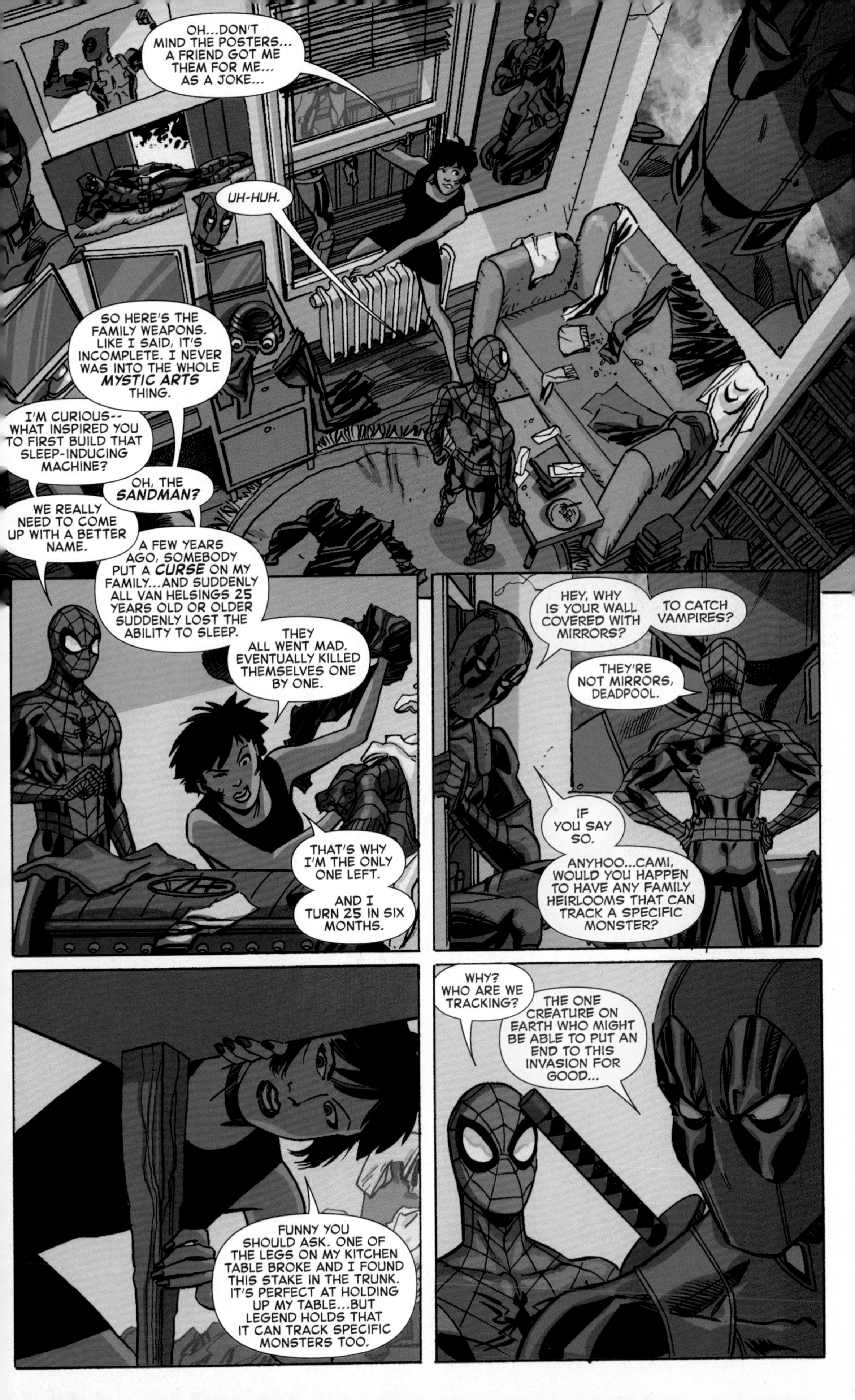
OH...DON'T MIND THE POSTERS... A FRIEND GOT ME THEM FOR ME... AS A JOKE...
UH-HUH.
SO HERE'S THE FAMILY WEAPONS. LIKE I SAID, IT'S INCOMPLETE. I NEVER WAS INTO THE WHOLE MYSTIC ARTS THING.
I'M CURIOUS-- WHAT INSPIRED YOU TO FIRST BUILD THAT SLEEP-INDUCING MACHINE?
OH, THE SANDMAN?
WE REALLY NEED TO COME UP WITH A BETTER NAME.
A FEW YEARS AGO, SOMEBODY PUT A CURSE ON MY FAMILY...AND SUDDENLY ALL VAN HELSINGS 25 YEARS OLD OR OLDER SUDDENLY LOST THE ABILITY TO SLEEP.
THEY ALL WENT MAD. EVENTUALLY KILLED THEMSELVES ONE BY ONE.
THAT'S WHY I'M THE ONLY ONE LEFT.
AND I TURN 25 IN SIX MONTHS.
HEY, WHY IS YOUR WALL COVERED WITH MIRRORS?
TO CATCH VAMPIRES?
THEY'RE NOT MIRRORS, DEADPOOL.
IF YOU SAY SO.
ANYHOO...CAMI, WOULD YOU HAPPEN TO HAVE ANY FAMILY HEIRLOOMS THAT CAN TRACK A SPECIFIC MONSTER?
FUNNY YOU SHOULD ASK. ONE OF THE LEGS ON MY KITCHEN TABLE BROKE AND I FOUND THIS STAKE IN THE TRUNK. IT'S PERFECT AT HOLDING UP MY TABLE...BUT LEGEND HOLDS THAT IT CAN TRACK SPECIFIC MONSTERS TOO.
WHY? WHO ARE WE TRACKING?
THE ONE CREATURE ON EARTH WHO MIGHT BE ABLE TO PUT AN END TO THIS INVASION FOR GOOD...

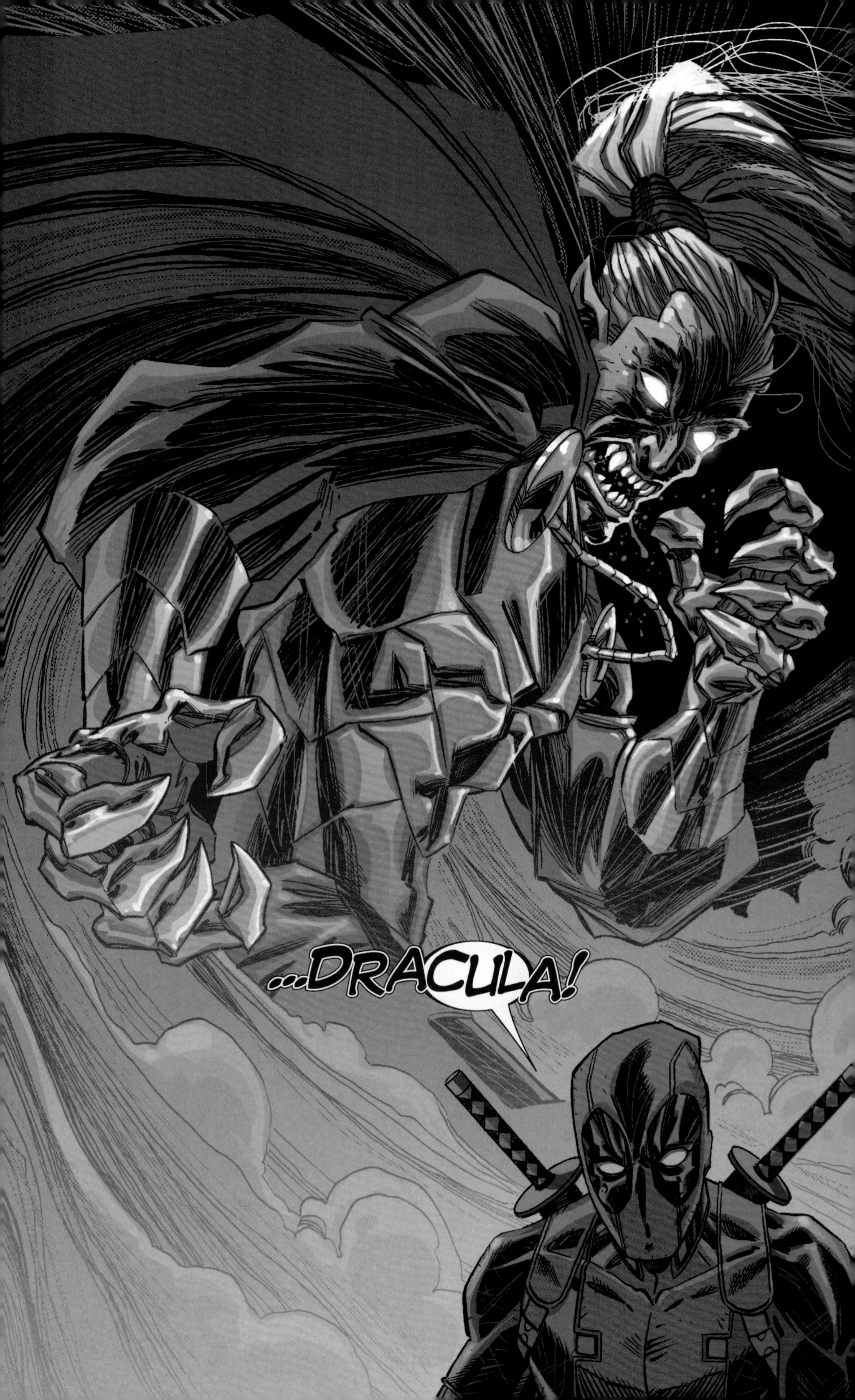
...DRACULA!

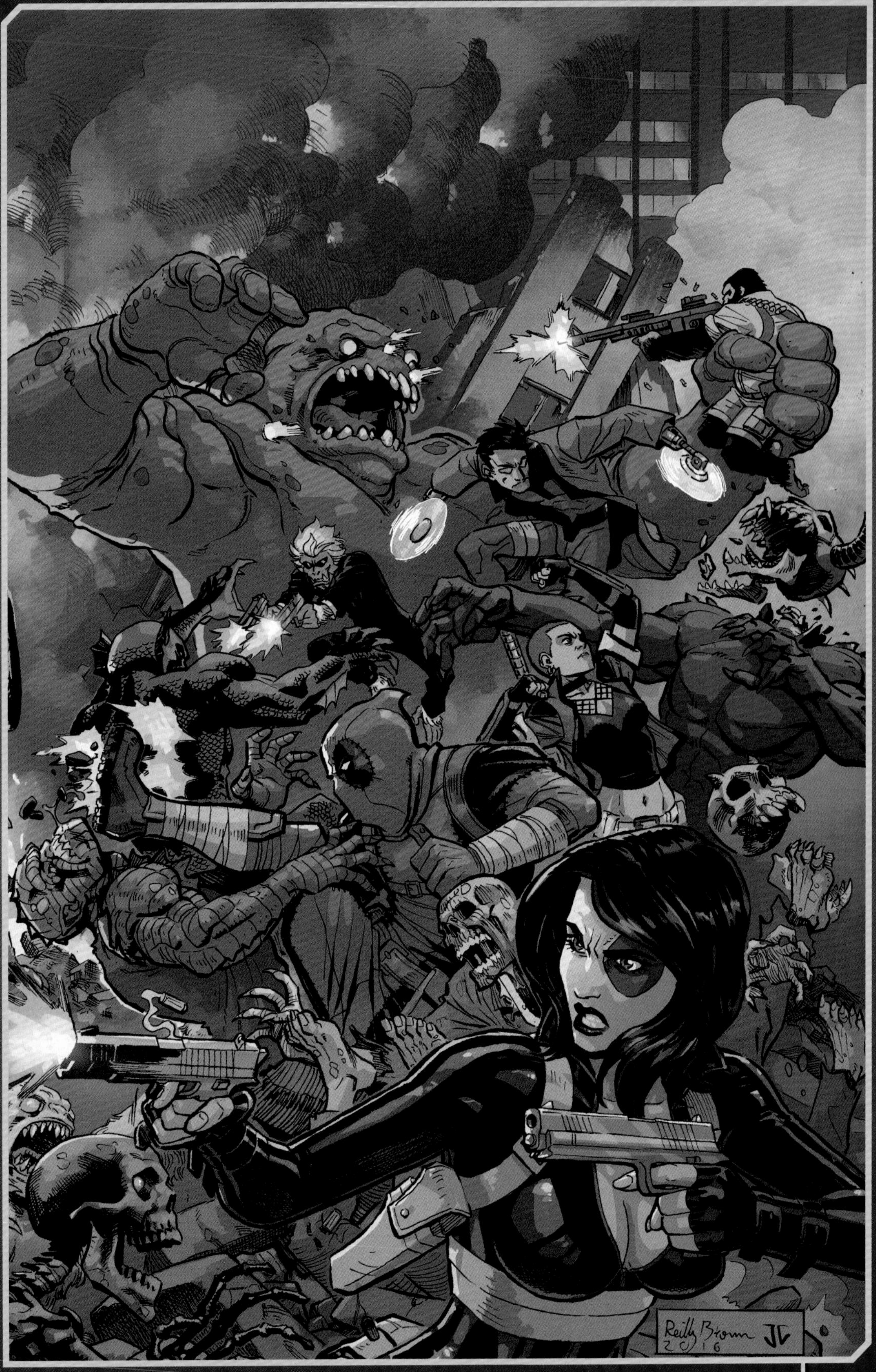
Reilly Brown
2016
JL

DEADPOOL & THE MERCS FOR MONEY

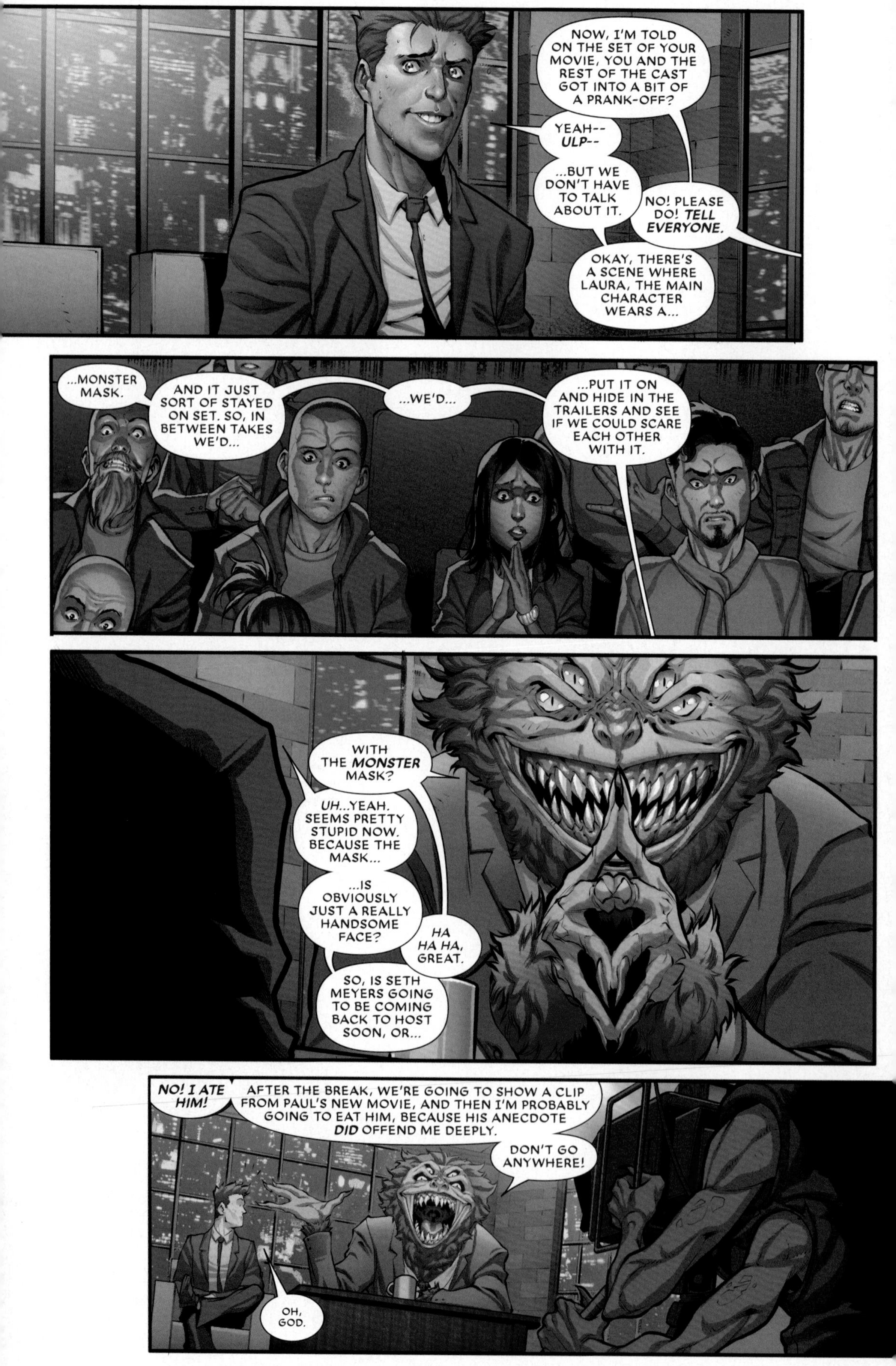
NOW, I'M TOLD ON THE SET OF YOUR MOVIE, YOU AND THE REST OF THE CAST GOT INTO A BIT OF A PRANK-OFF?
YEAH-- *ULP--*
...BUT WE DON'T HAVE TO TALK ABOUT IT.
NO! PLEASE DO! *TELL EVERYONE.*
OKAY, THERE'S A SCENE WHERE LAURA, THE MAIN CHARACTER WEARS A...
...MONSTER MASK.
AND IT JUST SORT OF STAYED ON SET. SO, IN BETWEEN TAKES WE'D...
...WE'D...
...PUT IT ON AND HIDE IN THE TRAILERS AND SEE IF WE COULD SCARE EACH OTHER WITH IT.
WITH THE *MONSTER* MASK?
UH...YEAH. SEEMS PRETTY STUPID NOW. BECAUSE THE MASK...
...IS OBVIOUSLY JUST A REALLY HANDSOME FACE?
HA HA HA, GREAT.
SO, IS SETH MEYERS GOING TO BE COMING BACK TO HOST SOON, OR...
NO! I ATE HIM!
AFTER THE BREAK, WE'RE GOING TO SHOW A CLIP FROM PAUL'S NEW MOVIE, AND THEN I'M PROBABLY GOING TO EAT HIM, BECAUSE HIS ANECDOTE *DID* OFFEND ME DEEPLY.
DON'T GO ANYWHERE!
OH, GOD.

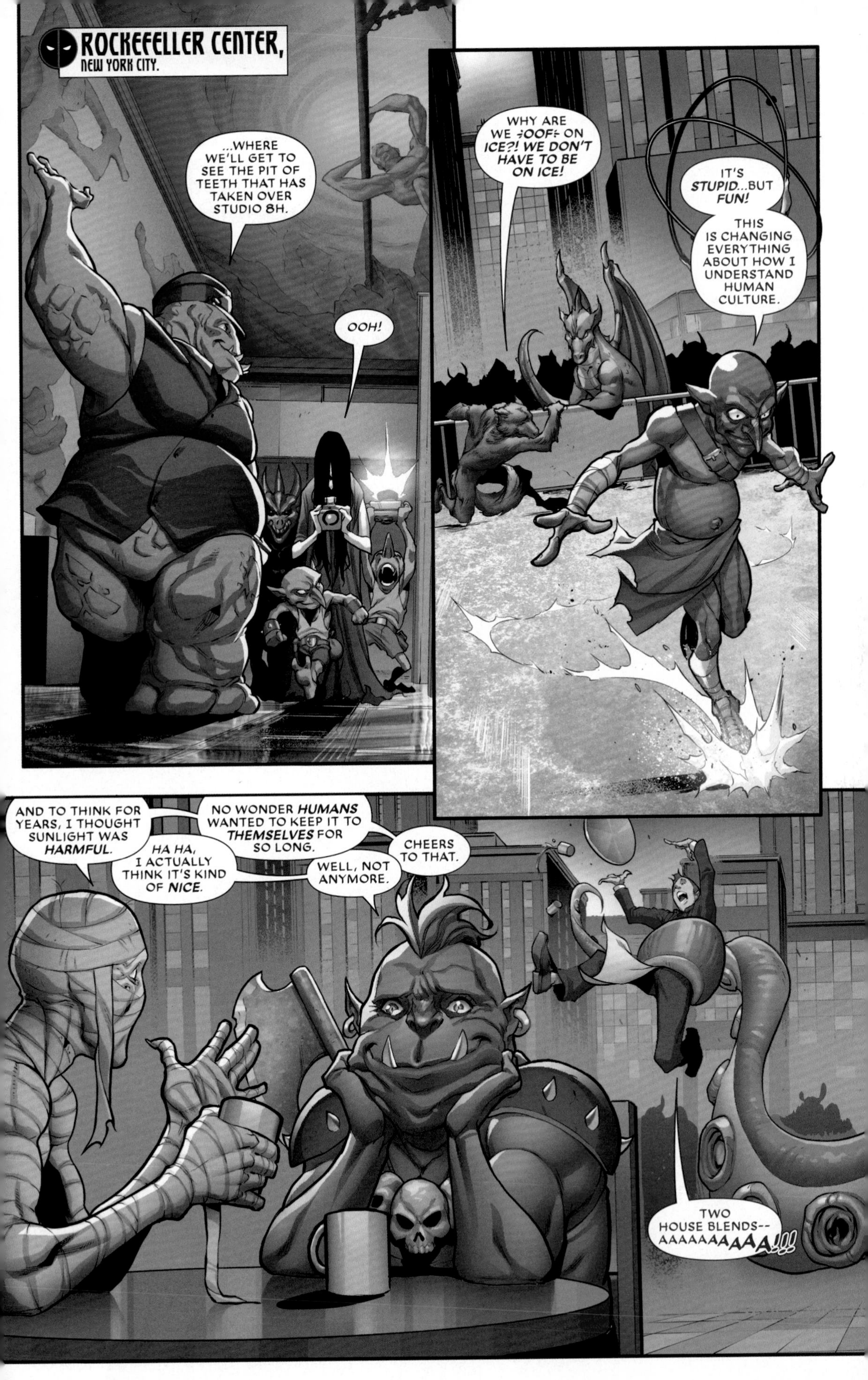
ROCKEFELLER CENTER, NEW YORK CITY.
...WHERE WE'LL GET TO SEE THE PIT OF TEETH THAT HAS TAKEN OVER STUDIO 8H.
OOH!
WHY ARE WE -OOF- ON ICE?! WE DON'T HAVE TO BE ON ICE!
IT'S STUPID...BUT FUN!
THIS IS CHANGING EVERYTHING ABOUT HOW I UNDERSTAND HUMAN CULTURE.
AND TO THINK FOR YEARS, I THOUGHT SUNLIGHT WAS HARMFUL.
HA HA, I ACTUALLY THINK IT'S KIND OF NICE.
NO WONDER HUMANS WANTED TO KEEP IT TO THEMSELVES FOR SO LONG.
WELL, NOT ANYMORE.
CHEERS TO THAT.
TWO HOUSE BLENDS--AAAAAAAAAA!!!

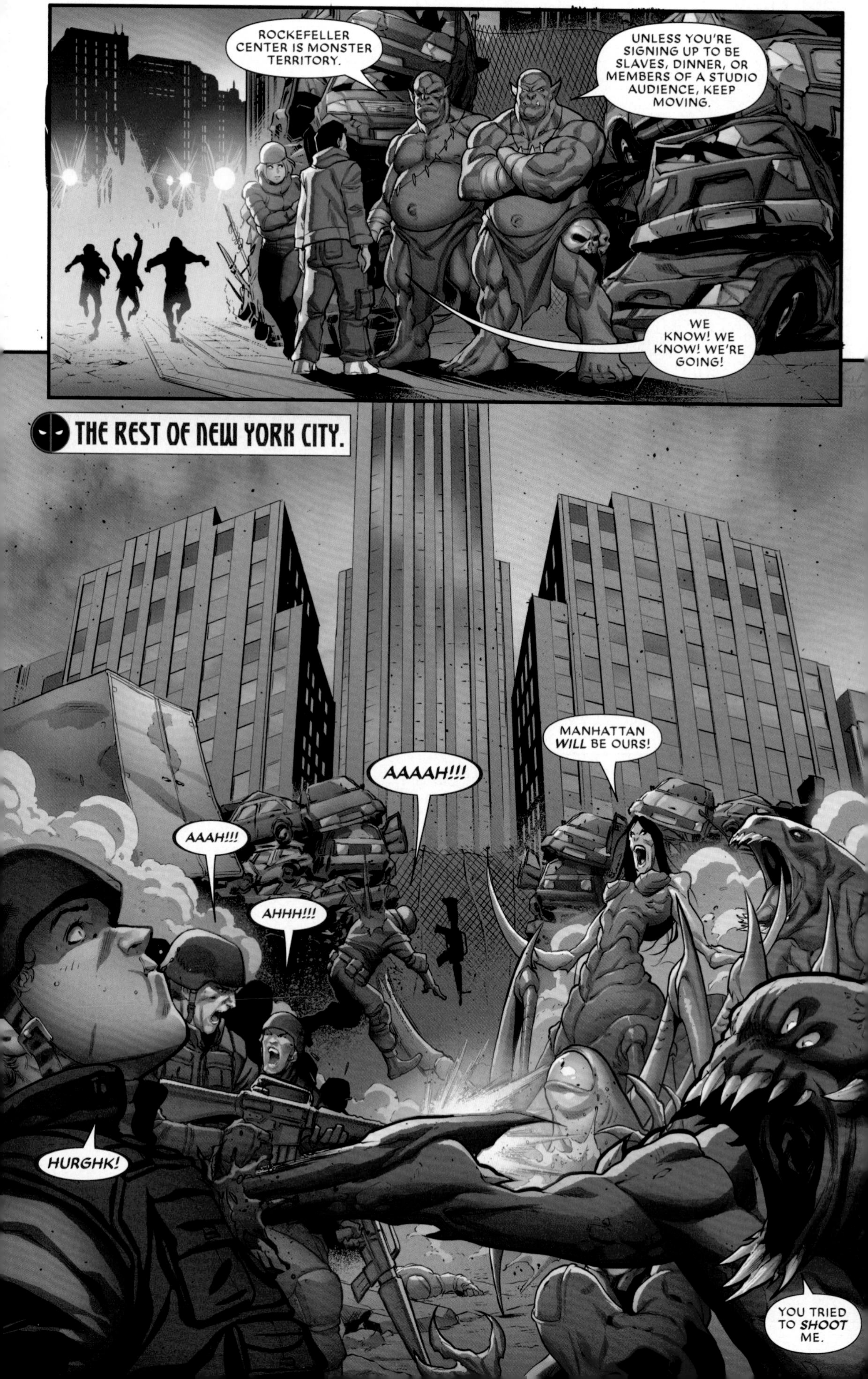
ROCKEFELLER CENTER IS MONSTER TERRITORY.
UNLESS YOU'RE SIGNING UP TO BE SLAVES, DINNER, OR MEMBERS OF A STUDIO AUDIENCE, KEEP MOVING.
WE KNOW! WE KNOW! WE'RE GOING!
THE REST OF NEW YORK CITY.
MANHATTAN WILL BE OURS!
AAAAH!!!
AAAH!!!
AHHH!!!
HURGHK!
YOU TRIED TO SHOOT ME.

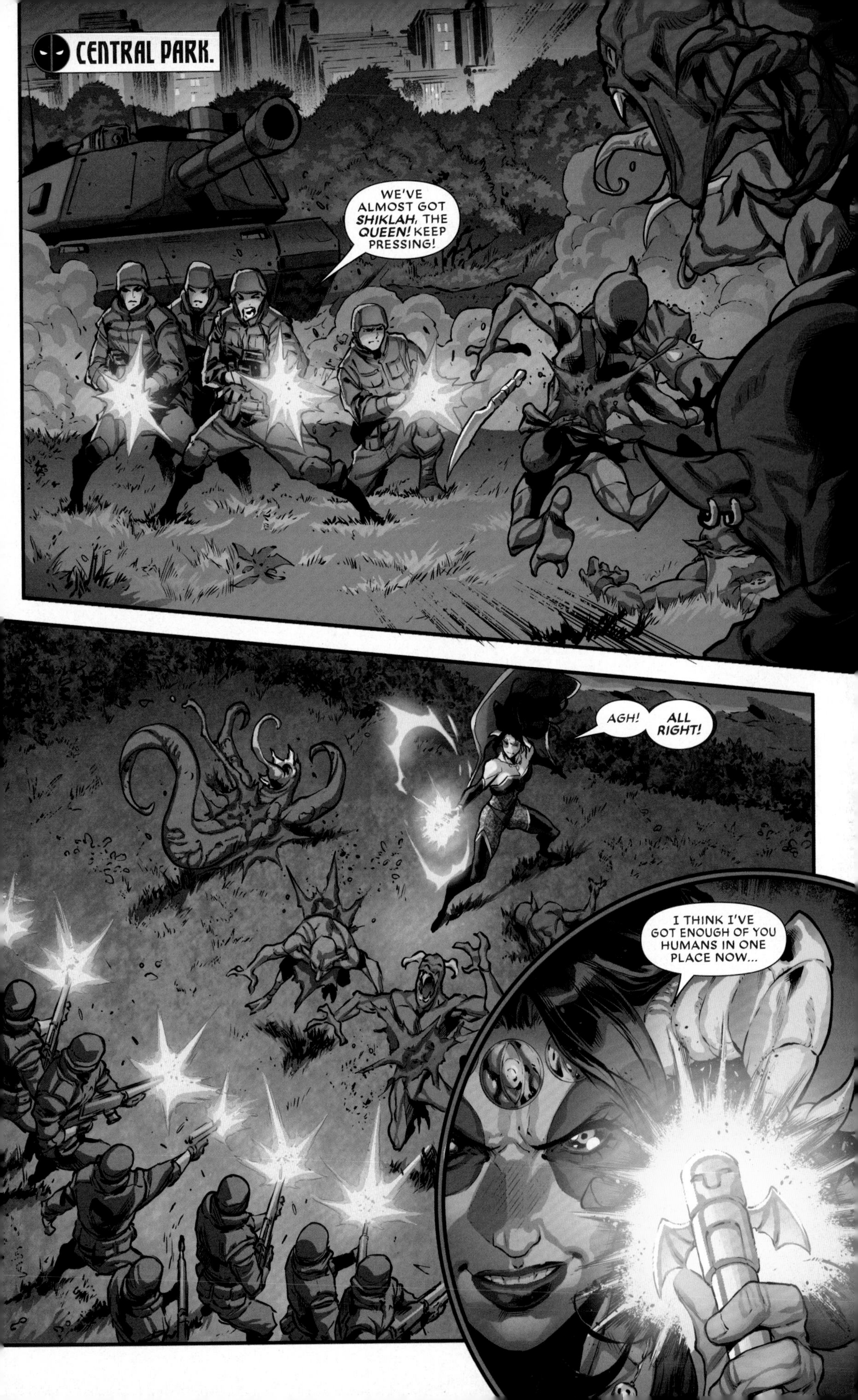
CENTRAL PARK.
WE'VE ALMOST GOT SHIKLAH, THE QUEEN! KEEP PRESSING!
AGH!
ALL RIGHT!
I THINK I'VE GOT ENOUGH OF YOU HUMANS IN ONE PLACE NOW...

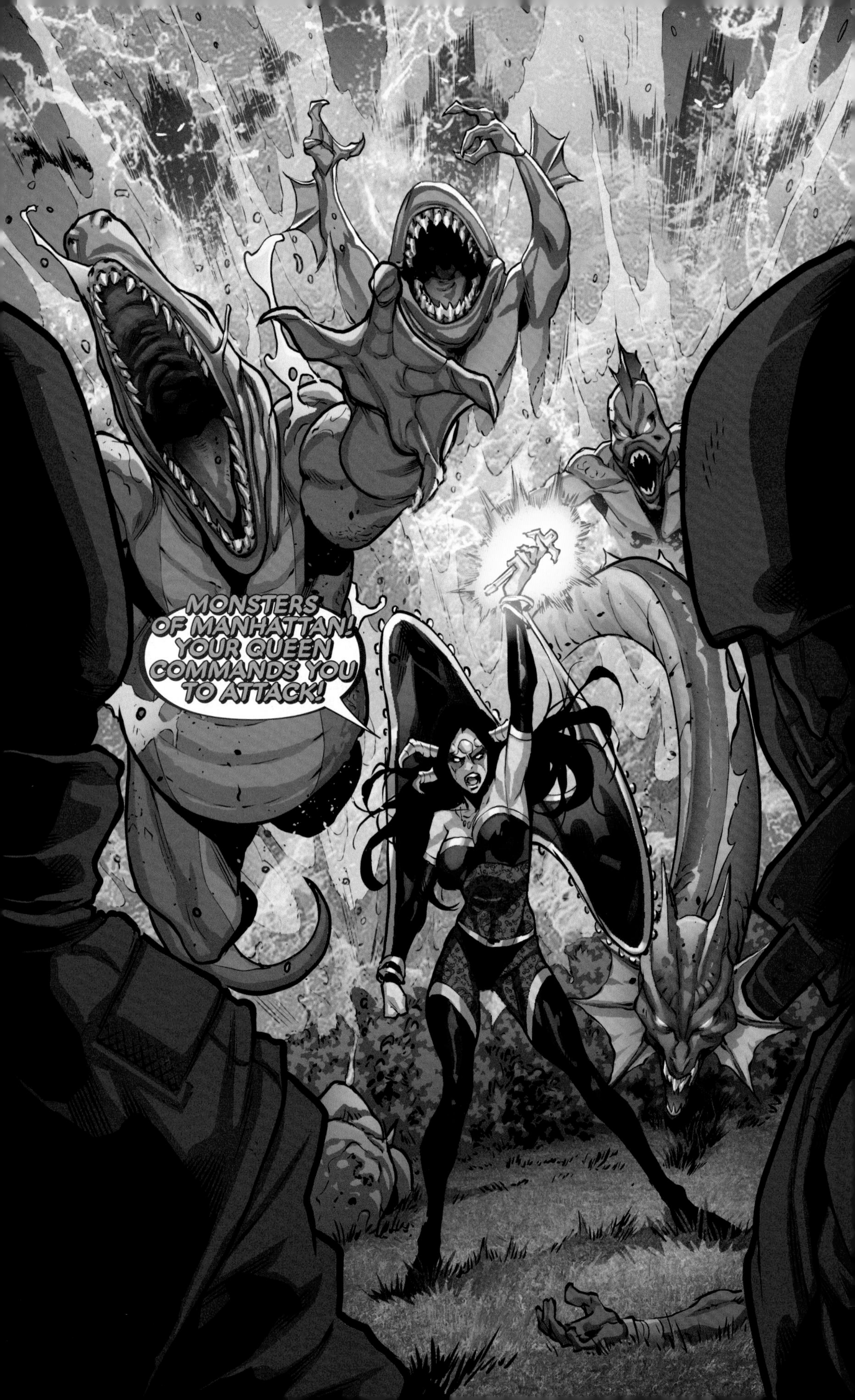
MONSTERS OF MANHATTAN! YOUR QUEEN COMMANDS YOU TO ATTACK!

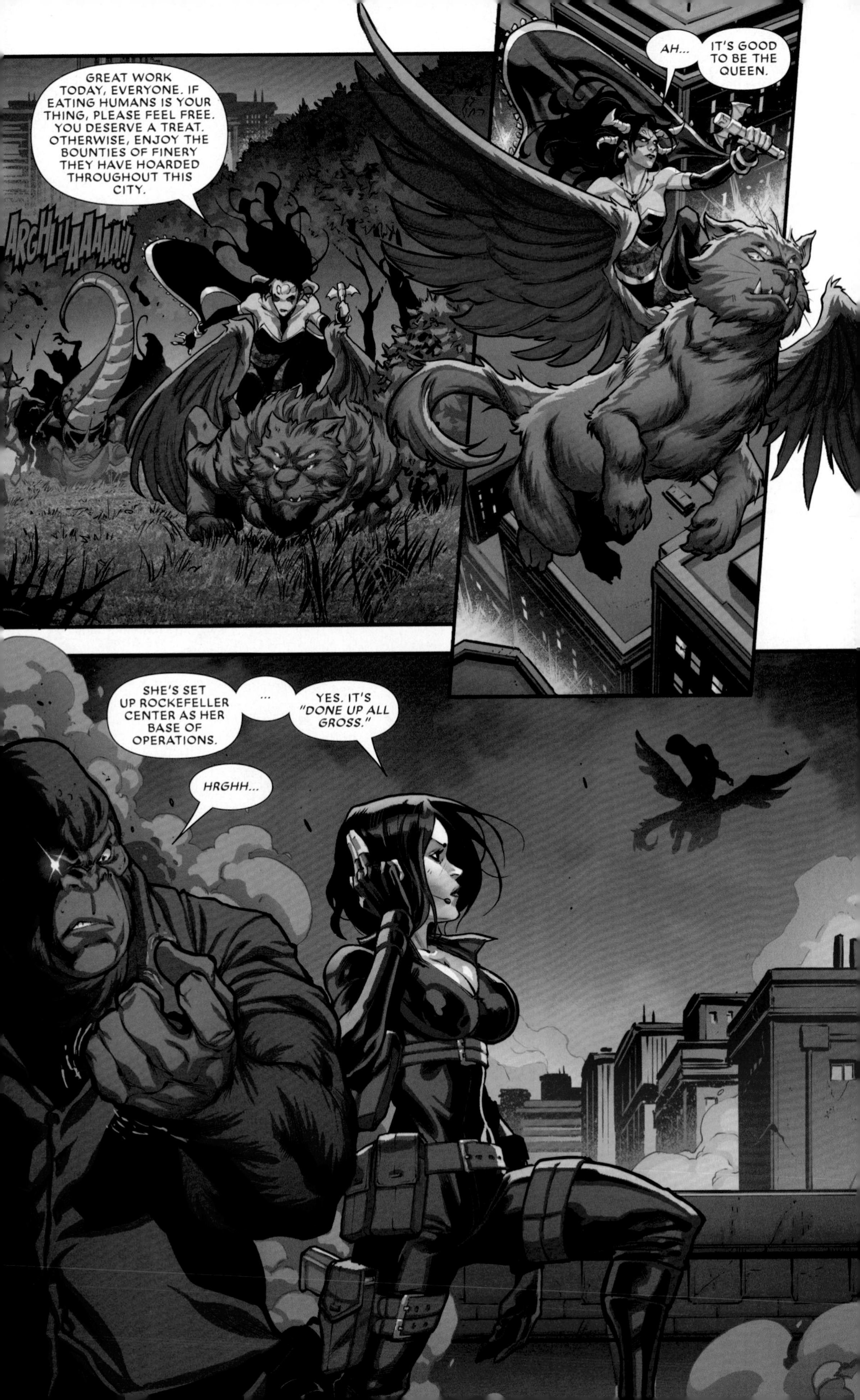
GREAT WORK TODAY, EVERYONE. IF EATING HUMANS IS YOUR THING, PLEASE FEEL FREE. YOU DESERVE A TREAT. OTHERWISE, ENJOY THE BOUNTIES OF FINERY THEY HAVE HOARDED THROUGHOUT THIS CITY.
ARGHLLLAAAAA!!
AH...
IT'S GOOD TO BE THE QUEEN.
SHE'S SET UP ROCKEFELLER CENTER AS HER BASE OF OPERATIONS.
...
YES. IT'S "DONE UP ALL GROSS."
HRGHH...

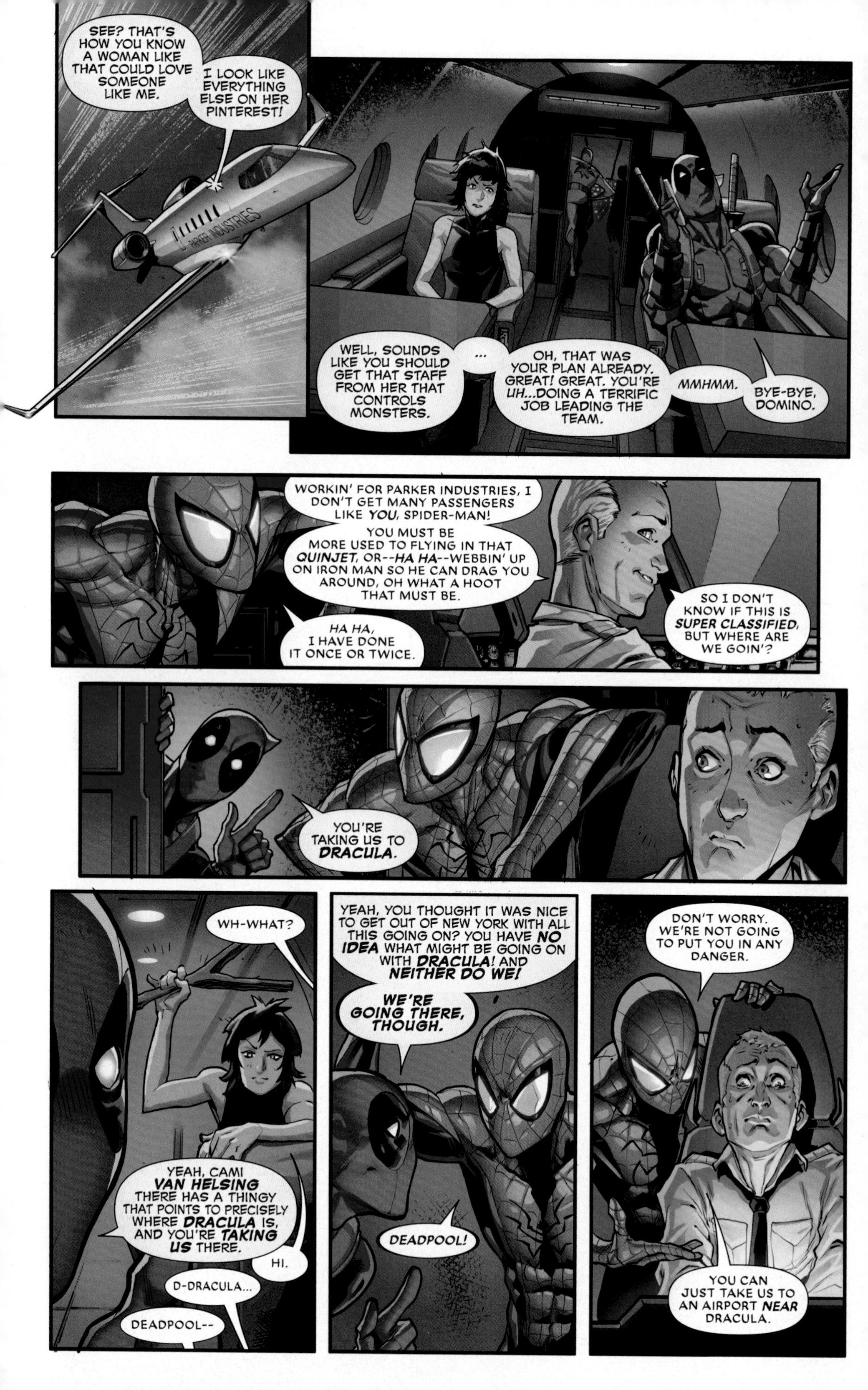
SEE? THAT'S HOW YOU KNOW A WOMAN LIKE THAT COULD LOVE SOMEONE LIKE ME.
I LOOK LIKE EVERYTHING ELSE ON HER PINTEREST!
PARKER INDUSTRIES
WELL, SOUNDS LIKE YOU SHOULD GET THAT STAFF FROM HER THAT CONTROLS MONSTERS.
...
OH, THAT WAS YOUR PLAN ALREADY. GREAT! GREAT. YOU'RE UH...DOING A TERRIFIC JOB LEADING THE TEAM.
MMHMM.
BYE-BYE, DOMINO.
WORKIN' FOR PARKER INDUSTRIES, I DON'T GET MANY PASSENGERS LIKE YOU, SPIDER-MAN!
YOU MUST BE MORE USED TO FLYING IN THAT QUINJET, OR--HA HA--WEBBIN' UP ON IRON MAN SO HE CAN DRAG YOU AROUND, OH WHAT A HOOT THAT MUST BE.
HA HA, I HAVE DONE IT ONCE OR TWICE.
SO I DON'T KNOW IF THIS IS SUPER CLASSIFIED, BUT WHERE ARE WE GOIN'?
YOU'RE TAKING US TO DRACULA.
WH-WHAT?
YEAH, CAMI VAN HELSING THERE HAS A THINGY THAT POINTS TO PRECISELY WHERE DRACULA IS, AND YOU'RE TAKING US THERE.
HI.
D-DRACULA...
DEADPOOL--
YEAH, YOU THOUGHT IT WAS NICE TO GET OUT OF NEW YORK WITH ALL THIS GOING ON? YOU HAVE NO IDEA WHAT MIGHT BE GOING ON WITH DRACULA! AND NEITHER DO WE!
WE'RE GOING THERE, THOUGH.
DEADPOOL!
DON'T WORRY. WE'RE NOT GOING TO PUT YOU IN ANY DANGER.
YOU CAN JUST TAKE US TO AN AIRPORT NEAR DRACULA.

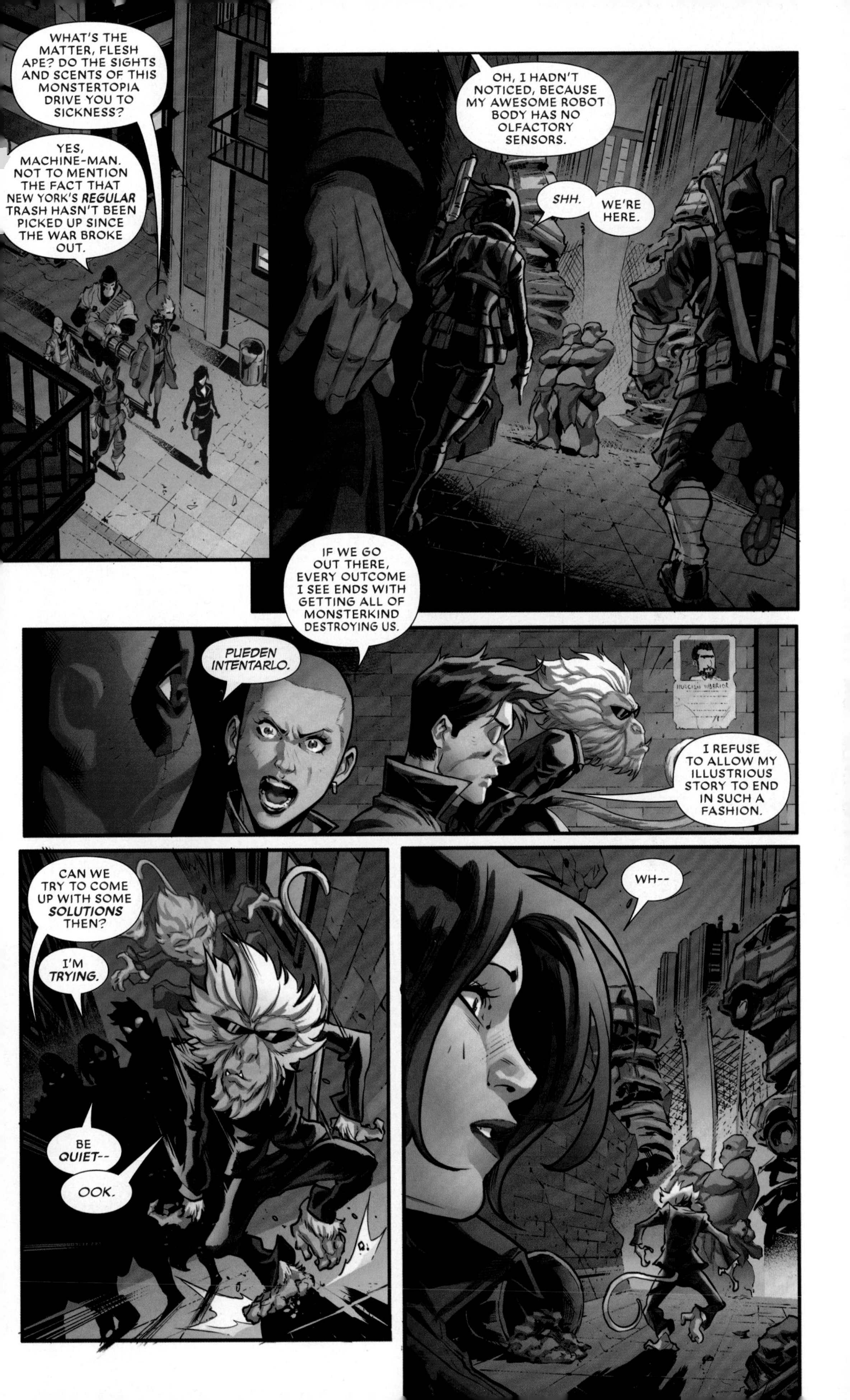
WHAT'S THE MATTER, FLESH APE? DO THE SIGHTS AND SCENTS OF THIS MONSTERTOPIA DRIVE YOU TO SICKNESS?
YES, MACHINE-MAN. NOT TO MENTION THE FACT THAT NEW YORK'S REGULAR TRASH HASN'T BEEN PICKED UP SINCE THE WAR BROKE OUT.
OH, I HADN'T NOTICED, BECAUSE MY AWESOME ROBOT BODY HAS NO OLFACTORY SENSORS.
SHH.
WE'RE HERE.
IF WE GO OUT THERE, EVERY OUTCOME I SEE ENDS WITH GETTING ALL OF MONSTERKIND DESTROYING US.
PUEDEN INTENTARLO.
I REFUSE TO ALLOW MY ILLUSTRIOUS STORY TO END IN SUCH A FASHION.
CAN WE TRY TO COME UP WITH SOME SOLUTIONS THEN?
I'M TRYING.
BE QUIET--
OOK.
WH--

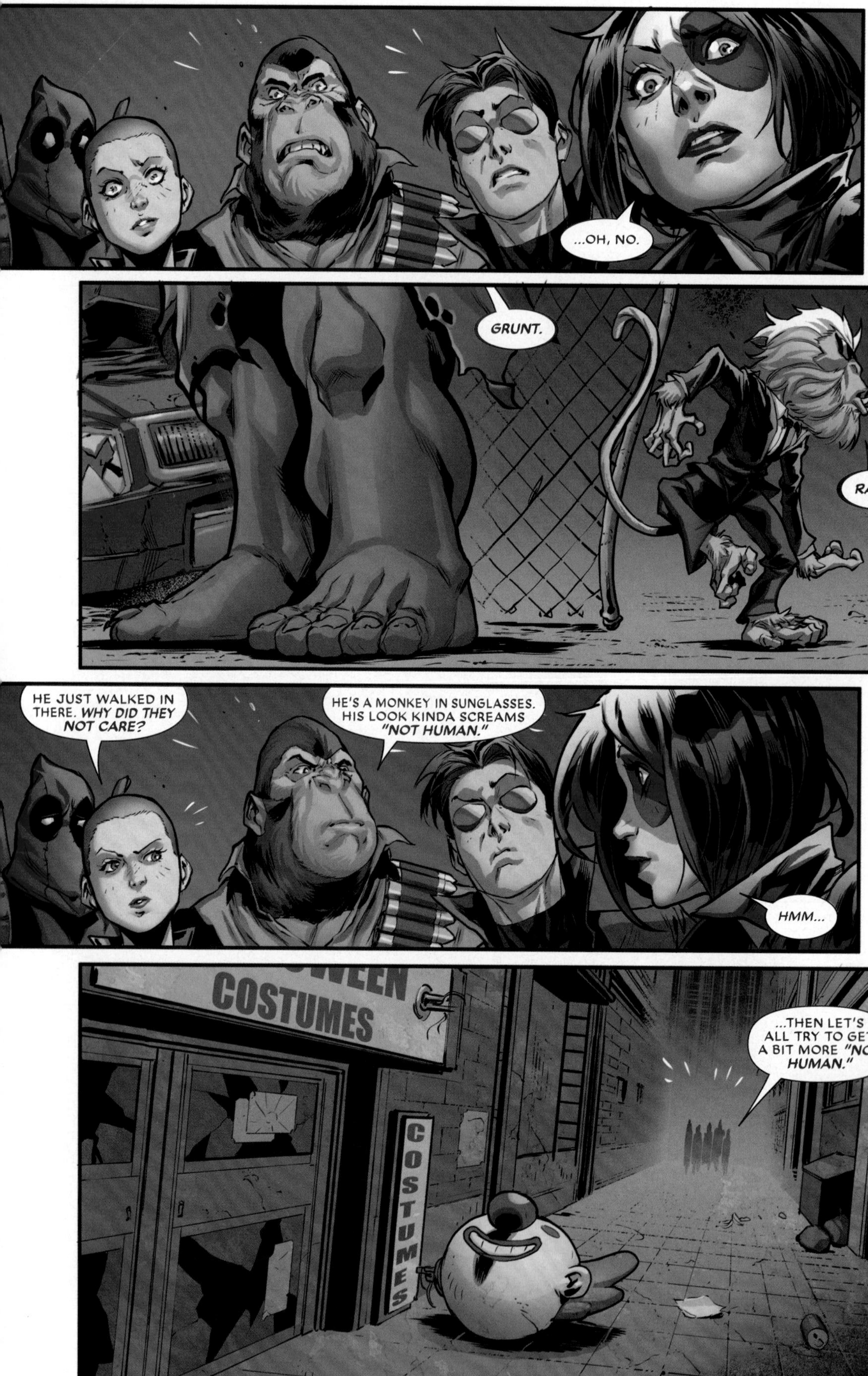
...OH, NO.
GRUNT.
RAAH.
HE JUST WALKED IN THERE. *WHY DID THEY NOT CARE?*
HE'S A MONKEY IN SUNGLASSES. HIS LOOK KINDA SCREAMS *"NOT HUMAN."*
HMM...
COSTUMES
COSTUMES
...THEN LET'S ALL TRY TO GET A BIT MORE *"NOT HUMAN."*

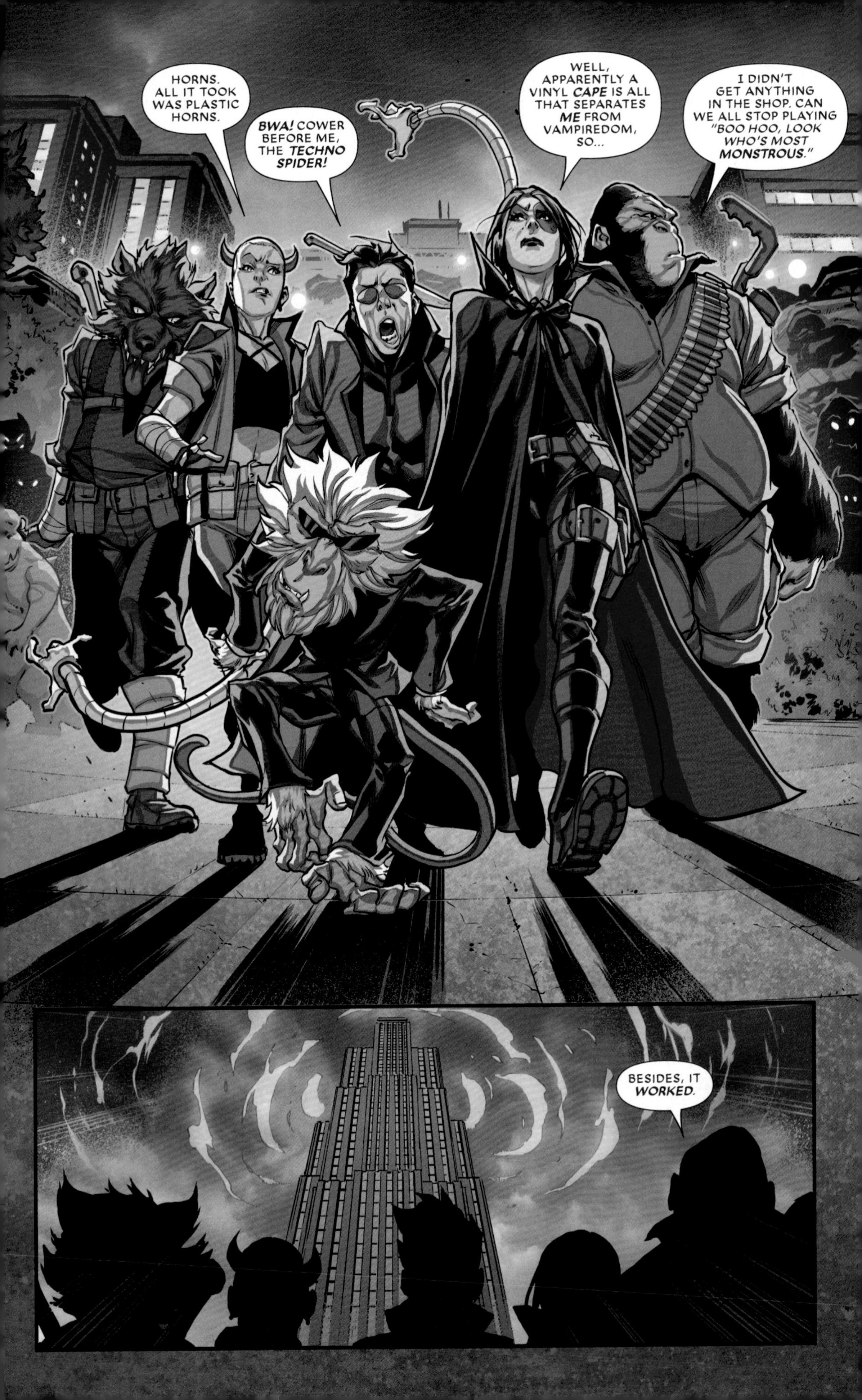

HORNS. ALL IT TOOK WAS PLASTIC HORNS.
BWA! COWER BEFORE ME, THE TECHNO SPIDER!
WELL, APPARENTLY A VINYL CAPE IS ALL THAT SEPARATES ME FROM VAMPIREDOM, SO...
I DIDN'T GET ANYTHING IN THE SHOP. CAN WE ALL STOP PLAYING "BOO HOO, LOOK WHO'S MOST MONSTROUS."
BESIDES, IT WORKED.

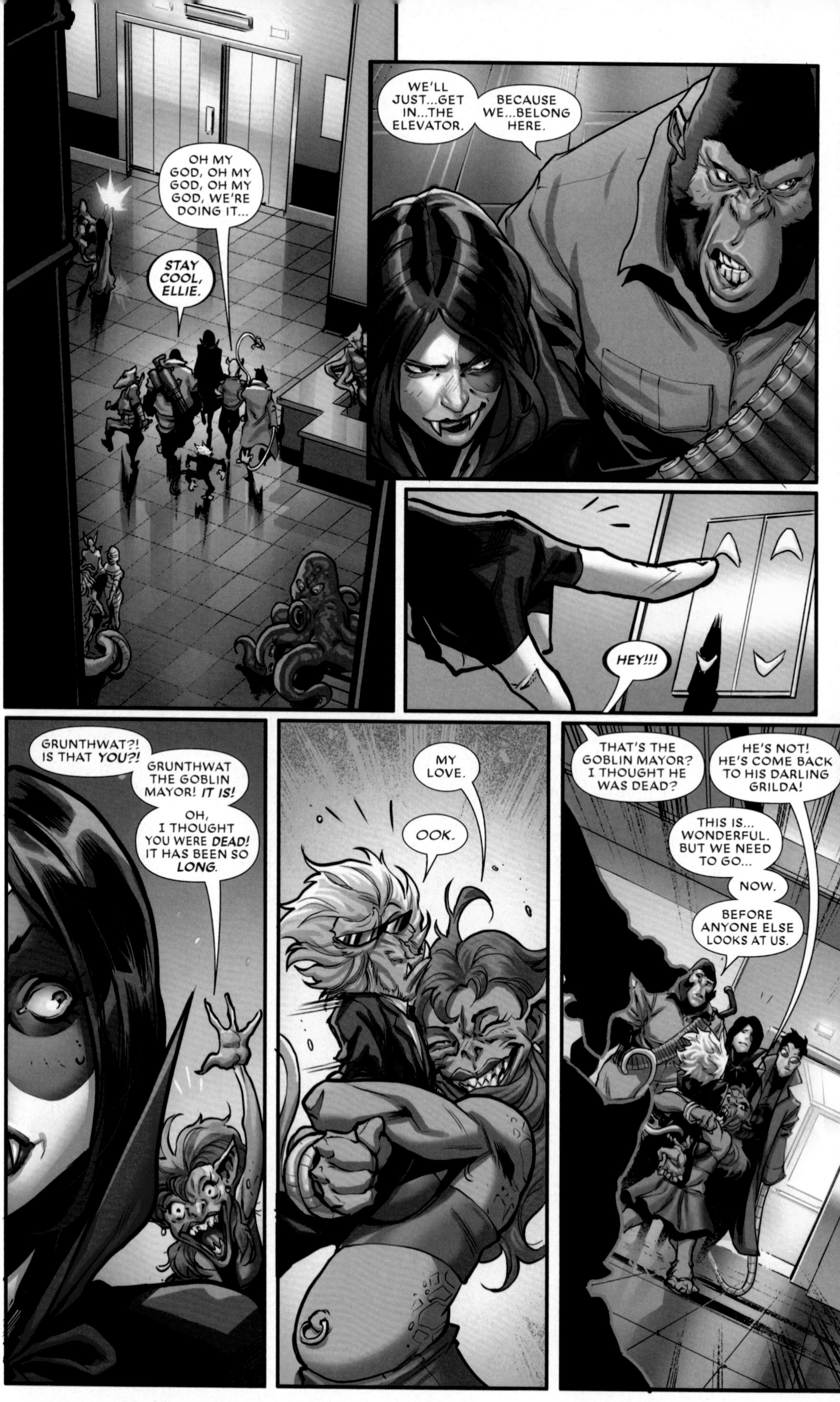
OH MY GOD, OH MY GOD, OH MY GOD, WE'RE DOING IT...
STAY COOL, ELLIE.
WE'LL JUST...GET IN...THE ELEVATOR.
BECAUSE WE...BELONG HERE.
HEY!!!
GRUNTHWAT?! IS THAT YOU?!
GRUNTHWAT THE GOBLIN MAYOR! IT IS!
OH, I THOUGHT YOU WERE DEAD! IT HAS BEEN SO LONG.
MY LOVE.
OOK.
THAT'S THE GOBLIN MAYOR? I THOUGHT HE WAS DEAD?
HE'S NOT! HE'S COME BACK TO HIS DARLING GRILDA!
THIS IS... WONDERFUL. BUT WE NEED TO GO...
NOW.
BEFORE ANYONE ELSE LOOKS AT US.

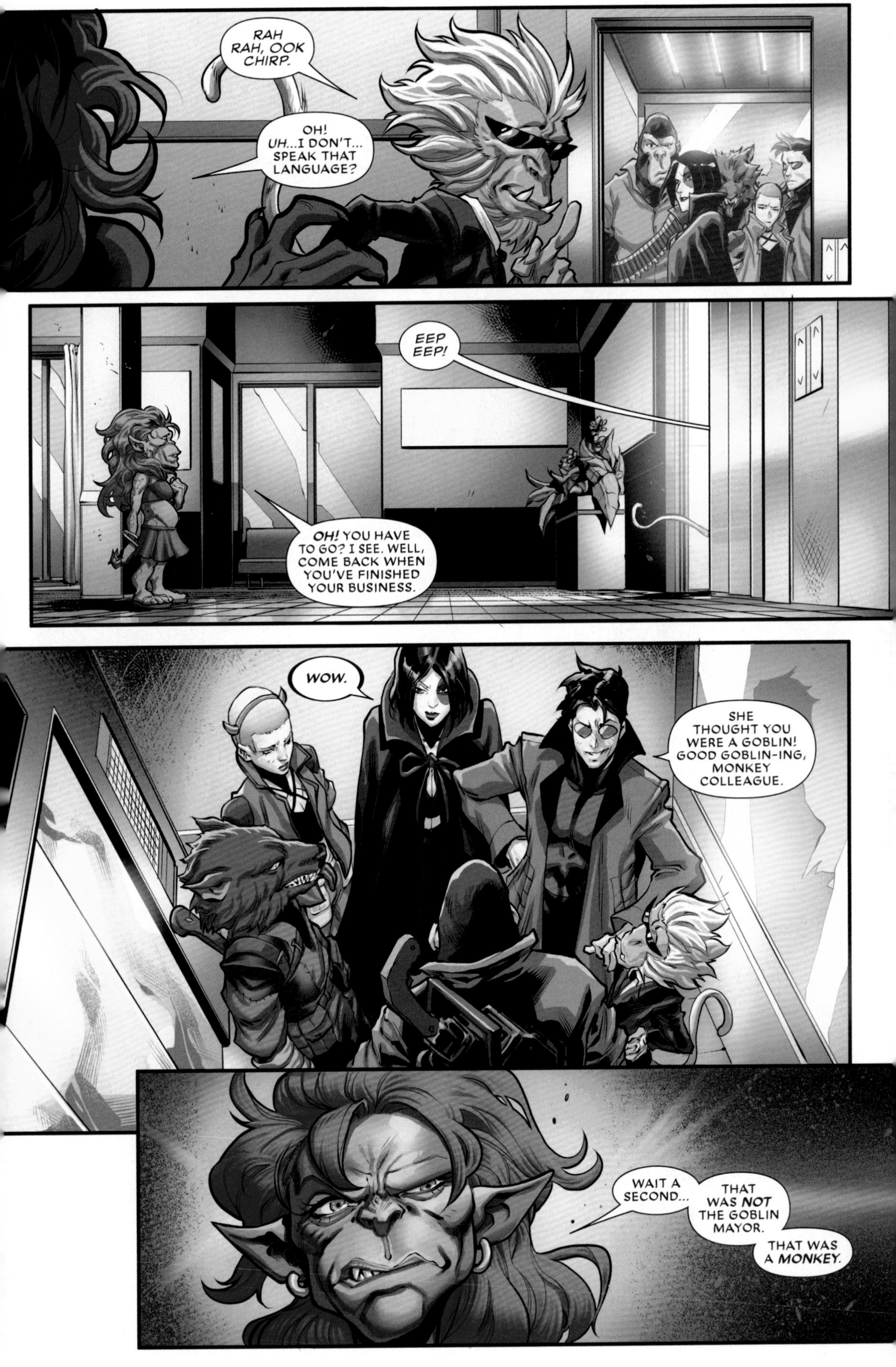
RAH RAH, OOK CHIRP.
OH! UH...I DON'T... SPEAK THAT LANGUAGE?
EEP EEP!
OH! YOU HAVE TO GO? I SEE. WELL, COME BACK WHEN YOU'VE FINISHED YOUR BUSINESS.
WOW.
SHE THOUGHT YOU WERE A GOBLIN! GOOD GOBLIN-ING, MONKEY COLLEAGUE.
WAIT A SECOND...
THAT WAS NOT THE GOBLIN MAYOR.
THAT WAS A MONKEY.

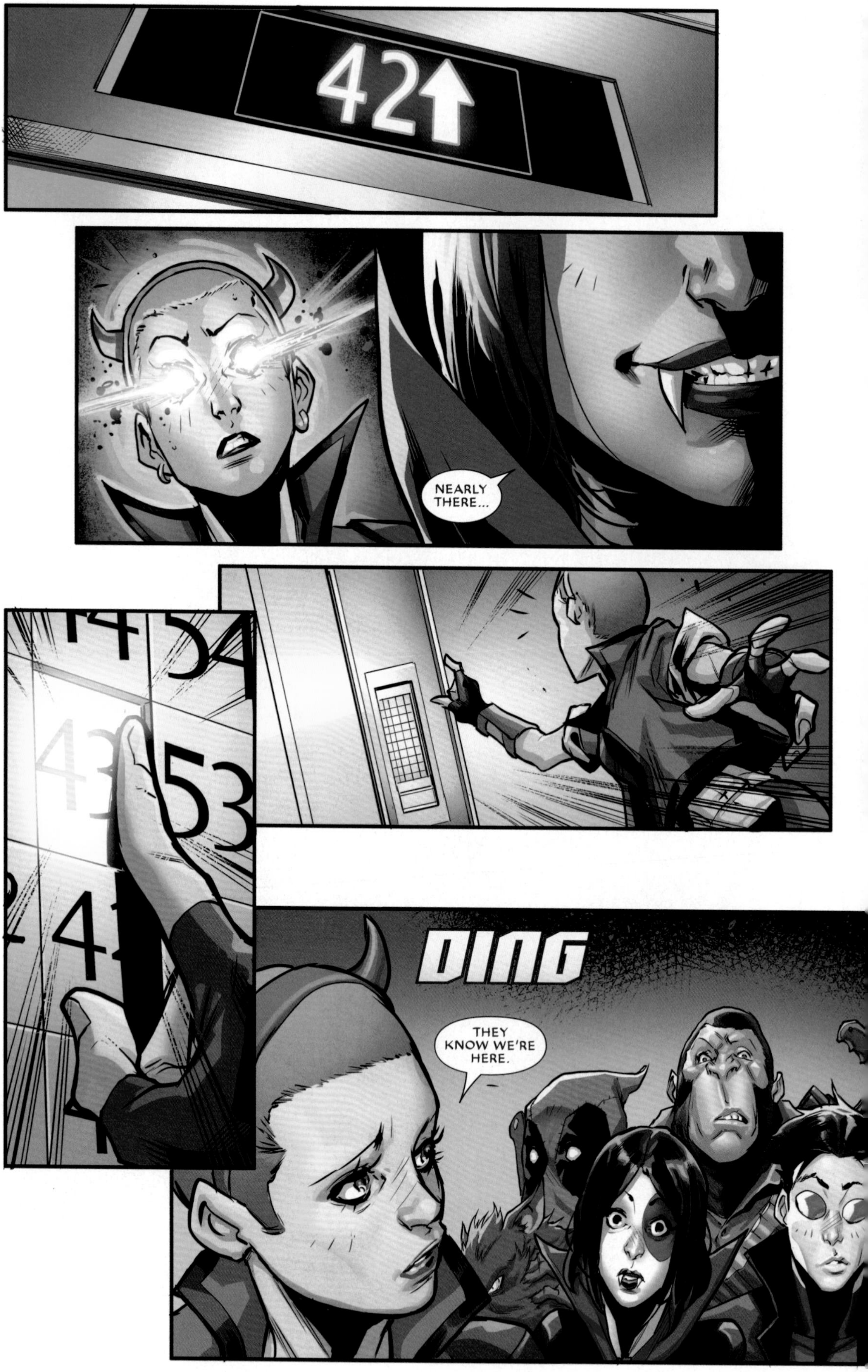
42
NEARLY THERE...
DING
THEY KNOW WE'RE HERE.

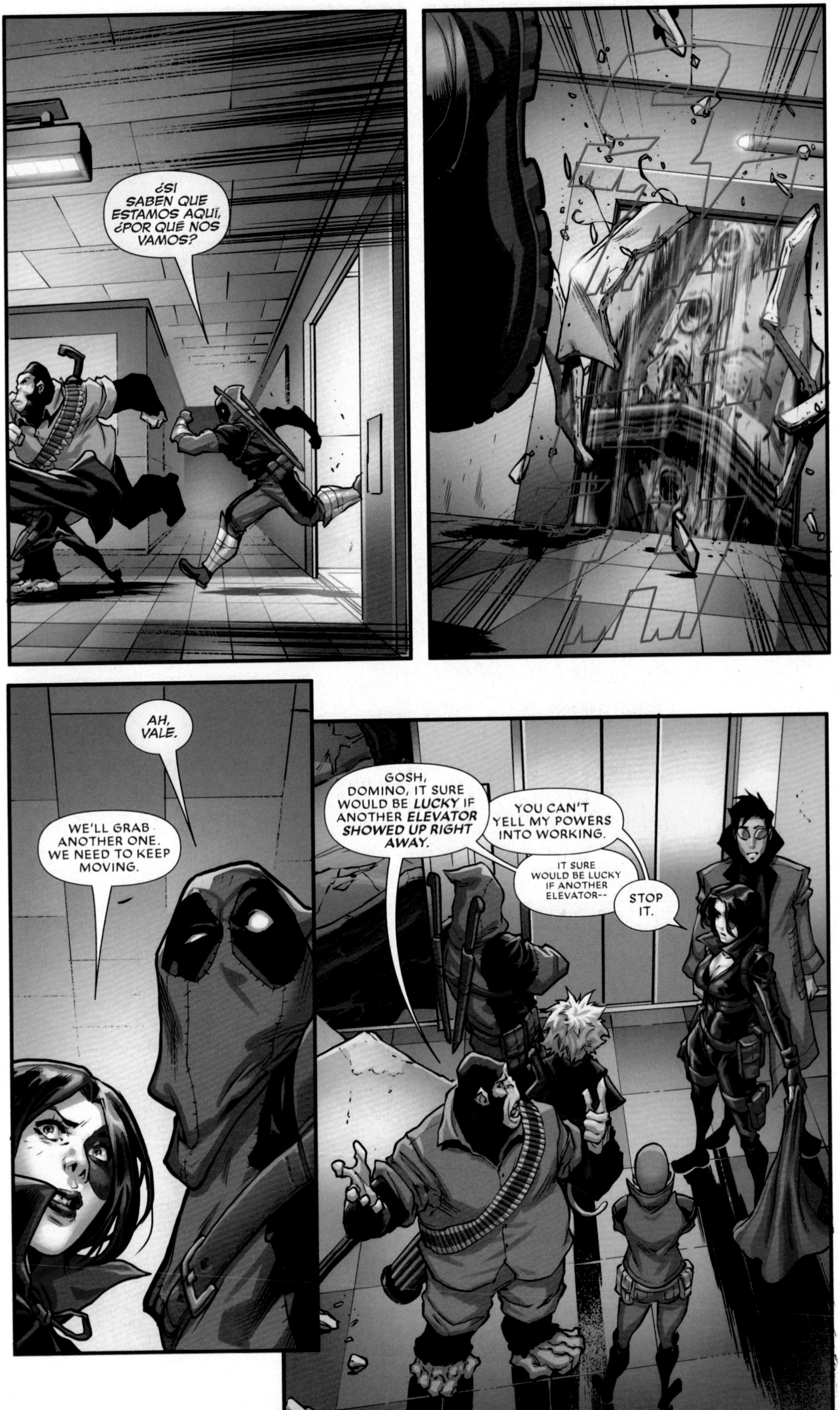
¿SI SABEN QUE ESTAMOS AQUÍ, ¿POR QUÉ NOS VAMOS?
AH, VALE.
WE'LL GRAB ANOTHER ONE. WE NEED TO KEEP MOVING.
GOSH, DOMINO, IT SURE WOULD BE LUCKY IF ANOTHER ELEVATOR SHOWED UP RIGHT AWAY.
YOU CAN'T YELL MY POWERS INTO WORKING.
IT SURE WOULD BE LUCKY IF ANOTHER ELEVATOR--
STOP IT.

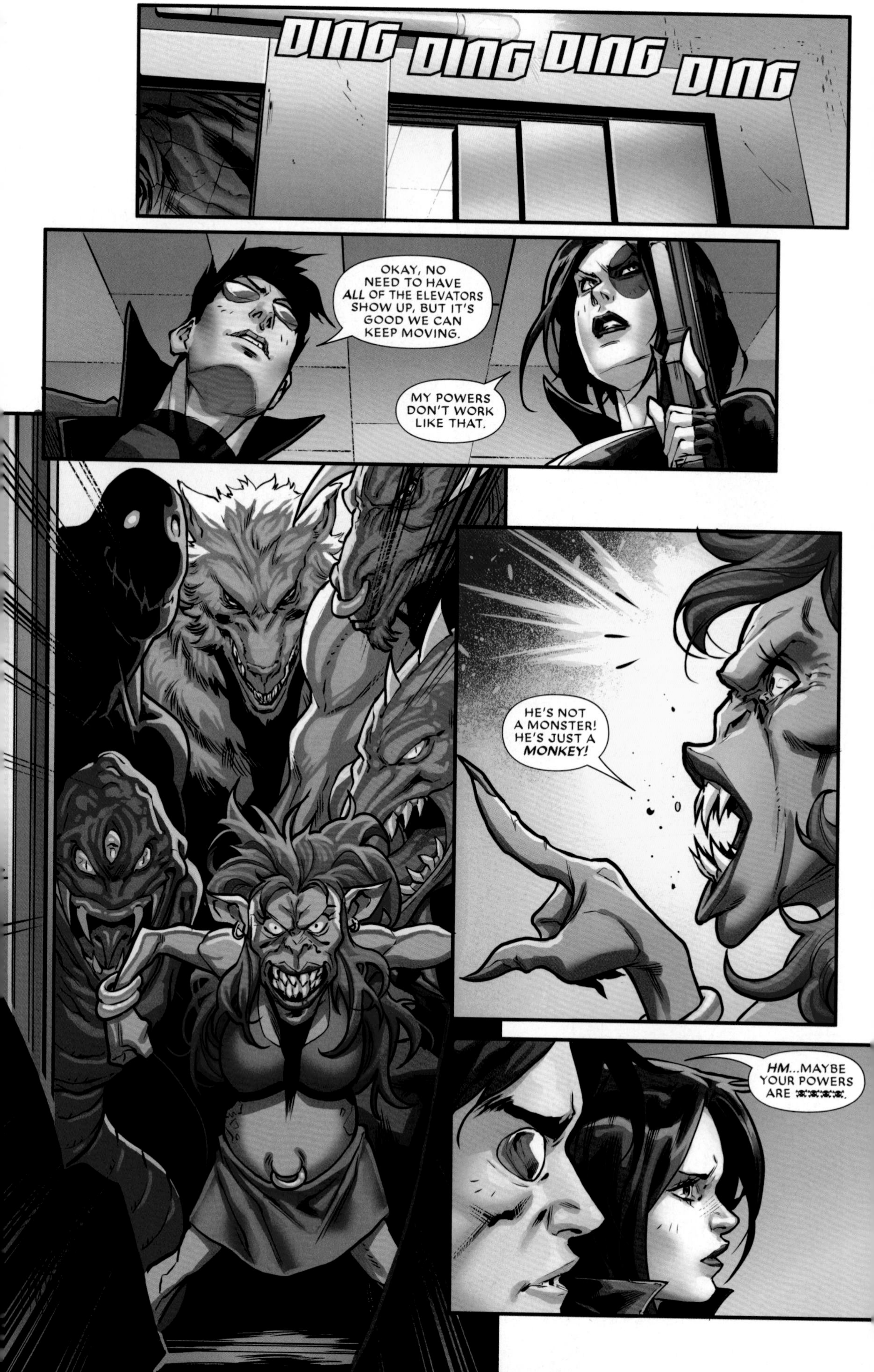

DING DING DING DING
OKAY, NO NEED TO HAVE *ALL* OF THE ELEVATORS SHOW UP, BUT IT'S GOOD WE CAN KEEP MOVING.
MY POWERS DON'T WORK LIKE THAT.
HE'S NOT A MONSTER! HE'S JUST A *MONKEY!*
HM...MAYBE YOUR POWERS ARE ☠☠☠☠.

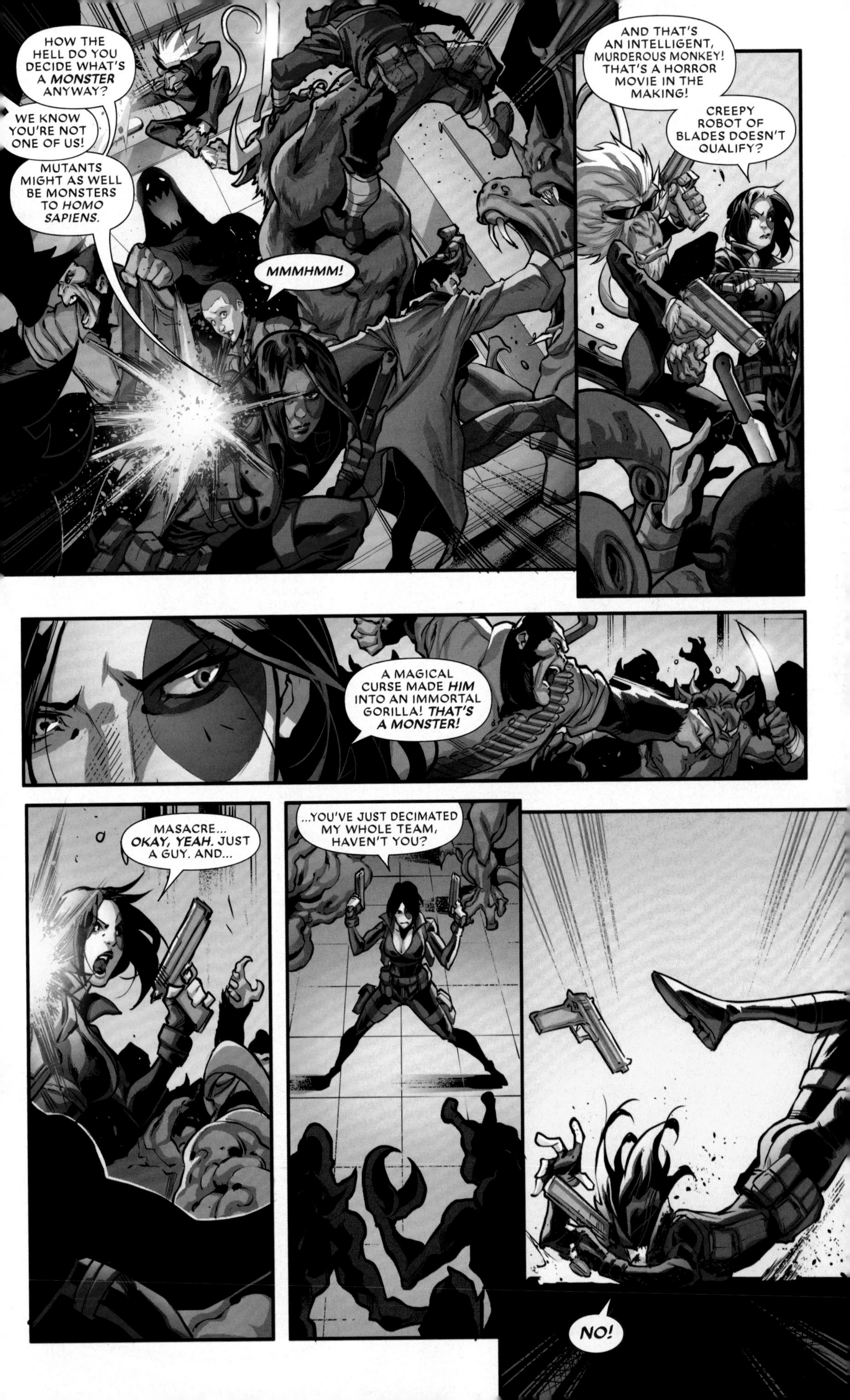
HOW THE HELL DO YOU DECIDE WHAT'S A *MONSTER* ANYWAY?
WE KNOW YOU'RE NOT ONE OF US!
MUTANTS MIGHT AS WELL BE MONSTERS TO *HOMO SAPIENS.*
MMMHMM!
AND THAT'S AN INTELLIGENT, MURDEROUS MONKEY! THAT'S A HORROR MOVIE IN THE MAKING!
CREEPY ROBOT OF BLADES DOESN'T QUALIFY?
A MAGICAL CURSE MADE *HIM* INTO AN IMMORTAL GORILLA! *THAT'S A MONSTER!*
MASACRE... *OKAY, YEAH.* JUST A GUY. AND...
...YOU'VE JUST DECIMATED MY WHOLE TEAM, HAVEN'T YOU?
NO!

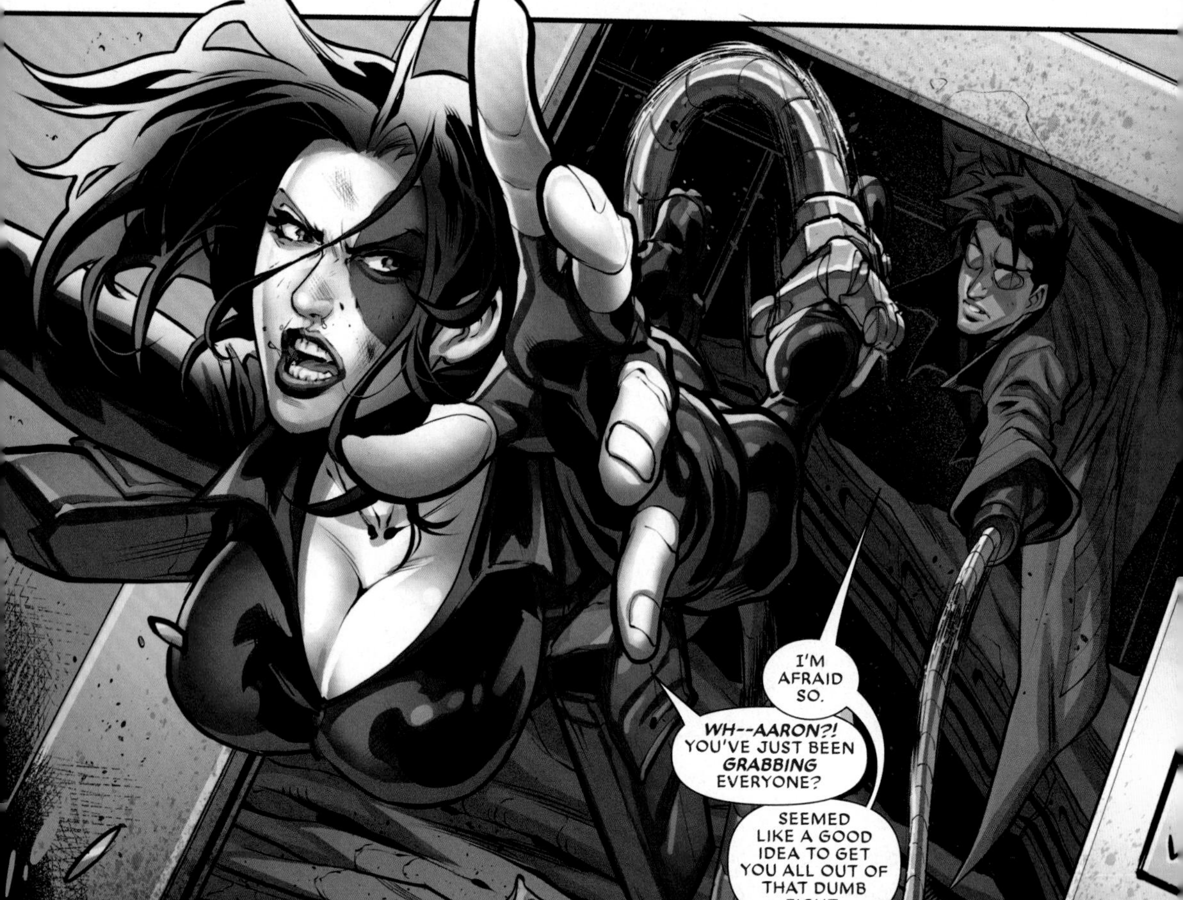
I'M AFRAID SO.
WH--AARON?! YOU'VE JUST BEEN GRABBING EVERYONE?
SEEMED LIKE A GOOD IDEA TO GET YOU ALL OUT OF THAT DUMB FIGHT.

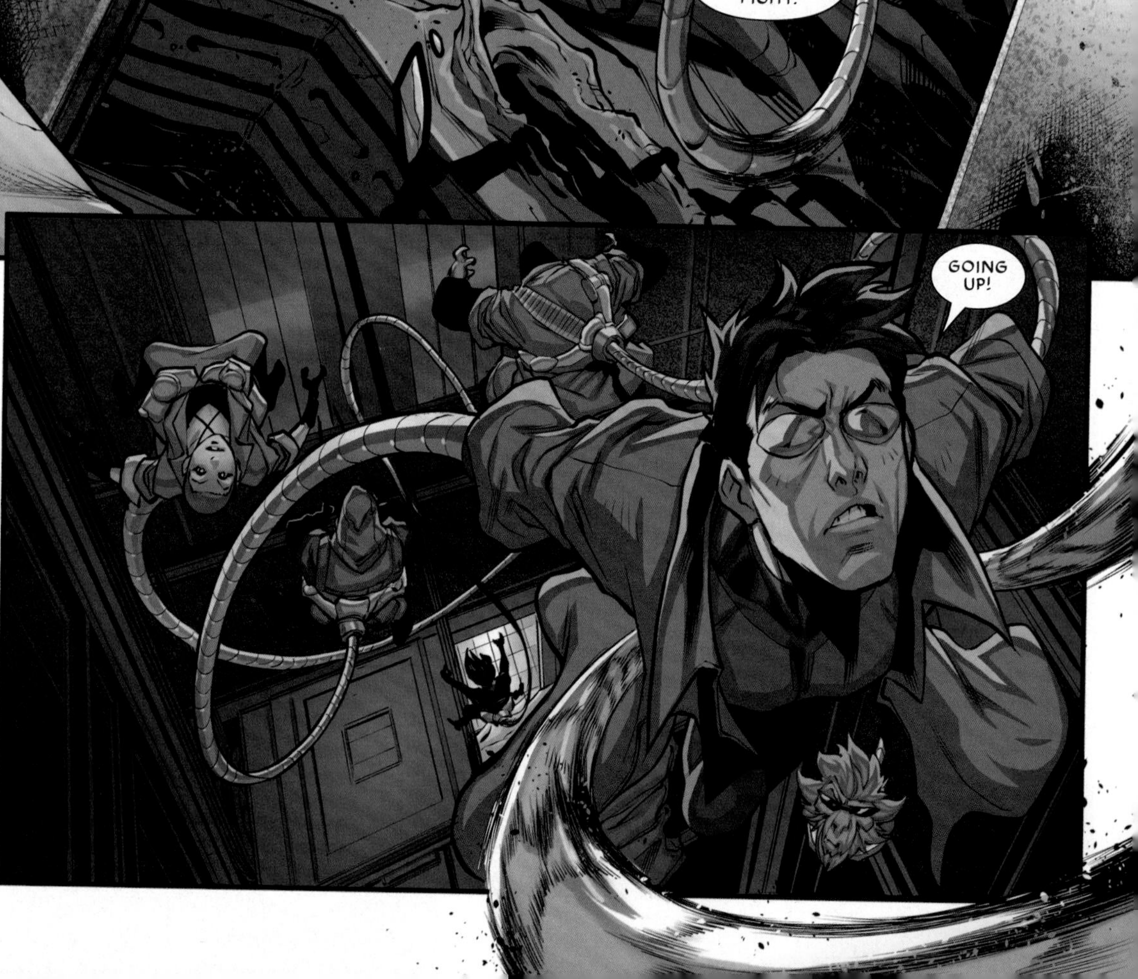
GOING UP!

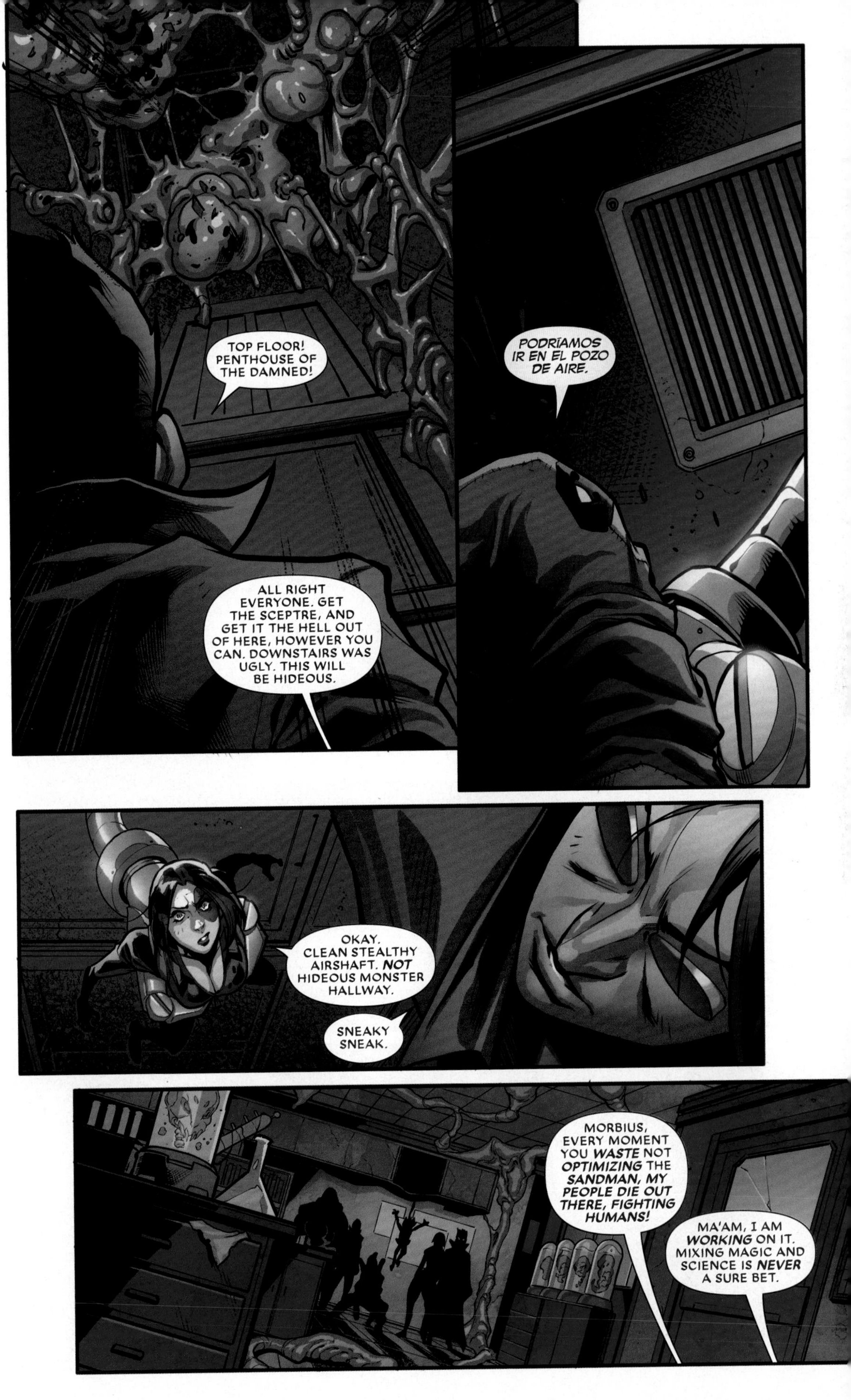

TOP FLOOR! PENTHOUSE OF THE DAMNED!
ALL RIGHT EVERYONE. GET THE SCEPTRE, AND GET IT THE HELL OUT OF HERE, HOWEVER YOU CAN. DOWNSTAIRS WAS UGLY. THIS WILL BE HIDEOUS.
PODRÍAMOS IR EN EL POZO DE AIRE.
OKAY. CLEAN STEALTHY AIRSHAFT. NOT HIDEOUS MONSTER HALLWAY.
SNEAKY SNEAK.
MORBIUS, EVERY MOMENT YOU WASTE NOT OPTIMIZING THE SANDMAN, MY PEOPLE DIE OUT THERE, FIGHTING HUMANS!
MA'AM, I AM WORKING ON IT. MIXING MAGIC AND SCIENCE IS NEVER A SURE BET.

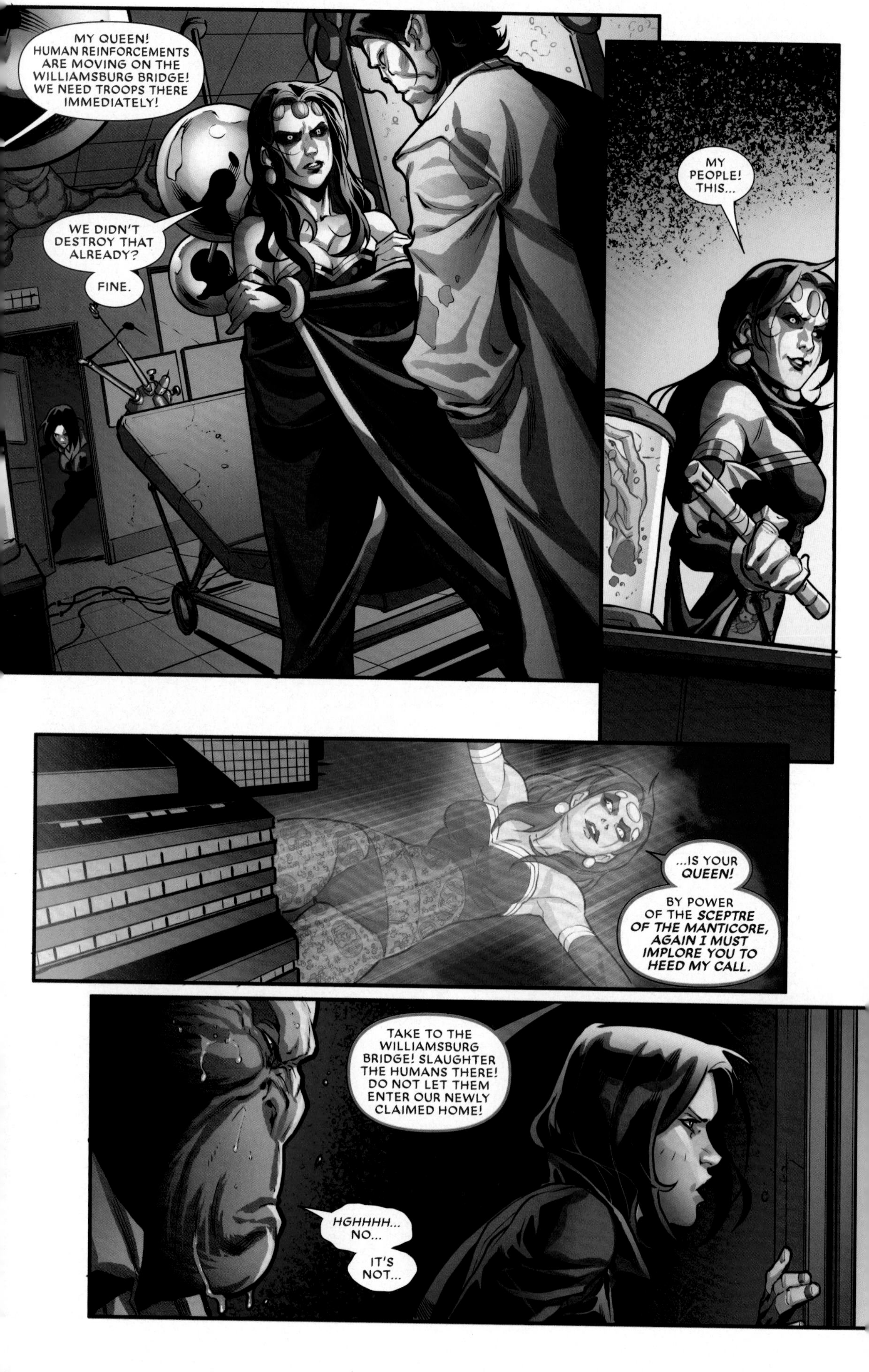
MY QUEEN! HUMAN REINFORCEMENTS ARE MOVING ON THE WILLIAMSBURG BRIDGE! WE NEED TROOPS THERE IMMEDIATELY!
WE DIDN'T DESTROY THAT ALREADY?
FINE.
MY PEOPLE! THIS...
...IS YOUR QUEEN!
BY POWER OF THE SCEPTRE OF THE MANTICORE, AGAIN I MUST IMPLORE YOU TO HEED MY CALL.
TAKE TO THE WILLIAMSBURG BRIDGE! SLAUGHTER THE HUMANS THERE! DO NOT LET THEM ENTER OUR NEWLY CLAIMED HOME!
HGHHHH... NO...
IT'S NOT...

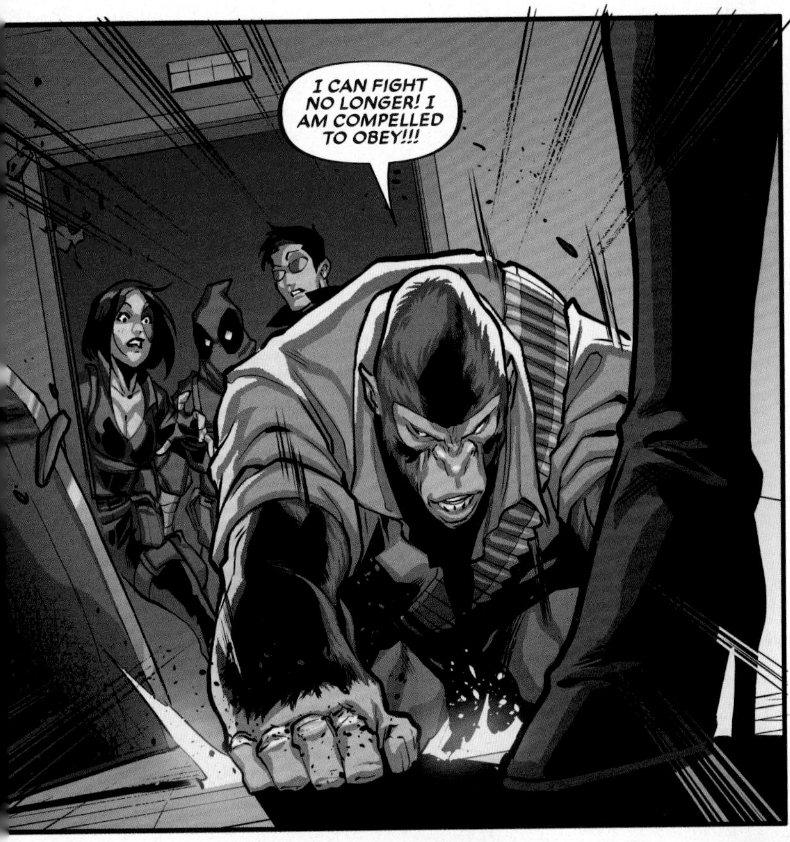
I CAN FIGHT NO LONGER! I AM COMPELLED TO OBEY!!!

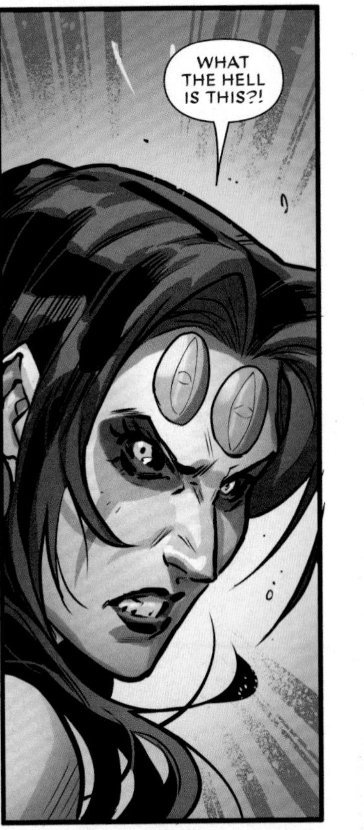
WHAT THE HELL IS THIS?!

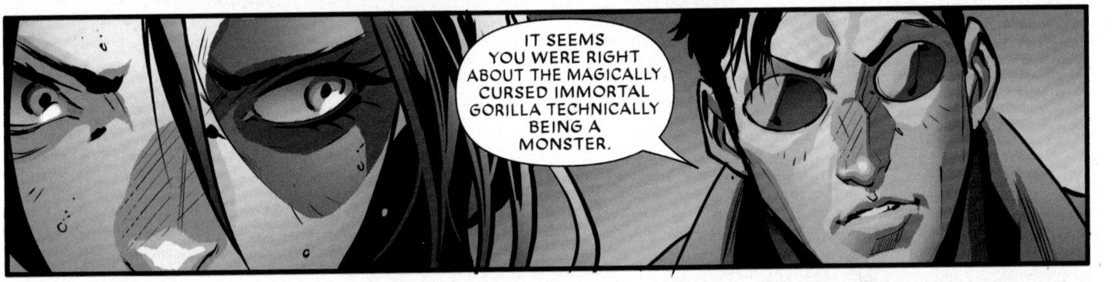
IT SEEMS YOU WERE RIGHT ABOUT THE MAGICALLY CURSED IMMORTAL GORILLA TECHNICALLY BEING A MONSTER.

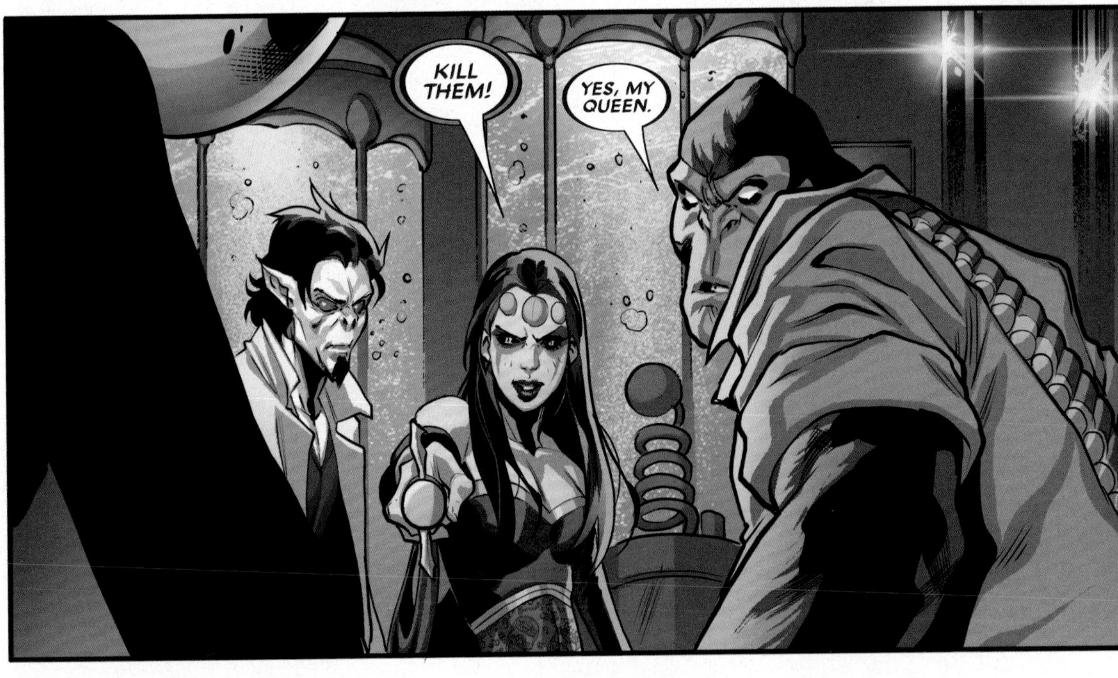
KILL THEM!
YES, MY QUEEN.

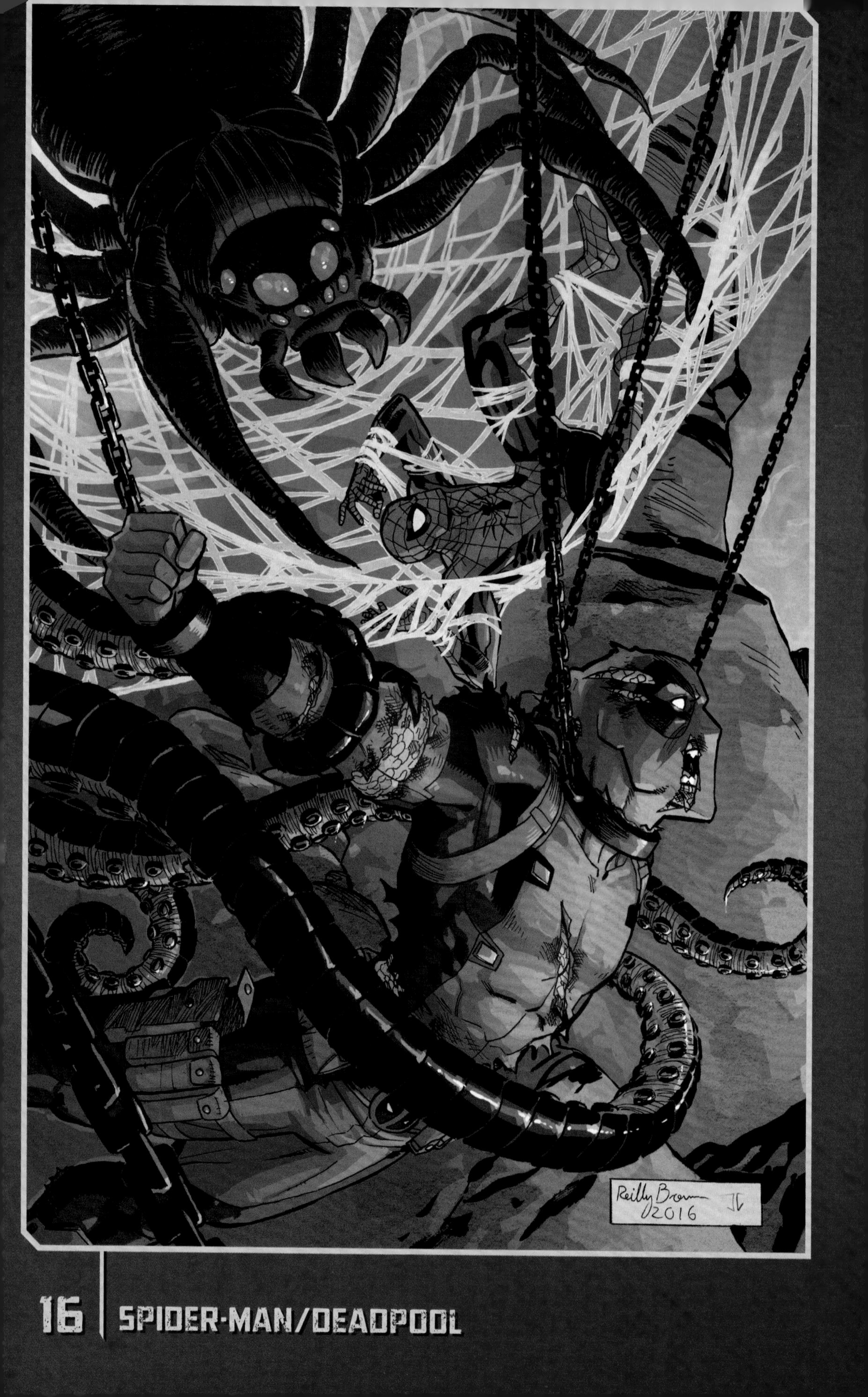

Reilly Brown
2016

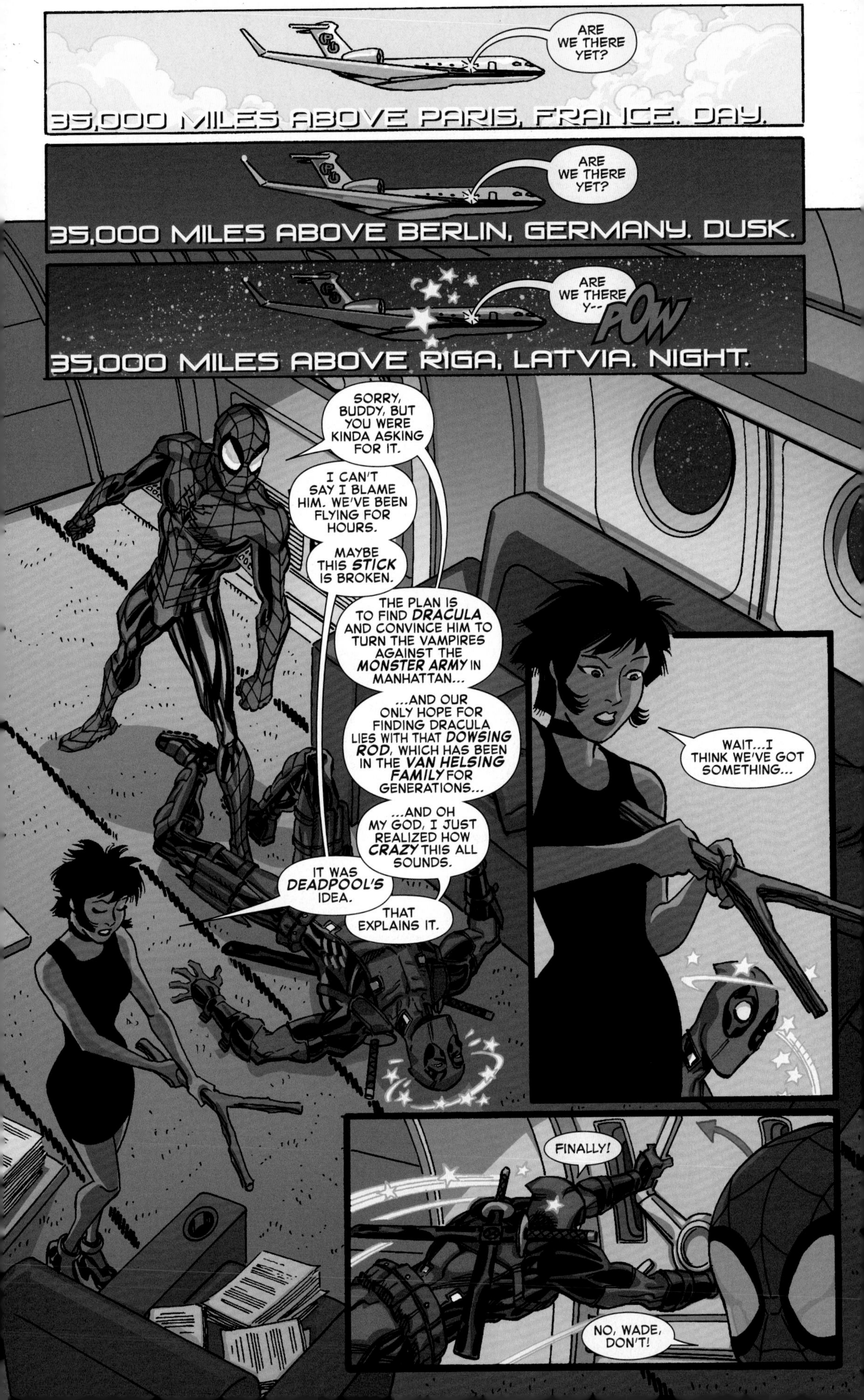
ARE WE THERE YET?
35,000 MILES ABOVE PARIS, FRANCE. DAY.
ARE WE THERE YET?
35,000 MILES ABOVE BERLIN, GERMANY. DUSK.
ARE WE THERE Y--
POW
35,000 MILES ABOVE RIGA, LATVIA. NIGHT.
SORRY, BUDDY, BUT YOU WERE KINDA ASKING FOR IT.
I CAN'T SAY I BLAME HIM. WE'VE BEEN FLYING FOR HOURS.
MAYBE THIS STICK IS BROKEN.
THE PLAN IS TO FIND DRACULA AND CONVINCE HIM TO TURN THE VAMPIRES AGAINST THE MONSTER ARMY IN MANHATTAN...
...AND OUR ONLY HOPE FOR FINDING DRACULA LIES WITH THAT DOWSING ROD, WHICH HAS BEEN IN THE VAN HELSING FAMILY FOR GENERATIONS...
...AND OH MY GOD, I JUST REALIZED HOW CRAZY THIS ALL SOUNDS.
IT WAS DEADPOOL'S IDEA.
THAT EXPLAINS IT.
WAIT...I THINK WE'VE GOT SOMETHING...
FINALLY!
NO, WADE, DON'T!

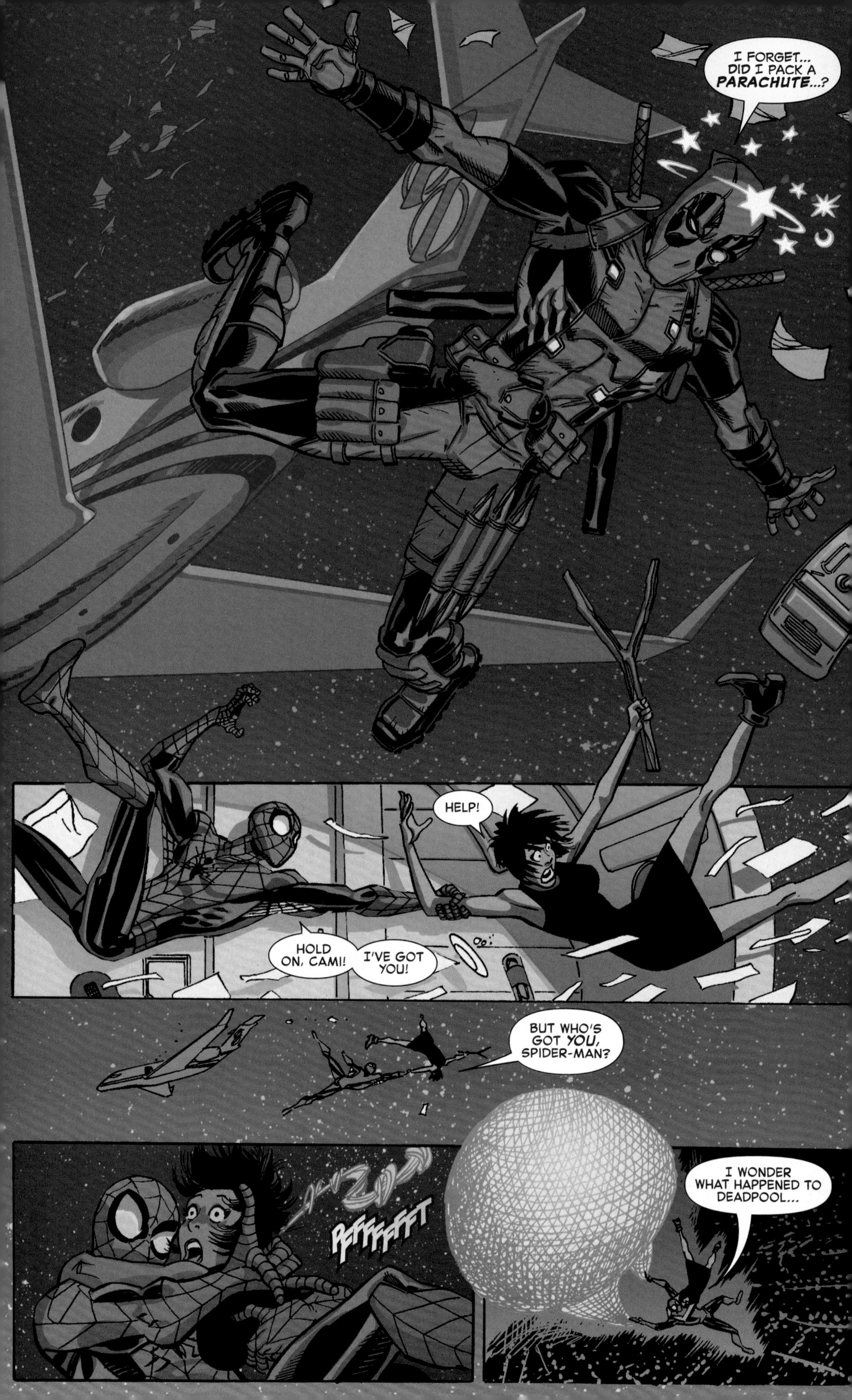
I FORGET... DID I PACK A PARACHUTE...?
HELP!
HOLD ON, CAMI!
I'VE GOT YOU!
BUT WHO'S GOT YOU, SPIDER-MAN?
ZIP
FFFFFFFT
I WONDER WHAT HAPPENED TO DEADPOOL...

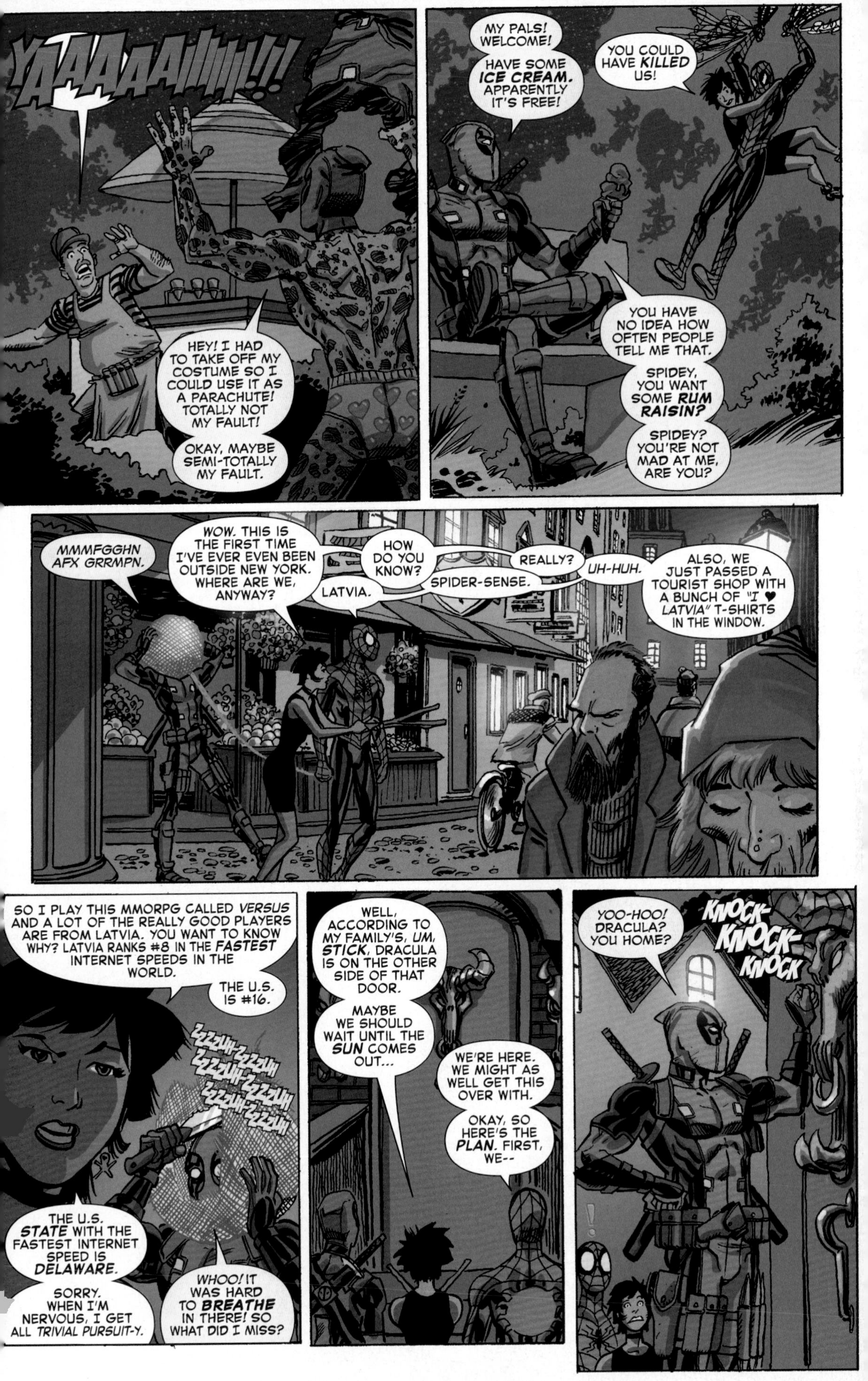
YAAAAAIIIIII!!!
HEY! I HAD TO TAKE OFF MY COSTUME SO I COULD USE IT AS A PARACHUTE! TOTALLY NOT MY FAULT!
OKAY, MAYBE SEMI-TOTALLY MY FAULT.
MY PALS! WELCOME!
HAVE SOME ICE CREAM. APPARENTLY IT'S FREE!
YOU COULD HAVE KILLED US!
YOU HAVE NO IDEA HOW OFTEN PEOPLE TELL ME THAT.
SPIDEY, YOU WANT SOME RUM RAISIN?
SPIDEY? YOU'RE NOT MAD AT ME, ARE YOU?
MMMFGGHN AFX GRRMPN.
WOW. THIS IS THE FIRST TIME I'VE EVER EVEN BEEN OUTSIDE NEW YORK. WHERE ARE WE, ANYWAY?
LATVIA.
HOW DO YOU KNOW?
SPIDER-SENSE.
REALLY?
UH-HUH.
ALSO, WE JUST PASSED A TOURIST SHOP WITH A BUNCH OF "I ♥ LATVIA" T-SHIRTS IN THE WINDOW.
SO I PLAY THIS MMORPG CALLED VERSUS AND A LOT OF THE REALLY GOOD PLAYERS ARE FROM LATVIA. YOU WANT TO KNOW WHY? LATVIA RANKS #8 IN THE FASTEST INTERNET SPEEDS IN THE WORLD.
THE U.S. IS #16.
ZZZZUH-ZZZZUH ZZZZUH-ZZZZUH ZZZZUH-ZZZZUH ZZZZUH-ZZZZUH
THE U.S. STATE WITH THE FASTEST INTERNET SPEED IS DELAWARE.
SORRY. WHEN I'M NERVOUS, I GET ALL TRIVIAL PURSUIT-Y.
WHOO! IT WAS HARD TO BREATHE IN THERE! SO WHAT DID I MISS?
WELL, ACCORDING TO MY FAMILY'S, UM, STICK, DRACULA IS ON THE OTHER SIDE OF THAT DOOR.
MAYBE WE SHOULD WAIT UNTIL THE SUN COMES OUT...
WE'RE HERE. WE MIGHT AS WELL GET THIS OVER WITH.
OKAY, SO HERE'S THE PLAN. FIRST, WE--
YOO-HOO! DRACULA? YOU HOME?
KNOCK-KNOCK-KNOCK
!

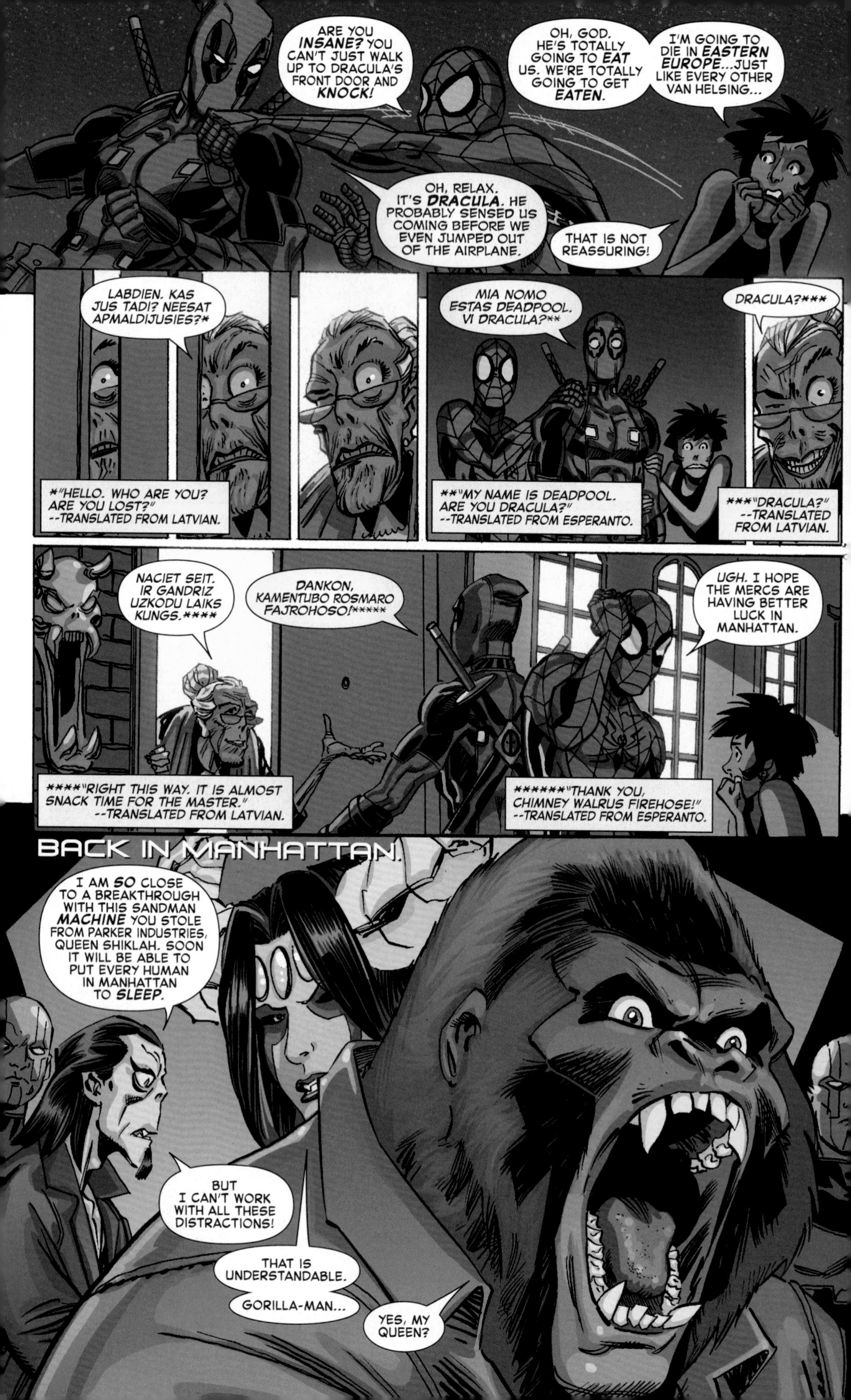
ARE YOU INSANE? YOU CAN'T JUST WALK UP TO DRACULA'S FRONT DOOR AND KNOCK!
OH, GOD. HE'S TOTALLY GOING TO EAT US. WE'RE TOTALLY GOING TO GET EATEN.
I'M GOING TO DIE IN EASTERN EUROPE...JUST LIKE EVERY OTHER VAN HELSING...
OH, RELAX. IT'S DRACULA. HE PROBABLY SENSED US COMING BEFORE WE EVEN JUMPED OUT OF THE AIRPLANE.
THAT IS NOT REASSURING!
LABDIEN. KAS JUS TADI? NEESAT APMALDIJUSIES?*
*"HELLO. WHO ARE YOU? ARE YOU LOST?" --TRANSLATED FROM LATVIAN.
MIA NOMO ESTAS DEADPOOL. VI DRACULA?**
**"MY NAME IS DEADPOOL. ARE YOU DRACULA?" --TRANSLATED FROM ESPERANTO.
DRACULA?***
***"DRACULA?" --TRANSLATED FROM LATVIAN.
NACIET SEIT. IR GANDRIZ UZKODU LAIKS KUNGS.****
DANKON, KAMENTUBO ROSMARO FAJROHOSO!*****
UGH. I HOPE THE MERCS ARE HAVING BETTER LUCK IN MANHATTAN.
****"RIGHT THIS WAY. IT IS ALMOST SNACK TIME FOR THE MASTER." --TRANSLATED FROM LATVIAN.
*****"THANK YOU, CHIMNEY WALRUS FIREHOSE!" --TRANSLATED FROM ESPERANTO.
BACK IN MANHATTAN.
I AM SO CLOSE TO A BREAKTHROUGH WITH THIS SANDMAN MACHINE YOU STOLE FROM PARKER INDUSTRIES, QUEEN SHIKLAH. SOON IT WILL BE ABLE TO PUT EVERY HUMAN IN MANHATTAN TO SLEEP.
BUT I CAN'T WORK WITH ALL THESE DISTRACTIONS!
THAT IS UNDERSTANDABLE.
GORILLA-MAN...
YES, MY QUEEN?

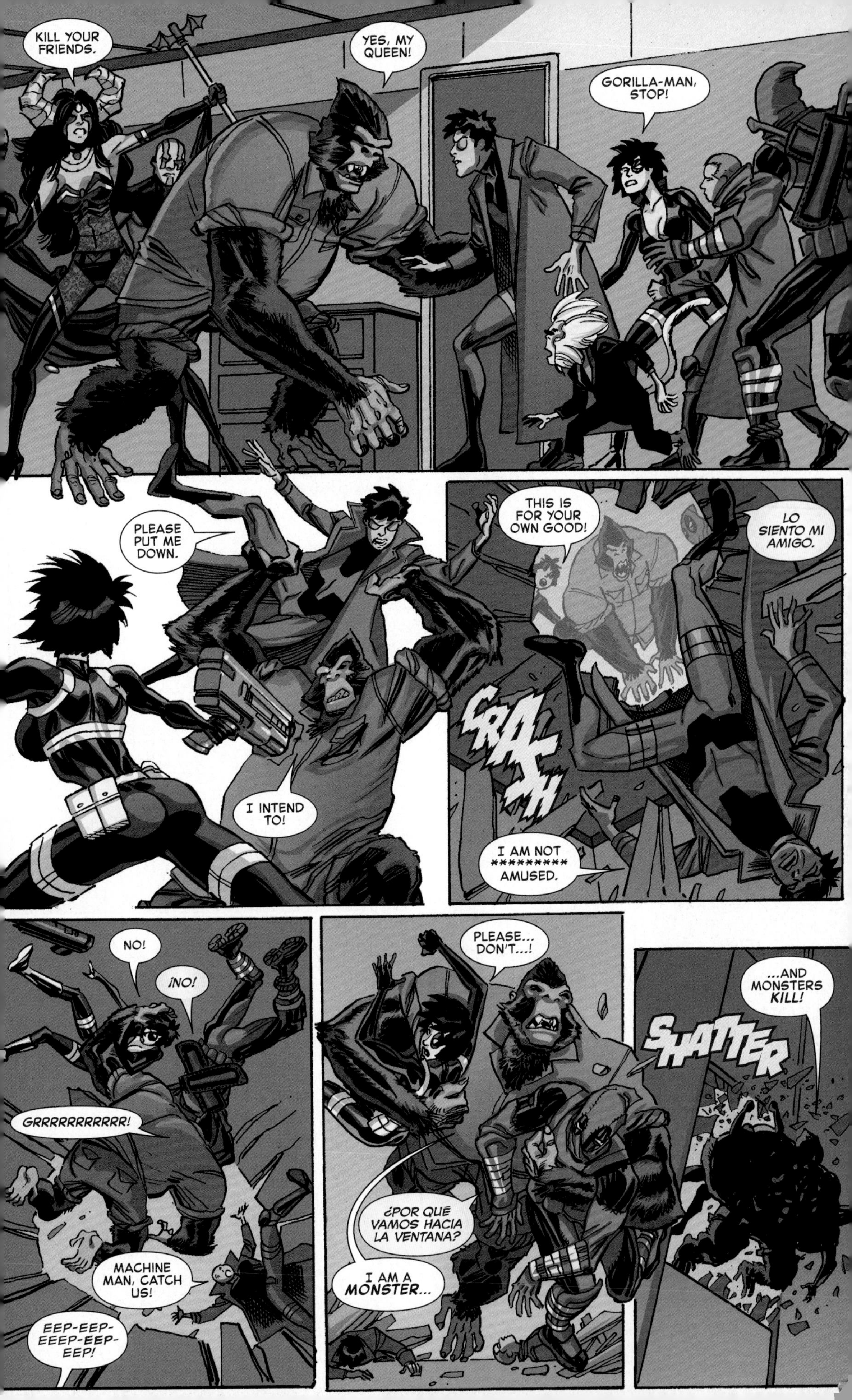
KILL YOUR FRIENDS.
YES, MY QUEEN!
GORILLA-MAN, STOP!
PLEASE PUT ME DOWN.
I INTEND TO!
THIS IS FOR YOUR OWN GOOD!
LO SIENTO MI AMIGO.
CRASH
I AM NOT ********* AMUSED.
NO!
¡NO!
GRRRRRRRRRR!
MACHINE MAN, CATCH US!
EEP-EEP-EEEP-EEP-EEP!
PLEASE... DON'T...!
¿POR QUÉ VAMOS HACIA LA VENTANA?
I AM A MONSTER...
...AND MONSTERS KILL!
SHATTER

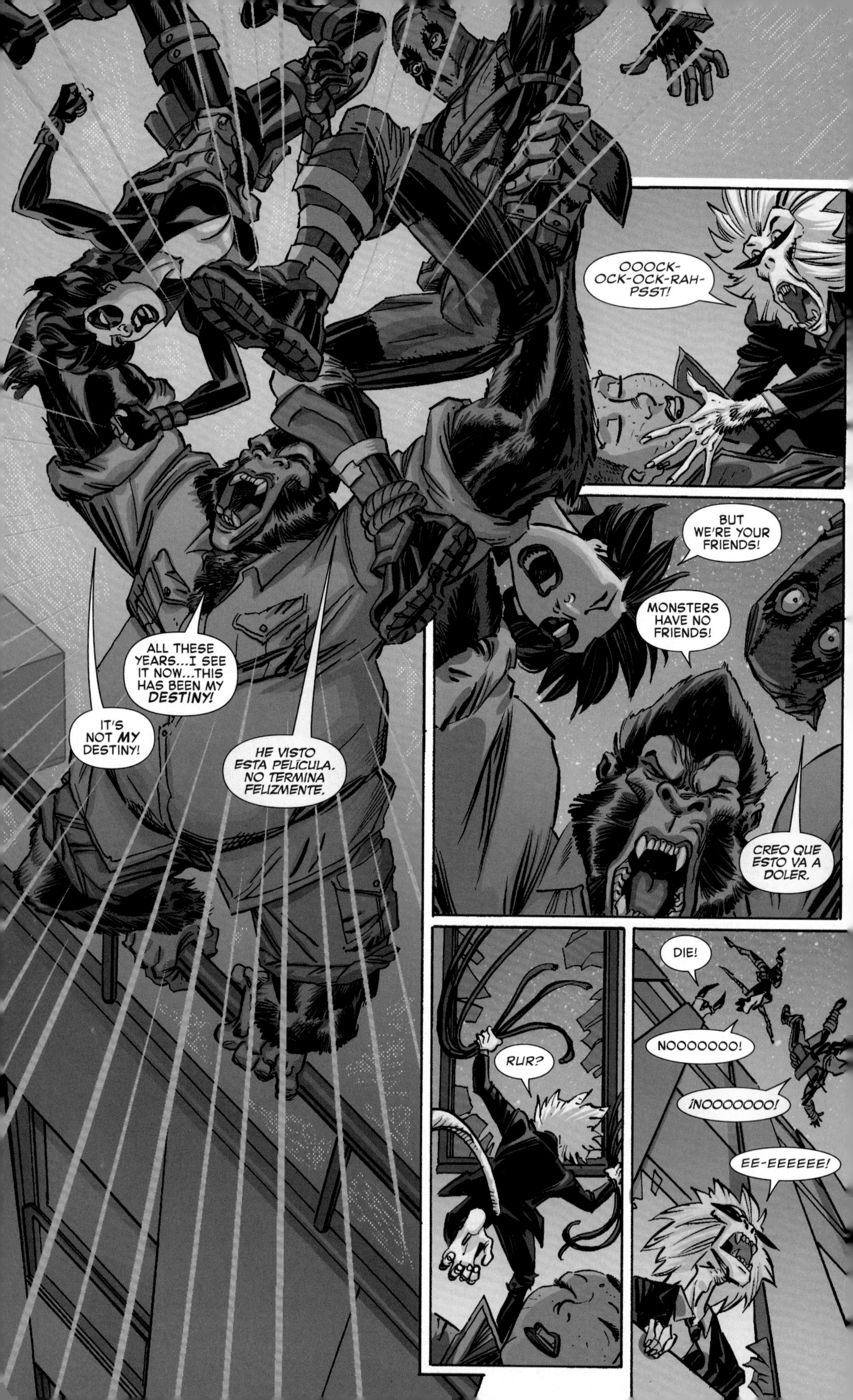
OOOCK-OCK-OCK-RAH-PSST!
ALL THESE YEARS...I SEE IT NOW...THIS HAS BEEN MY DESTINY!
IT'S NOT MY DESTINY!
HE VISTO ESTA PELÍCULA. NO TERMINA FELIZMENTE.
BUT WE'RE YOUR FRIENDS!
MONSTERS HAVE NO FRIENDS!
CREO QUE ESTO VA A DOLER.
RUR?
DIE!
NOOOOOOO!
¡NOOOOOOO!
EE-EEEEEE!

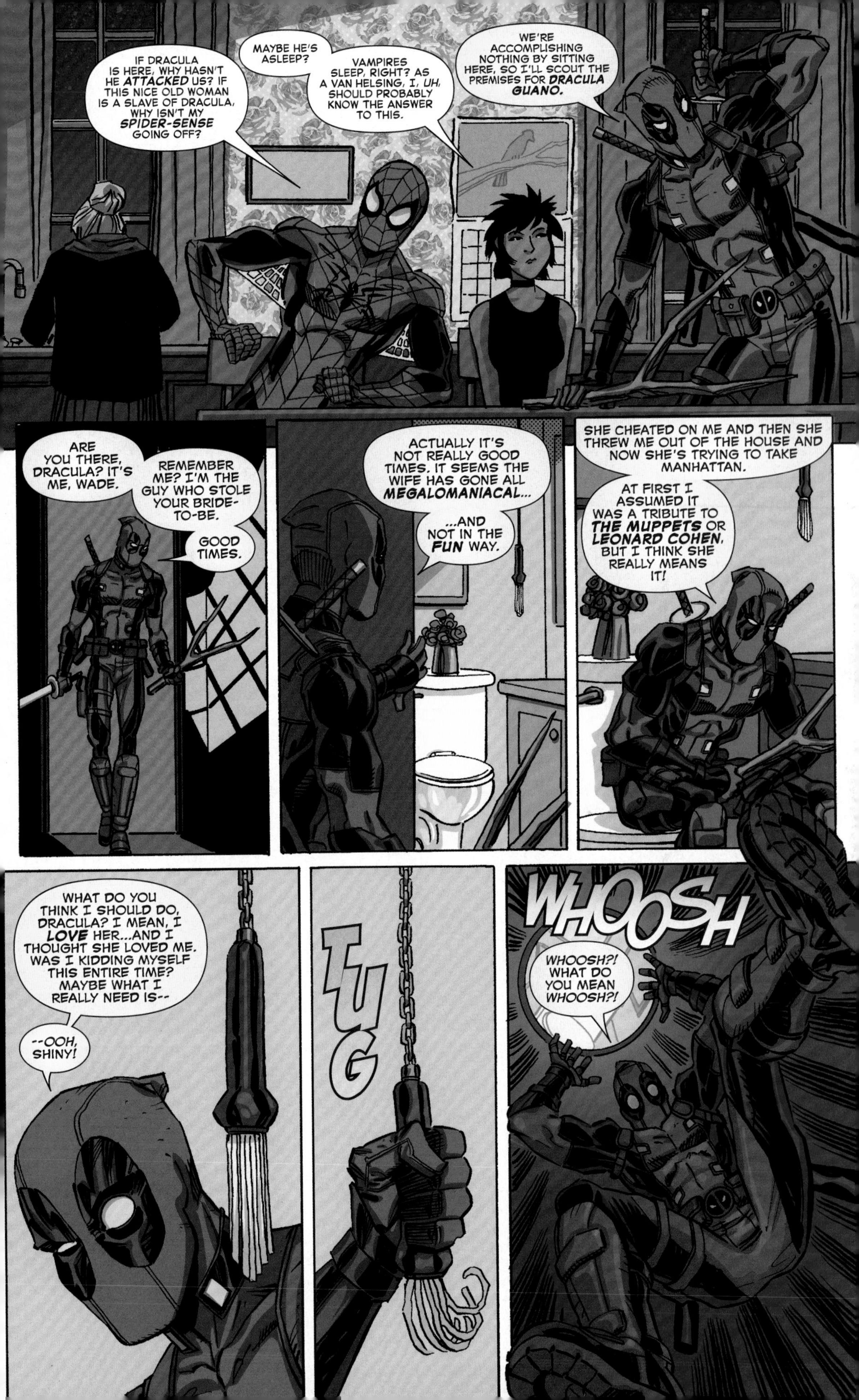
IF DRACULA IS HERE, WHY HASN'T HE ATTACKED US? IF THIS NICE OLD WOMAN IS A SLAVE OF DRACULA, WHY ISN'T MY SPIDER-SENSE GOING OFF?
MAYBE HE'S ASLEEP?
VAMPIRES SLEEP, RIGHT? AS A VAN HELSING, I, UH, SHOULD PROBABLY KNOW THE ANSWER TO THIS.
WE'RE ACCOMPLISHING NOTHING BY SITTING HERE, SO I'LL SCOUT THE PREMISES FOR DRACULA GUANO.
ARE YOU THERE, DRACULA? IT'S ME, WADE.
REMEMBER ME? I'M THE GUY WHO STOLE YOUR BRIDE-TO-BE.
GOOD TIMES.
ACTUALLY IT'S NOT REALLY GOOD TIMES. IT SEEMS THE WIFE HAS GONE ALL MEGALOMANIACAL...
...AND NOT IN THE FUN WAY.
SHE CHEATED ON ME AND THEN SHE THREW ME OUT OF THE HOUSE AND NOW SHE'S TRYING TO TAKE MANHATTAN.
AT FIRST I ASSUMED IT WAS A TRIBUTE TO THE MUPPETS OR LEONARD COHEN, BUT I THINK SHE REALLY MEANS IT!
WHAT DO YOU THINK I SHOULD DO, DRACULA? I MEAN, I LOVE HER...AND I THOUGHT SHE LOVED ME. WAS I KIDDING MYSELF THIS ENTIRE TIME? MAYBE WHAT I REALLY NEED IS--
--OOH, SHINY!
TUG
WHOOSH
WHOOSH?! WHAT DO YOU MEAN WHOOSH?!

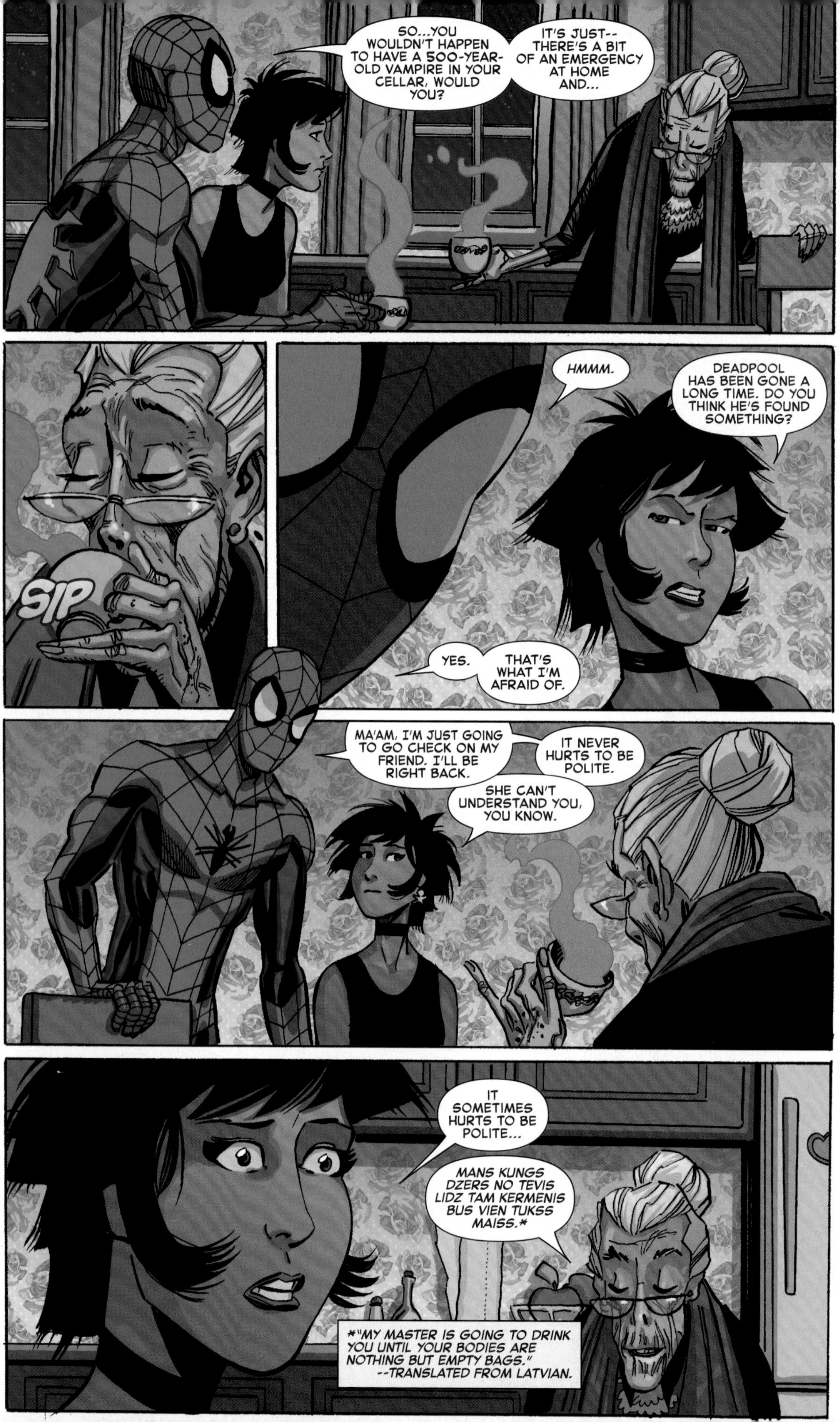
SO...YOU WOULDN'T HAPPEN TO HAVE A 500-YEAR-OLD VAMPIRE IN YOUR CELLAR, WOULD YOU?
IT'S JUST-- THERE'S A BIT OF AN EMERGENCY AT HOME AND...
SIP
HMMM.
DEADPOOL HAS BEEN GONE A LONG TIME. DO YOU THINK HE'S FOUND SOMETHING?
YES.
THAT'S WHAT I'M AFRAID OF.
MA'AM, I'M JUST GOING TO GO CHECK ON MY FRIEND. I'LL BE RIGHT BACK.
IT NEVER HURTS TO BE POLITE.
SHE CAN'T UNDERSTAND YOU, YOU KNOW.
IT SOMETIMES HURTS TO BE POLITE...
MANS KUNGS DZERS NO TEVIS LIDZ TAM KERMENIS BUS VIEN TUKSS MAISS.*
*"MY MASTER IS GOING TO DRINK YOU UNTIL YOUR BODIES ARE NOTHING BUT EMPTY BAGS." --TRANSLATED FROM LATVIAN.

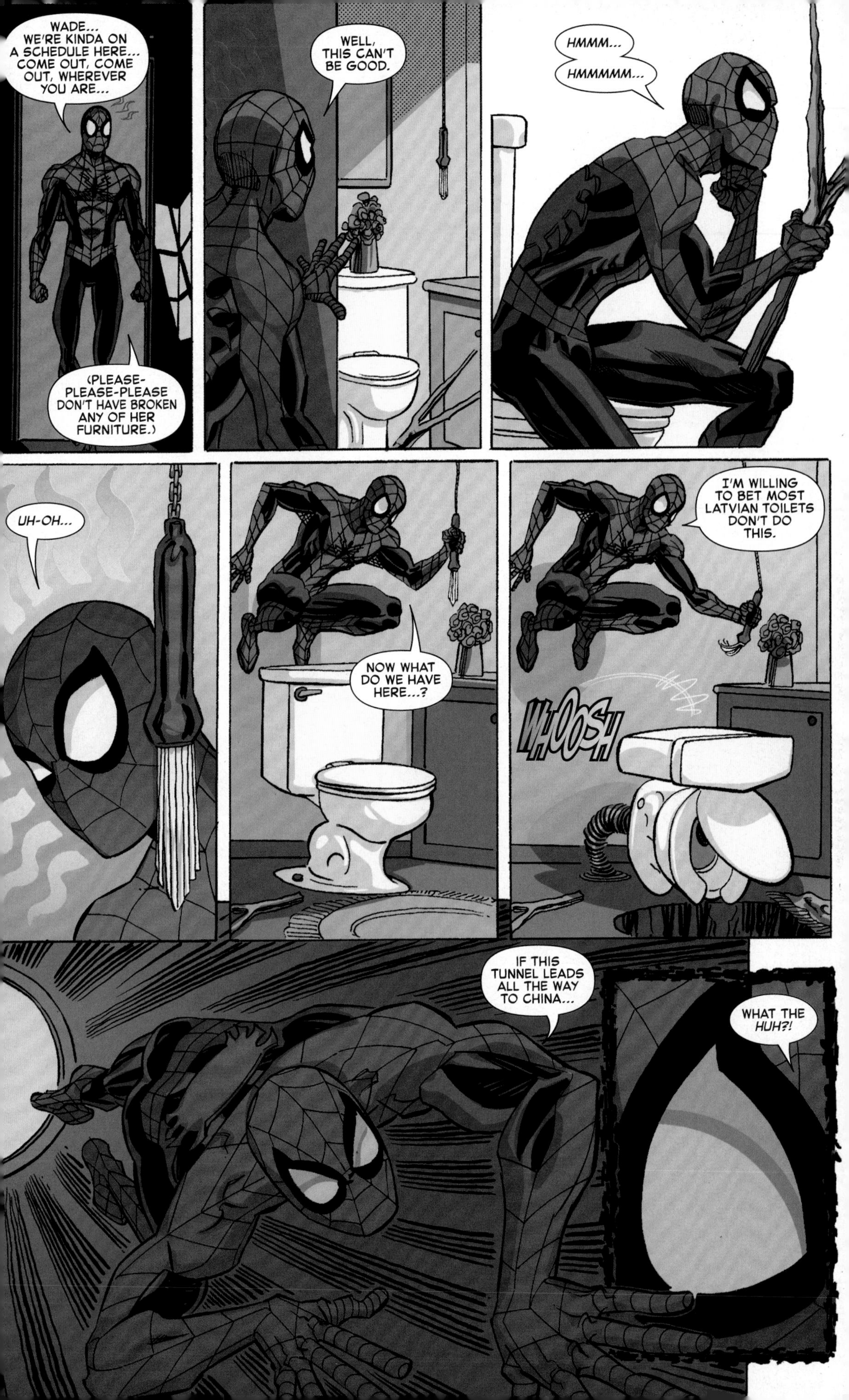
WADE... WE'RE KINDA ON A SCHEDULE HERE... COME OUT, COME OUT, WHEREVER YOU ARE...
(PLEASE-PLEASE-PLEASE DON'T HAVE BROKEN ANY OF HER FURNITURE.)
WELL, THIS CAN'T BE GOOD.
HMMM...
HMMMMM...
UH-OH...
NOW WHAT DO WE HAVE HERE...?
I'M WILLING TO BET MOST LATVIAN TOILETS DON'T DO THIS.
WHOOSH
IF THIS TUNNEL LEADS ALL THE WAY TO CHINA...
WHAT THE HUH?!

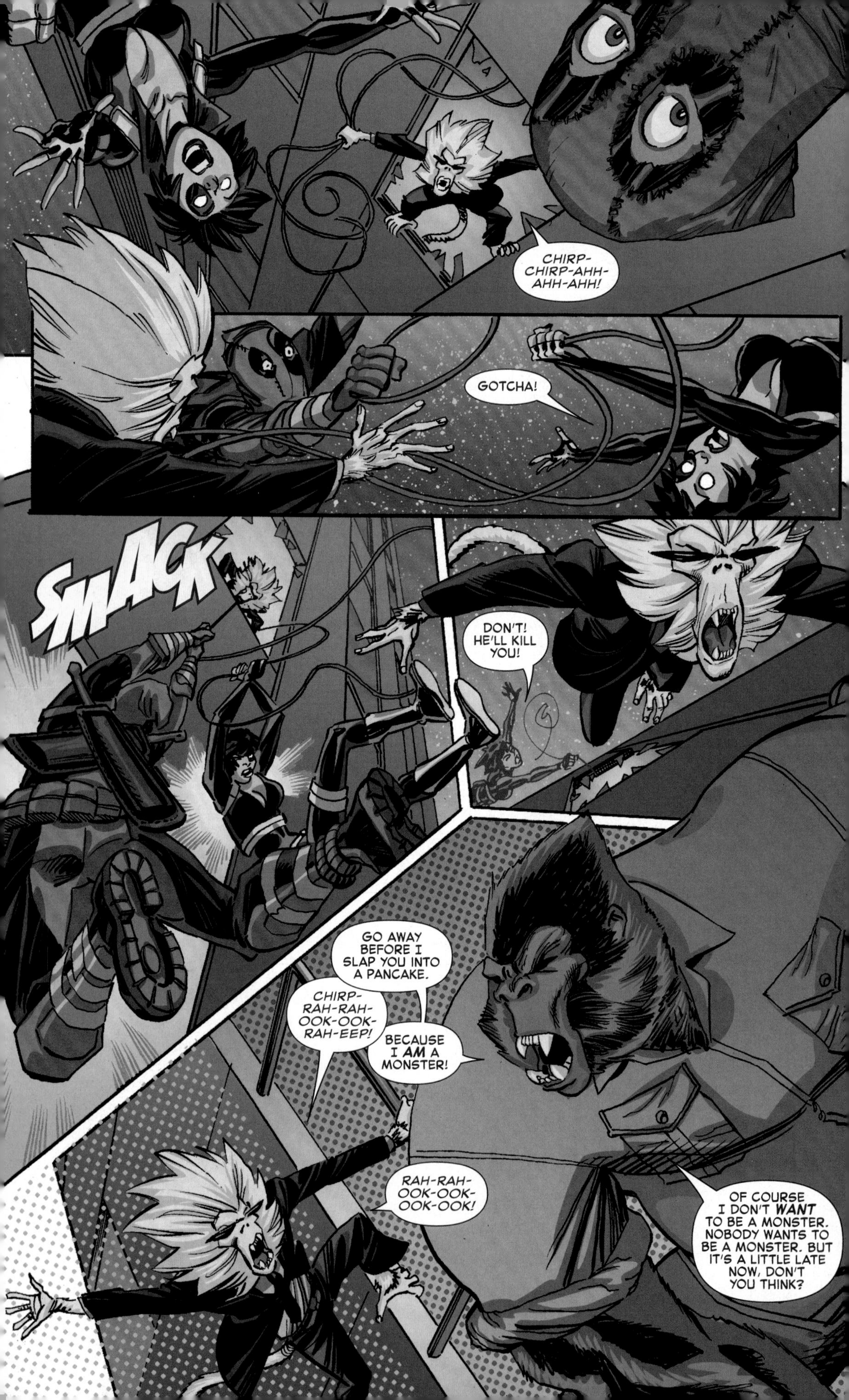

CHIRP-CHIRP-AHH-AHH-AHH!
GOTCHA!
SMACK
DON'T! HE'LL KILL YOU!
GO AWAY BEFORE I SLAP YOU INTO A PANCAKE.
CHIRP-RAH-RAH-OOK-OOK-RAH-EEP!
BECAUSE I AM A MONSTER!
RAH-RAH-OOK-OOK-OOK-OOK!
OF COURSE I DON'T WANT TO BE A MONSTER. NOBODY WANTS TO BE A MONSTER. BUT IT'S A LITTLE LATE NOW, DON'T YOU THINK?

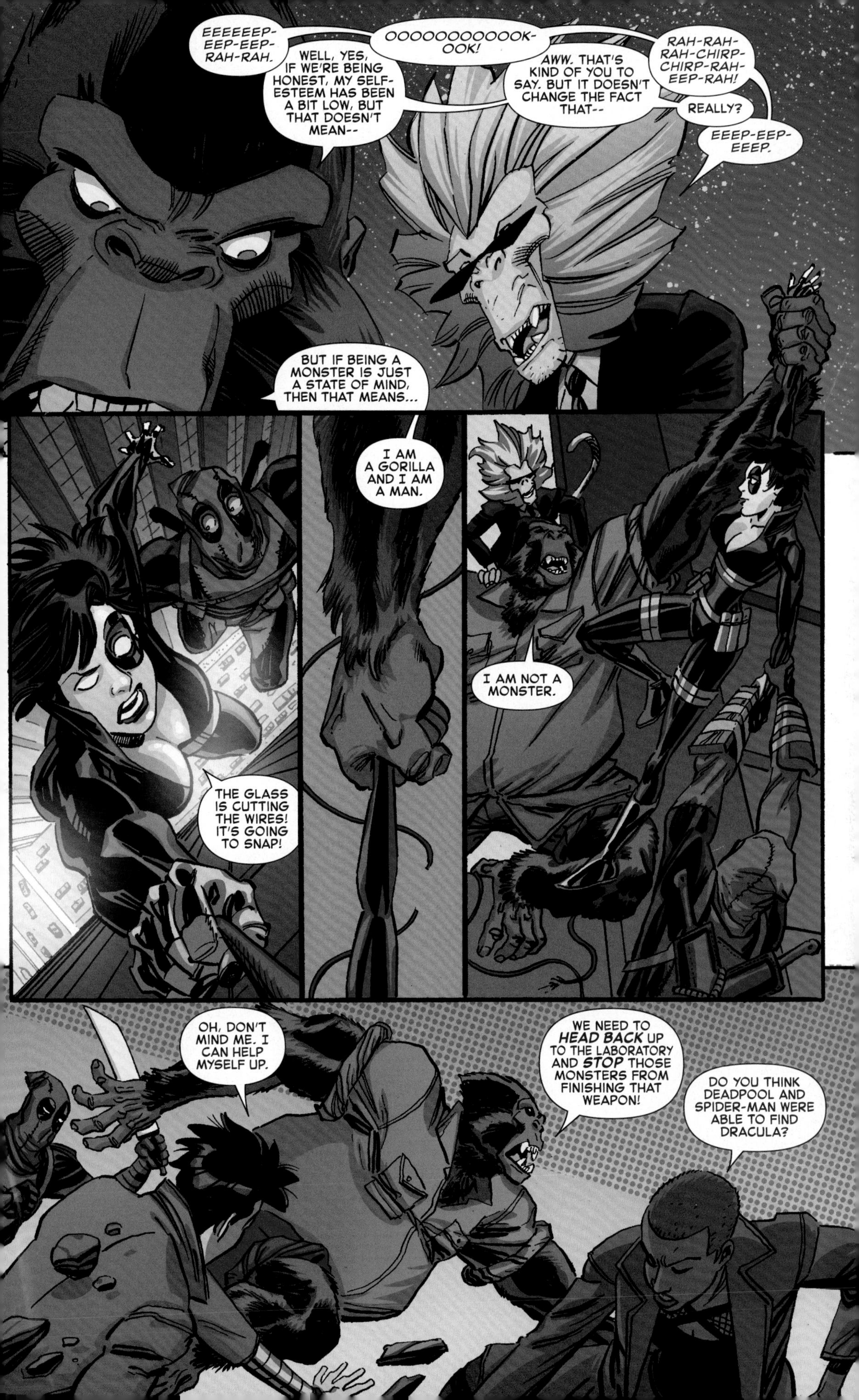
EEEEEEP-EEP-EEP-RAH-RAH.
OOOOOOOOOOOK-OOK!
WELL, YES, IF WE'RE BEING HONEST, MY SELF-ESTEEM HAS BEEN A BIT LOW, BUT THAT DOESN'T MEAN--
AWW. THAT'S KIND OF YOU TO SAY. BUT IT DOESN'T CHANGE THE FACT THAT--
RAH-RAH-RAH-CHIRP-CHIRP-RAH-EEP-RAH!
REALLY?
EEEP-EEP-EEEP.
BUT IF BEING A MONSTER IS JUST A STATE OF MIND, THEN THAT MEANS...
THE GLASS IS CUTTING THE WIRES! IT'S GOING TO SNAP!
I AM A GORILLA AND I AM A MAN.
I AM NOT A MONSTER.
OH, DON'T MIND ME. I CAN HELP MYSELF UP.
WE NEED TO HEAD BACK UP TO THE LABORATORY AND STOP THOSE MONSTERS FROM FINISHING THAT WEAPON!
DO YOU THINK DEADPOOL AND SPIDER-MAN WERE ABLE TO FIND DRACULA?

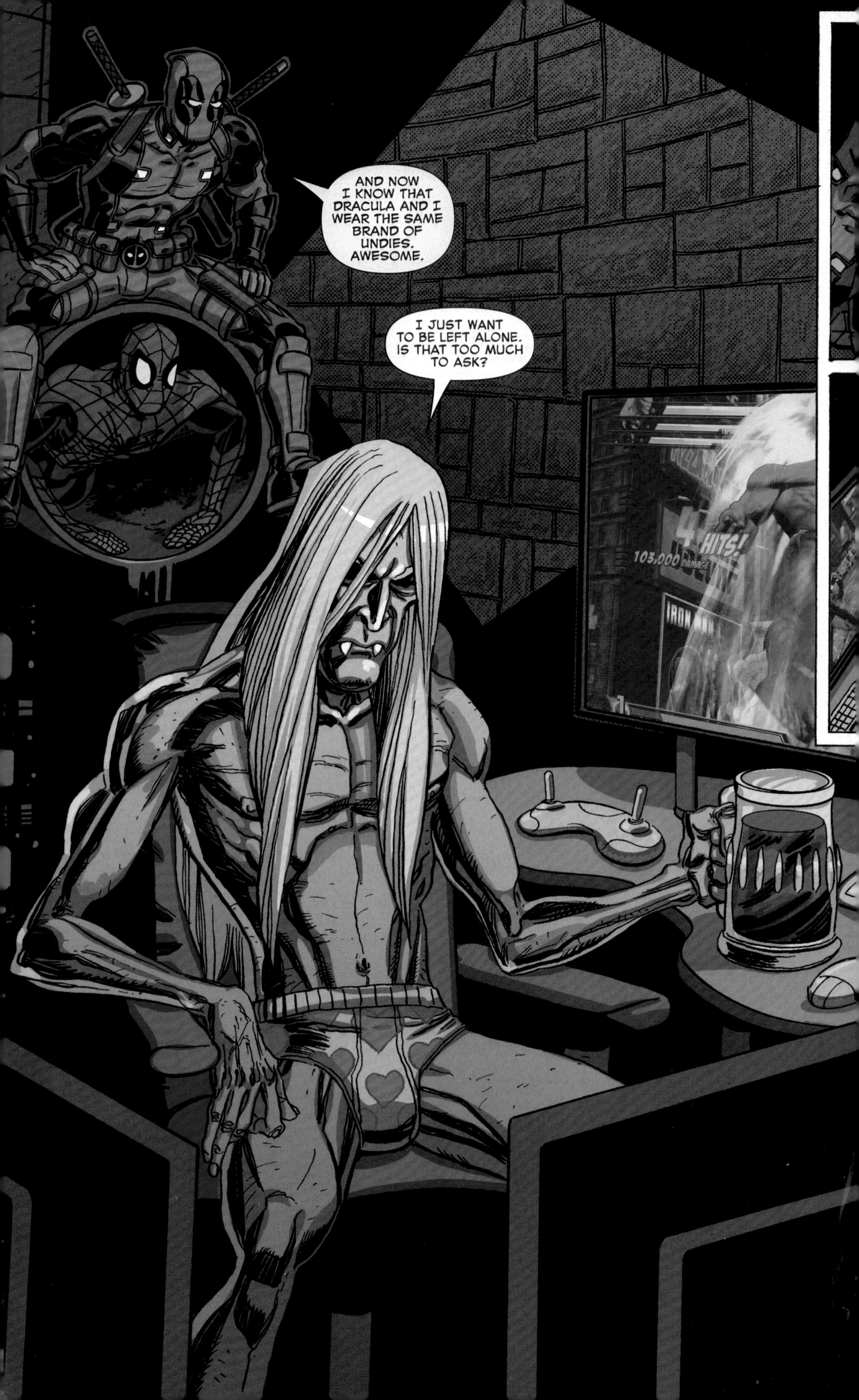
AND NOW I KNOW THAT DRACULA AND I WEAR THE SAME BRAND OF UNDIES. AWESOME.
I JUST WANT TO BE LEFT ALONE. IS THAT TOO MUCH TO ASK?
4 HITS!
IRON MAN

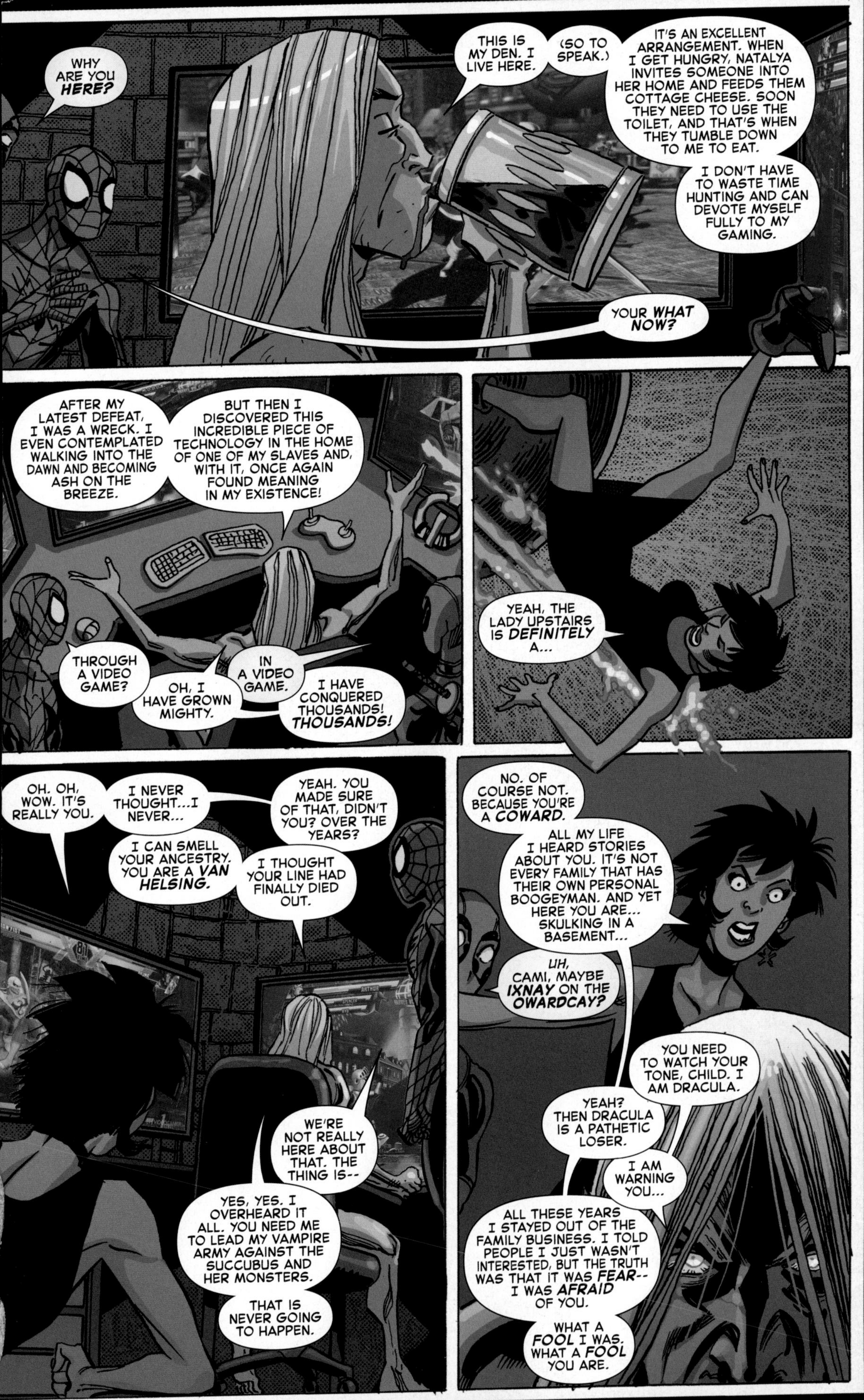
WHY ARE YOU HERE?
THIS IS MY DEN. I LIVE HERE.
(SO TO SPEAK.)
IT'S AN EXCELLENT ARRANGEMENT. WHEN I GET HUNGRY, NATALYA INVITES SOMEONE INTO HER HOME AND FEEDS THEM COTTAGE CHEESE. SOON THEY NEED TO USE THE TOILET, AND THAT'S WHEN THEY TUMBLE DOWN TO ME TO EAT.
I DON'T HAVE TO WASTE TIME HUNTING AND CAN DEVOTE MYSELF FULLY TO MY GAMING.
YOUR WHAT NOW?
AFTER MY LATEST DEFEAT, I WAS A WRECK. I EVEN CONTEMPLATED WALKING INTO THE DAWN AND BECOMING ASH ON THE BREEZE.
BUT THEN I DISCOVERED THIS INCREDIBLE PIECE OF TECHNOLOGY IN THE HOME OF ONE OF MY SLAVES AND, WITH IT, ONCE AGAIN FOUND MEANING IN MY EXISTENCE!
THROUGH A VIDEO GAME?
OH, I HAVE GROWN MIGHTY.
IN A VIDEO GAME.
I HAVE CONQUERED THOUSANDS! THOUSANDS!
YEAH, THE LADY UPSTAIRS IS DEFINITELY A...
OH. OH, WOW. IT'S REALLY YOU.
I NEVER THOUGHT...I NEVER...
YEAH. YOU MADE SURE OF THAT, DIDN'T YOU? OVER THE YEARS?
I CAN SMELL YOUR ANCESTRY. YOU ARE A VAN HELSING.
I THOUGHT YOUR LINE HAD FINALLY DIED OUT.
WE'RE NOT REALLY HERE ABOUT THAT. THE THING IS--
YES, YES. I OVERHEARD IT ALL. YOU NEED ME TO LEAD MY VAMPIRE ARMY AGAINST THE SUCCUBUS AND HER MONSTERS.
THAT IS NEVER GOING TO HAPPEN.
NO. OF COURSE NOT. BECAUSE YOU'RE A COWARD.
ALL MY LIFE I HEARD STORIES ABOUT YOU. IT'S NOT EVERY FAMILY THAT HAS THEIR OWN PERSONAL BOOGEYMAN. AND YET HERE YOU ARE... SKULKING IN A BASEMENT...
UH, CAMI, MAYBE IXNAY ON THE OWARDCAY?
YOU NEED TO WATCH YOUR TONE, CHILD. I AM DRACULA.
YEAH? THEN DRACULA IS A PATHETIC LOSER.
I AM WARNING YOU...
ALL THESE YEARS I STAYED OUT OF THE FAMILY BUSINESS. I TOLD PEOPLE I JUST WASN'T INTERESTED, BUT THE TRUTH WAS THAT IT WAS FEAR-- I WAS AFRAID OF YOU.
WHAT A FOOL I WAS. WHAT A FOOL YOU ARE.

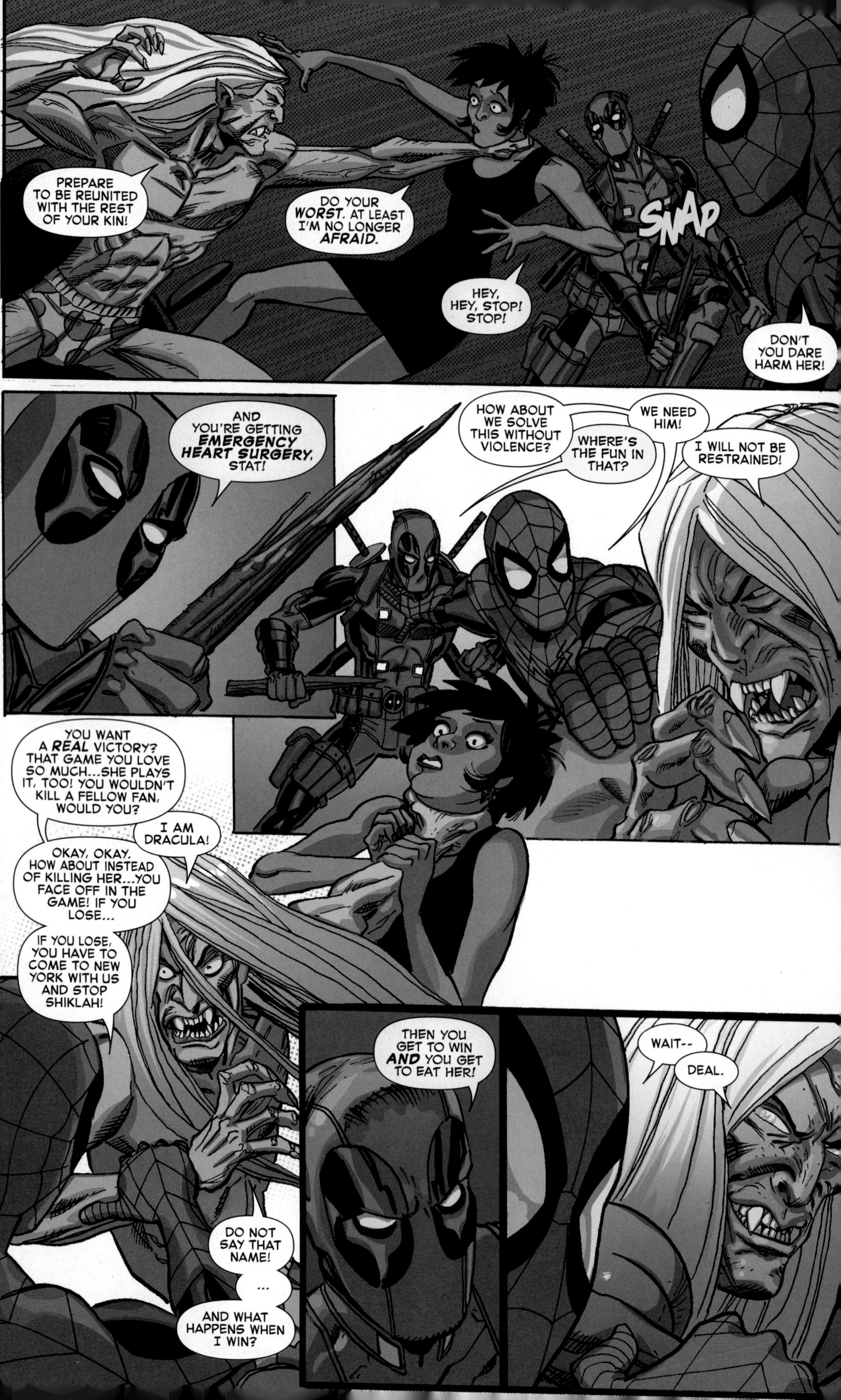
PREPARE TO BE REUNITED WITH THE REST OF YOUR KIN!
DO YOUR WORST. AT LEAST I'M NO LONGER AFRAID.
SNAP
HEY, HEY, STOP! STOP!
DON'T YOU DARE HARM HER!
AND YOU'RE GETTING EMERGENCY HEART SURGERY, STAT!
HOW ABOUT WE SOLVE THIS WITHOUT VIOLENCE?
WE NEED HIM!
WHERE'S THE FUN IN THAT?
I WILL NOT BE RESTRAINED!
YOU WANT A REAL VICTORY? THAT GAME YOU LOVE SO MUCH...SHE PLAYS IT, TOO! YOU WOULDN'T KILL A FELLOW FAN, WOULD YOU?
I AM DRACULA!
OKAY, OKAY. HOW ABOUT INSTEAD OF KILLING HER...YOU FACE OFF IN THE GAME! IF YOU LOSE...
IF YOU LOSE, YOU HAVE TO COME TO NEW YORK WITH US AND STOP SHIKLAH!
DO NOT SAY THAT NAME!
...
AND WHAT HAPPENS WHEN I WIN?
THEN YOU GET TO WIN AND YOU GET TO EAT HER!
WAIT--
DEAL.

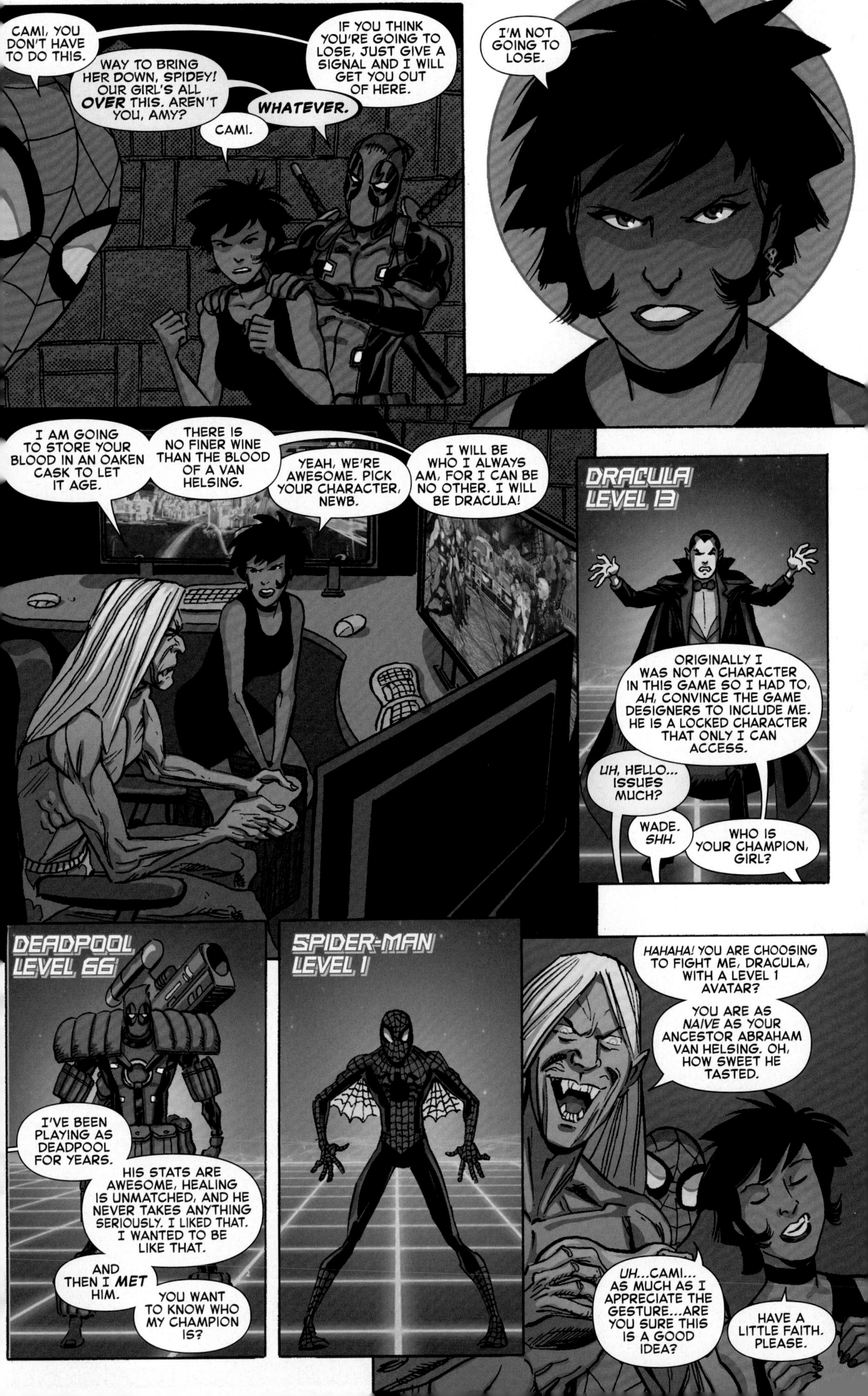
CAMI, YOU DON'T HAVE TO DO THIS.
IF YOU THINK YOU'RE GOING TO LOSE, JUST GIVE A SIGNAL AND I WILL GET YOU OUT OF HERE.
WAY TO BRING HER DOWN, SPIDEY! OUR GIRL'S ALL OVER THIS. AREN'T YOU, AMY?
WHATEVER.
CAMI.
I'M NOT GOING TO LOSE.
I AM GOING TO STORE YOUR BLOOD IN AN OAKEN CASK TO LET IT AGE.
THERE IS NO FINER WINE THAN THE BLOOD OF A VAN HELSING.
YEAH, WE'RE AWESOME. PICK YOUR CHARACTER, NEWB.
I WILL BE WHO I ALWAYS AM, FOR I CAN BE NO OTHER. I WILL BE DRACULA!
DRACULA LEVEL 13
ORIGINALLY I WAS NOT A CHARACTER IN THIS GAME SO I HAD TO, AH, CONVINCE THE GAME DESIGNERS TO INCLUDE ME. HE IS A LOCKED CHARACTER THAT ONLY I CAN ACCESS.
UH, HELLO... ISSUES MUCH?
WADE. SHH.
WHO IS YOUR CHAMPION, GIRL?
DEADPOOL LEVEL 66
I'VE BEEN PLAYING AS DEADPOOL FOR YEARS.
HIS STATS ARE AWESOME, HEALING IS UNMATCHED, AND HE NEVER TAKES ANYTHING SERIOUSLY. I LIKED THAT. I WANTED TO BE LIKE THAT.
AND THEN I MET HIM.
YOU WANT TO KNOW WHO MY CHAMPION IS?
SPIDER-MAN LEVEL 1
HAHAHA! YOU ARE CHOOSING TO FIGHT ME, DRACULA, WITH A LEVEL 1 AVATAR?
YOU ARE AS NAIVE AS YOUR ANCESTOR ABRAHAM VAN HELSING. OH, HOW SWEET HE TASTED.
UH...CAMI... AS MUCH AS I APPRECIATE THE GESTURE...ARE YOU SURE THIS IS A GOOD IDEA?
HAVE A LITTLE FAITH. PLEASE.

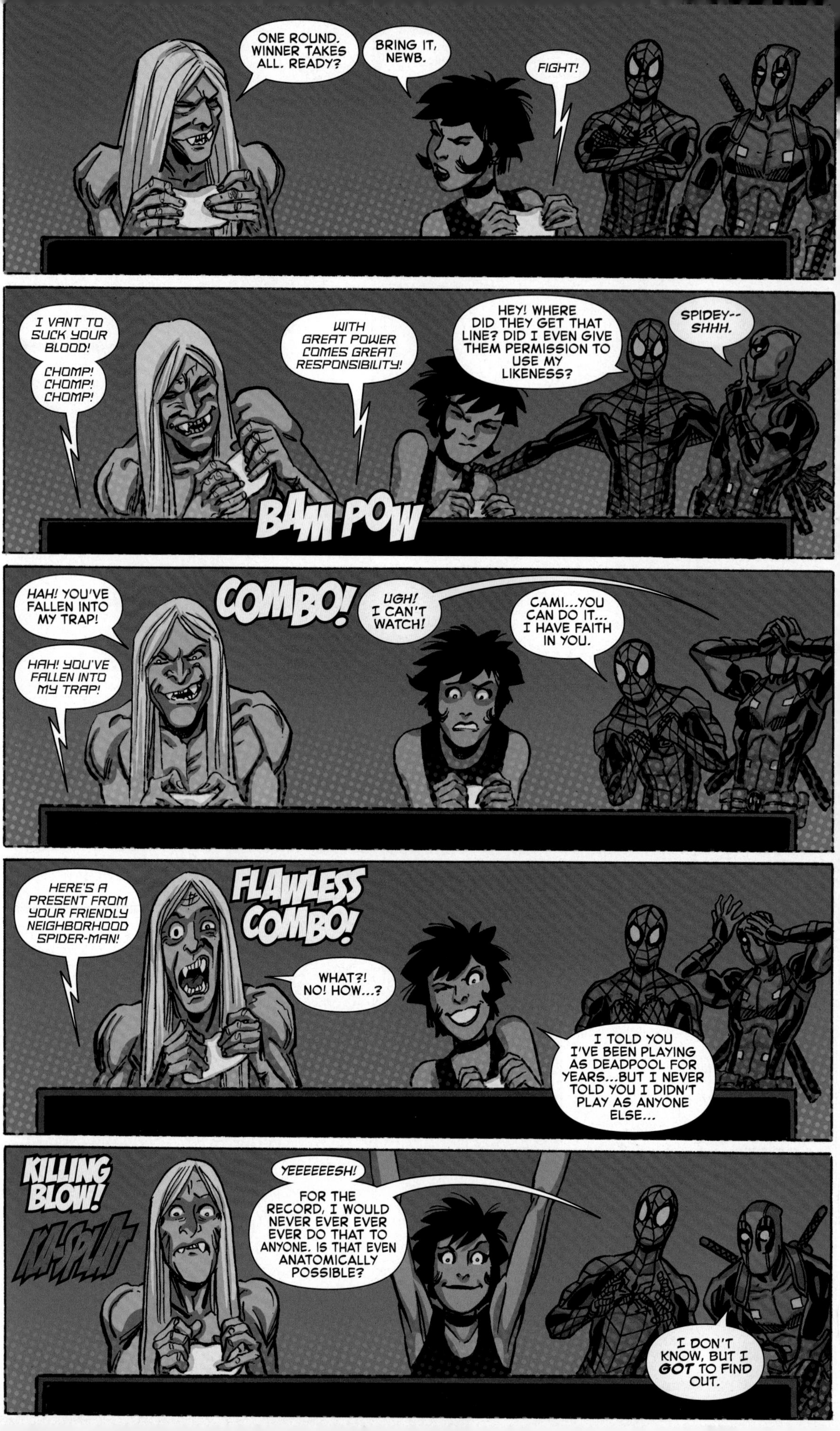

ONE ROUND. WINNER TAKES ALL. READY?
BRING IT, NEWB.
FIGHT!
I VANT TO SUCK YOUR BLOOD!
CHOMP! CHOMP! CHOMP!
WITH GREAT POWER COMES GREAT RESPONSIBILITY!
HEY! WHERE DID THEY GET THAT LINE? DID I EVEN GIVE THEM PERMISSION TO USE MY LIKENESS?
SPIDEY-- SHHH.
BAM POW
HAH! YOU'VE FALLEN INTO MY TRAP!
HAH! YOU'VE FALLEN INTO MY TRAP!
COMBO!
UGH! I CAN'T WATCH!
CAMI...YOU CAN DO IT... I HAVE FAITH IN YOU.
HERE'S A PRESENT FROM YOUR FRIENDLY NEIGHBORHOOD SPIDER-MAN!
FLAWLESS COMBO!
WHAT?! NO! HOW...?
I TOLD YOU I'VE BEEN PLAYING AS DEADPOOL FOR YEARS...BUT I NEVER TOLD YOU I DIDN'T PLAY AS ANYONE ELSE...
KILLING BLOW!
KA-SPLAT
YEEEEEESH!
FOR THE RECORD, I WOULD NEVER EVER EVER EVER DO THAT TO ANYONE. IS THAT EVEN ANATOMICALLY POSSIBLE?
I DON'T KNOW, BUT I GOT TO FIND OUT.

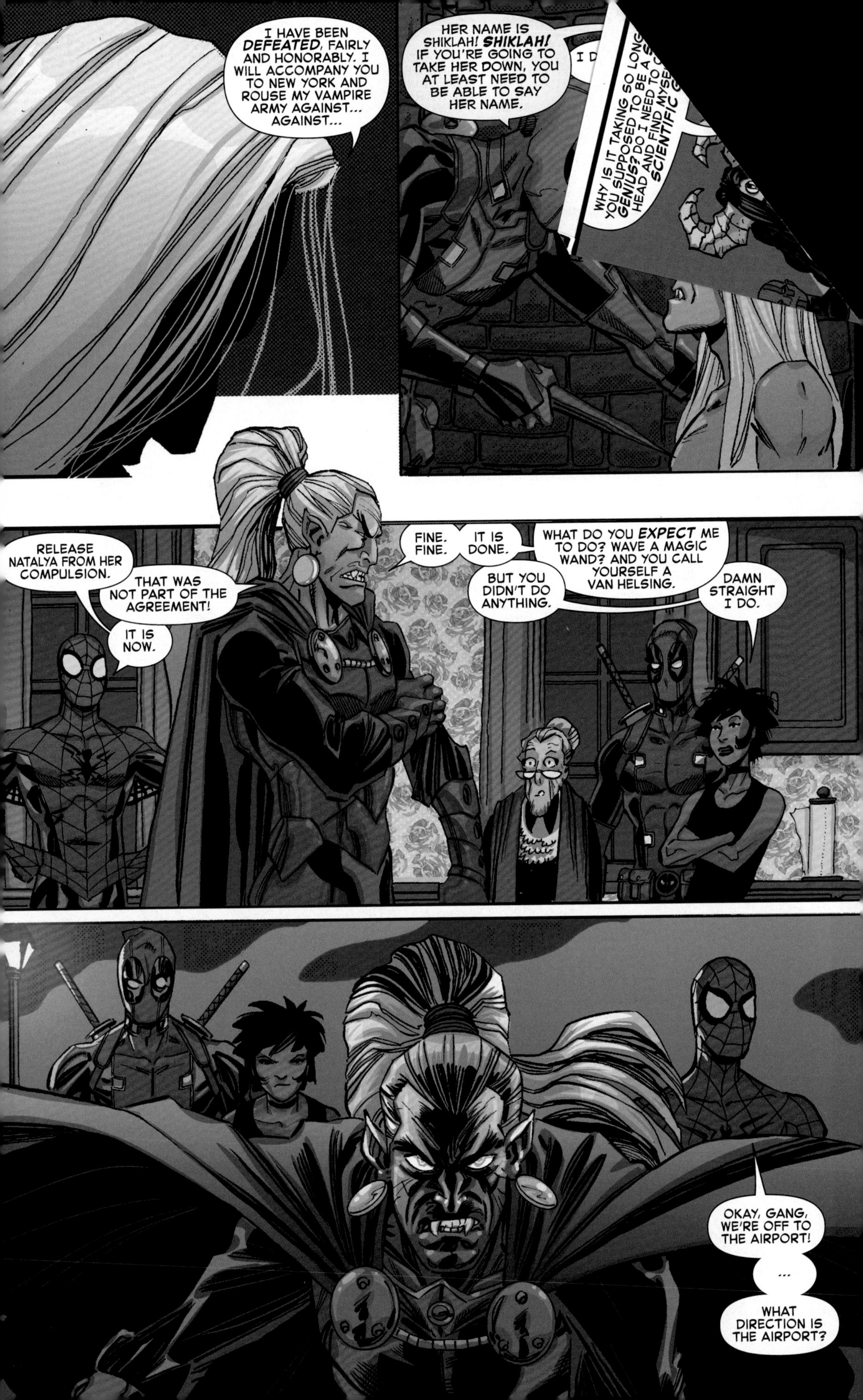
I HAVE BEEN *DEFEATED*, FAIRLY AND HONORABLY. I WILL ACCOMPANY YOU TO NEW YORK AND ROUSE MY VAMPIRE ARMY AGAINST... AGAINST...
HER NAME IS SHIKLAH! *SHIKLAH!* IF YOU'RE GOING TO TAKE HER DOWN, YOU AT LEAST NEED TO BE ABLE TO SAY HER NAME.
WHY IS IT TAKING SO LONG
YOU SUPPOSED TO BE A
GENIUS? DO I NEED TO
HEAD AND FIND MYSE
SCIENTIFIC
RELEASE NATALYA FROM HER COMPULSION.
THAT WAS NOT PART OF THE AGREEMENT!
IT IS NOW.
FINE. FINE.
IT IS DONE.
BUT YOU DIDN'T DO ANYTHING.
WHAT DO YOU *EXPECT* ME TO DO? WAVE A MAGIC WAND? AND YOU CALL YOURSELF A VAN HELSING.
DAMN STRAIGHT I DO.
OKAY, GANG, WE'RE OFF TO THE AIRPORT!
...
WHAT DIRECTION IS THE AIRPORT?

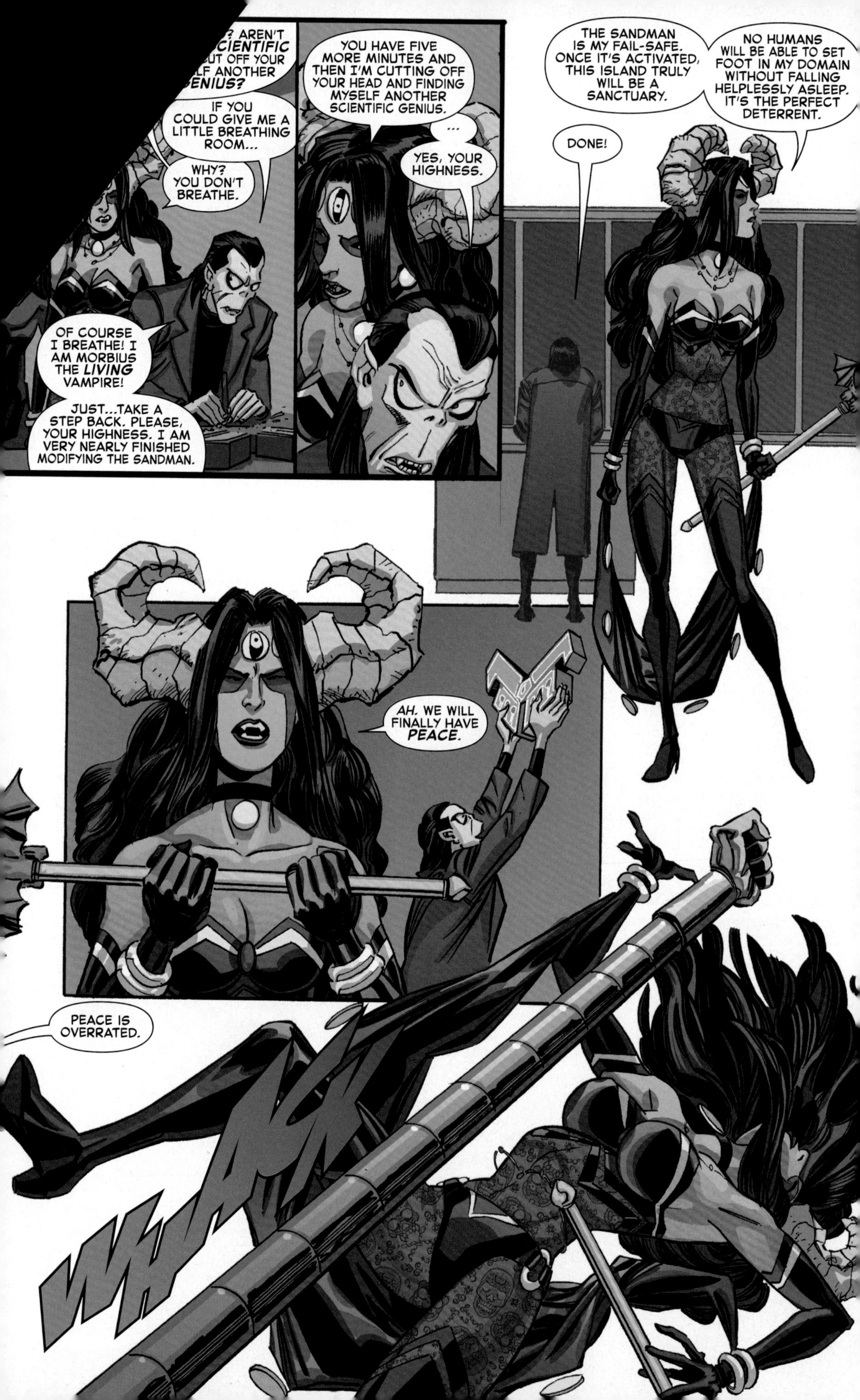

IF YOU COULD GIVE ME A LITTLE BREATHING ROOM...
WHY? YOU DON'T BREATHE.
OF COURSE I BREATHE! I AM MORBIUS THE *LIVING* VAMPIRE!
JUST...TAKE A STEP BACK. PLEASE, YOUR HIGHNESS. I AM VERY NEARLY FINISHED MODIFYING THE SANDMAN.
YOU HAVE FIVE MORE MINUTES AND THEN I'M CUTTING OFF YOUR HEAD AND FINDING MYSELF ANOTHER SCIENTIFIC GENIUS.
...
YES, YOUR HIGHNESS.
DONE!
THE SANDMAN IS MY FAIL-SAFE. ONCE IT'S ACTIVATED, THIS ISLAND TRULY WILL BE A SANCTUARY.
NO HUMANS WILL BE ABLE TO SET FOOT IN MY DOMAIN WITHOUT FALLING HELPLESSLY ASLEEP. IT'S THE PERFECT DETERRENT.
AH. WE WILL FINALLY HAVE *PEACE.*
PEACE IS OVERRATED.
WHAM

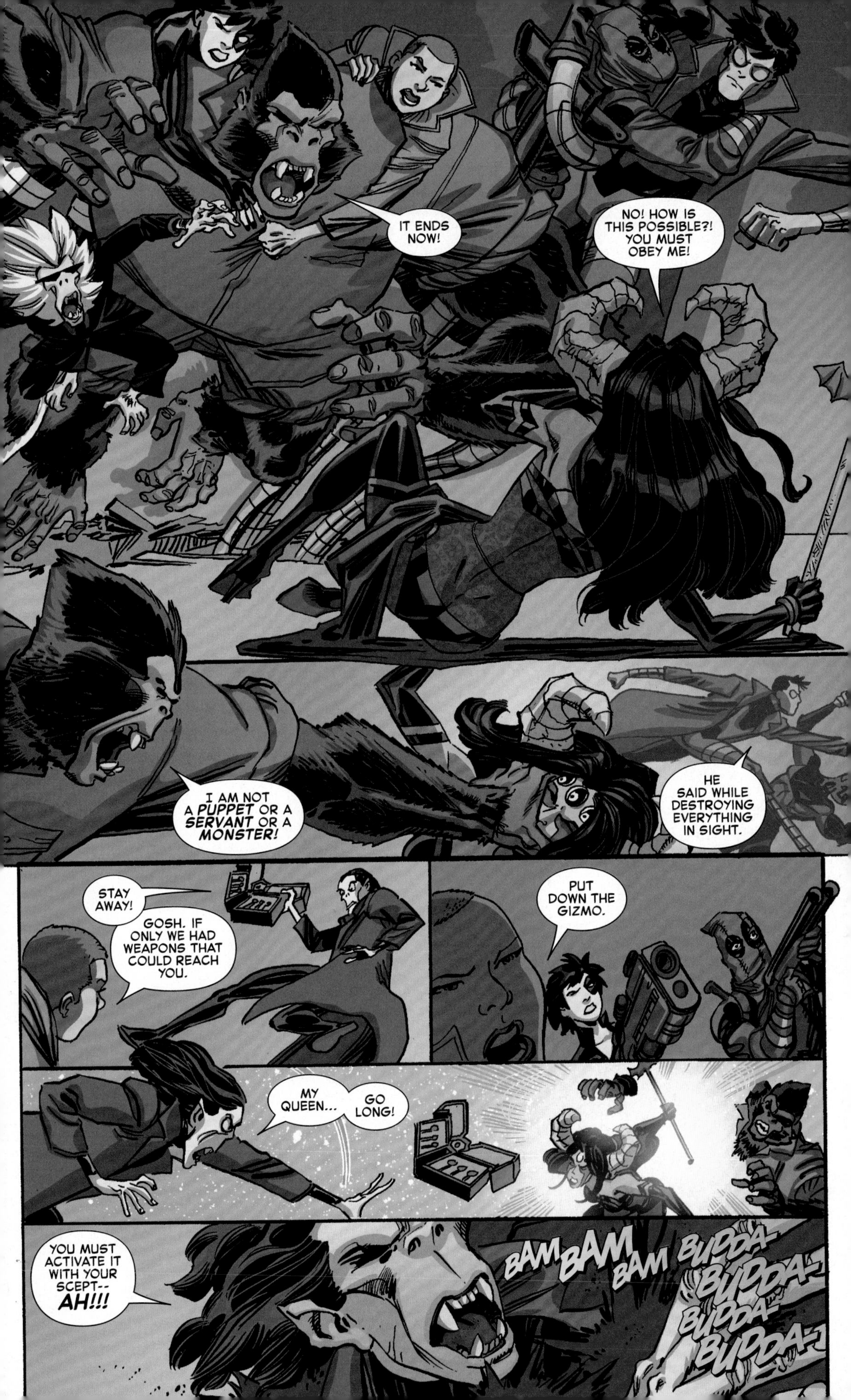
IT ENDS NOW!
NO! HOW IS THIS POSSIBLE?! YOU MUST OBEY ME!
I AM NOT A *PUPPET* OR A *SERVANT* OR A *MONSTER*!
HE SAID WHILE DESTROYING EVERYTHING IN SIGHT.
STAY AWAY!
GOSH. IF ONLY WE HAD WEAPONS THAT COULD REACH YOU.
PUT DOWN THE GIZMO.
MY QUEEN...
GO LONG!
YOU MUST ACTIVATE IT WITH YOUR SCEPT-- **AH!!!**
BAM BAM BAM BUDDA-BUDDA-BUDDA-BUDDA-

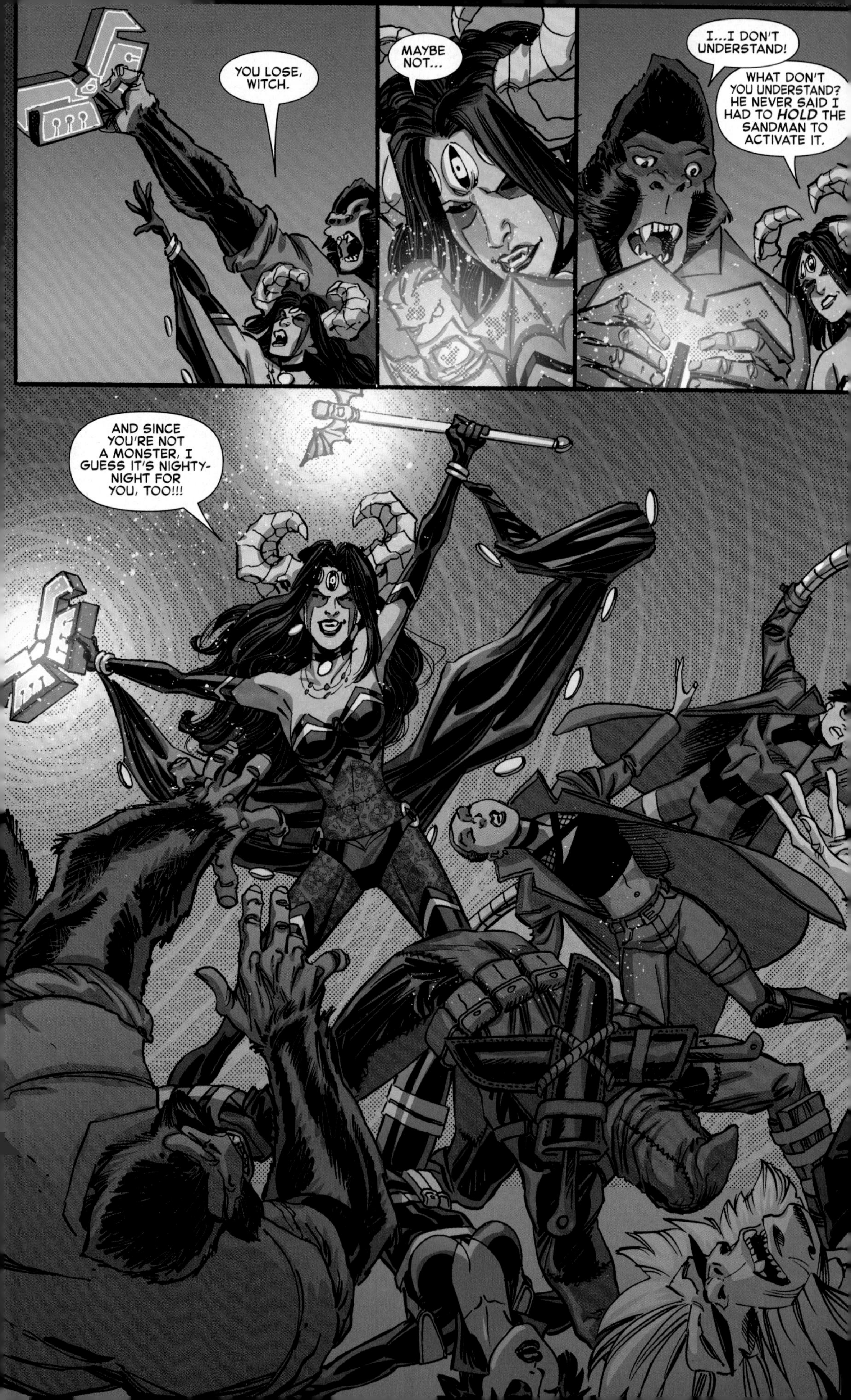
YOU LOSE, WITCH.
MAYBE NOT...
I...I DON'T UNDERSTAND!
WHAT DON'T YOU UNDERSTAND? HE NEVER SAID I HAD TO *HOLD* THE SANDMAN TO ACTIVATE IT.
AND SINCE YOU'RE NOT A MONSTER, I GUESS IT'S NIGHTY-NIGHT FOR YOU, TOO!!!

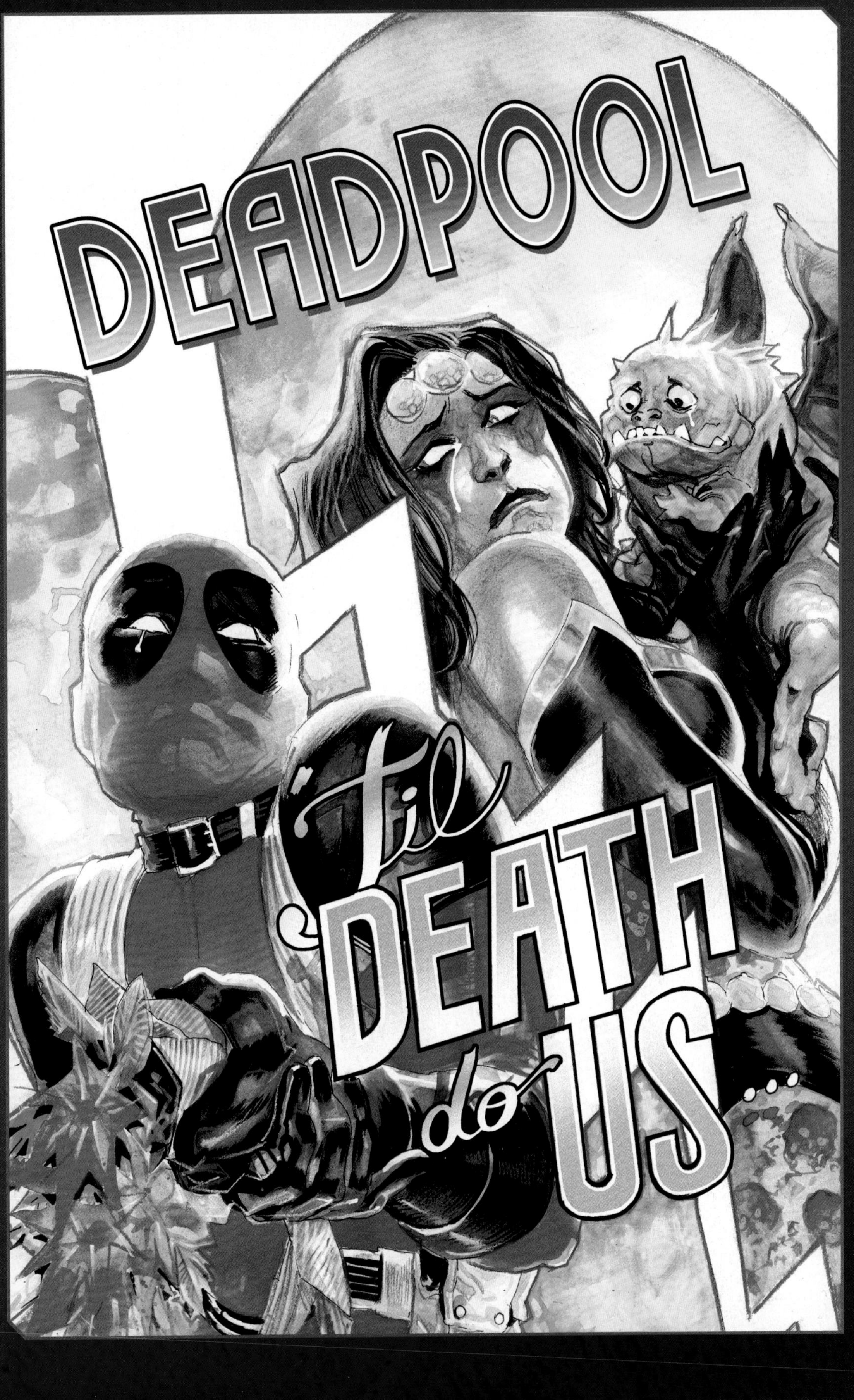
DEADPOOL
'til DEATH do US...

Deadpool #29 variant by RAFAEL ALBUQUERQUE

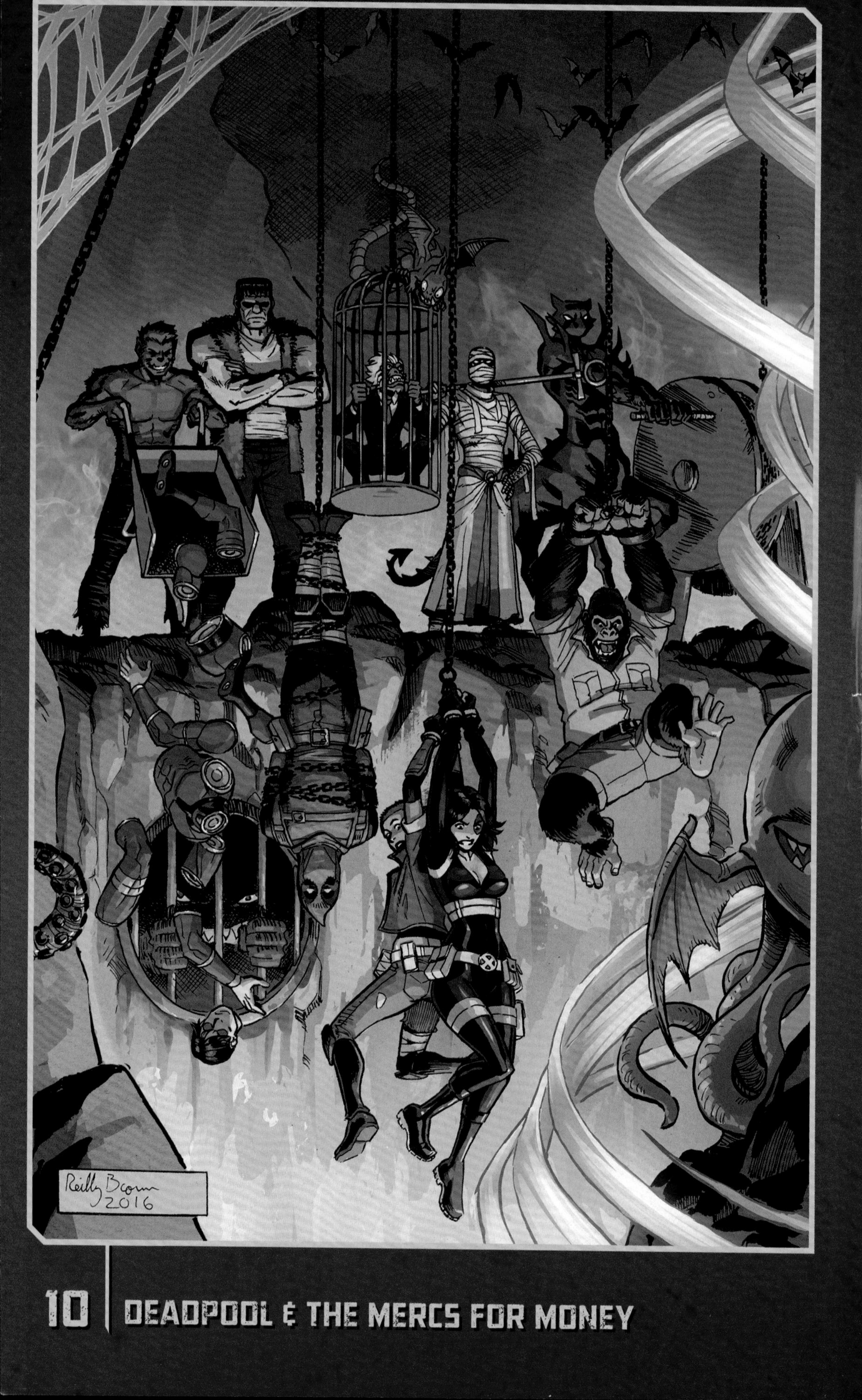
Reilly Brown
2016

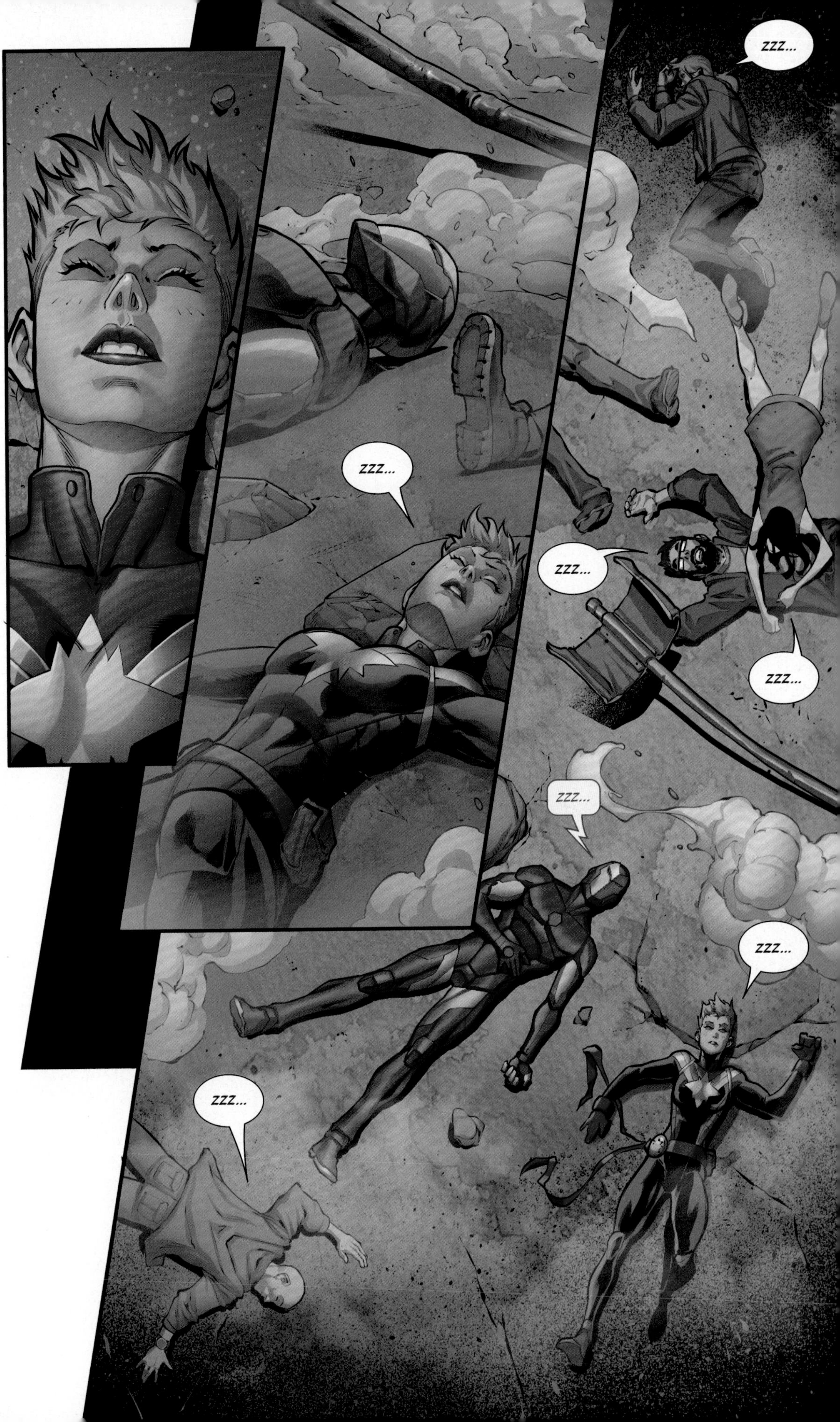
ZZZ...
ZZZ...
ZZZ...
ZZZ...
ZZZ...
ZZZ...
ZZZ...

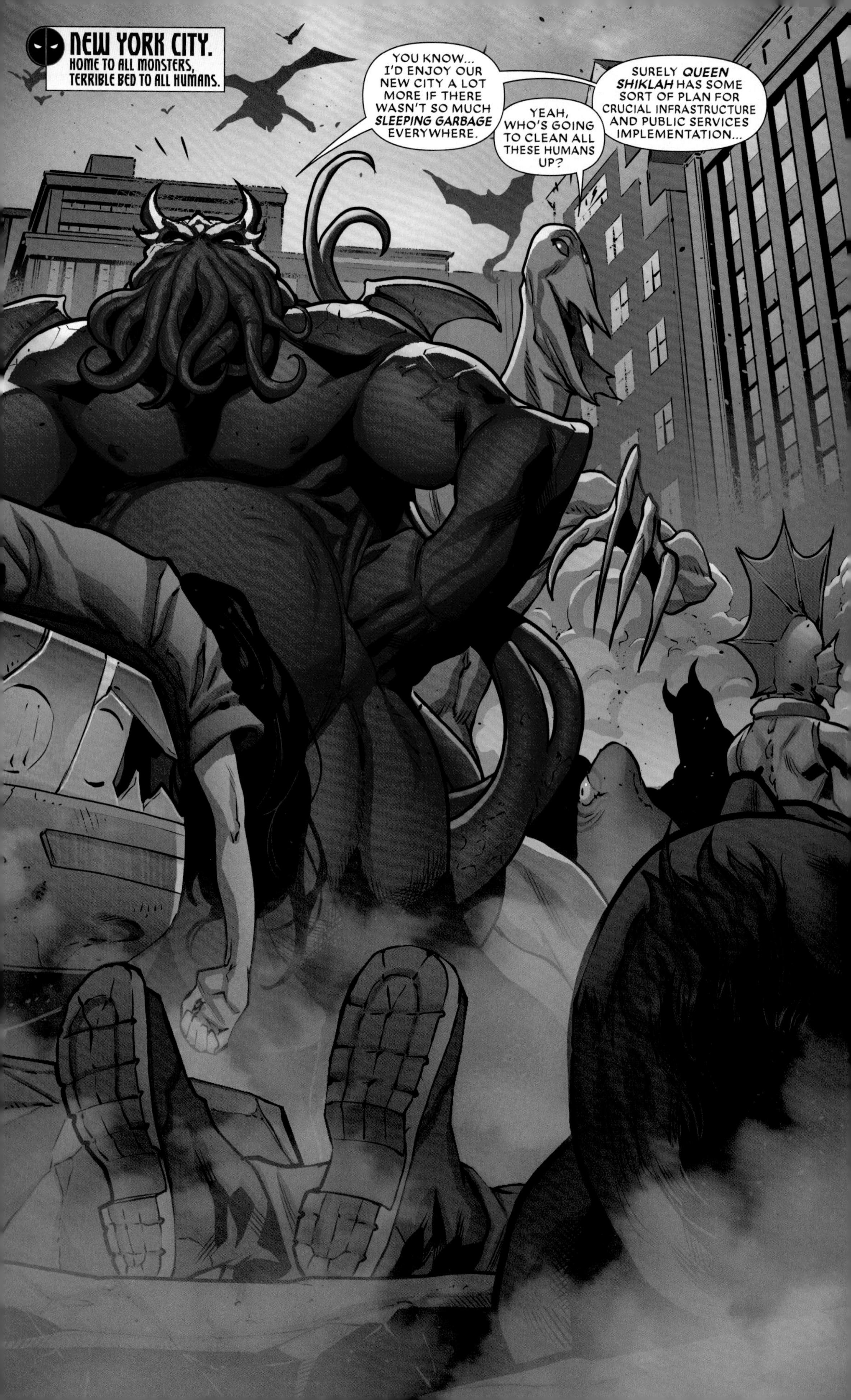
NEW YORK CITY.
HOME TO ALL MONSTERS, TERRIBLE BED TO ALL HUMANS.
YOU KNOW... I'D ENJOY OUR NEW CITY A LOT MORE IF THERE WASN'T SO MUCH SLEEPING GARBAGE EVERYWHERE.
YEAH, WHO'S GOING TO CLEAN ALL THESE HUMANS UP?
SURELY QUEEN SHIKLAH HAS SOME SORT OF PLAN FOR CRUCIAL INFRASTRUCTURE AND PUBLIC SERVICES IMPLEMENTATION...

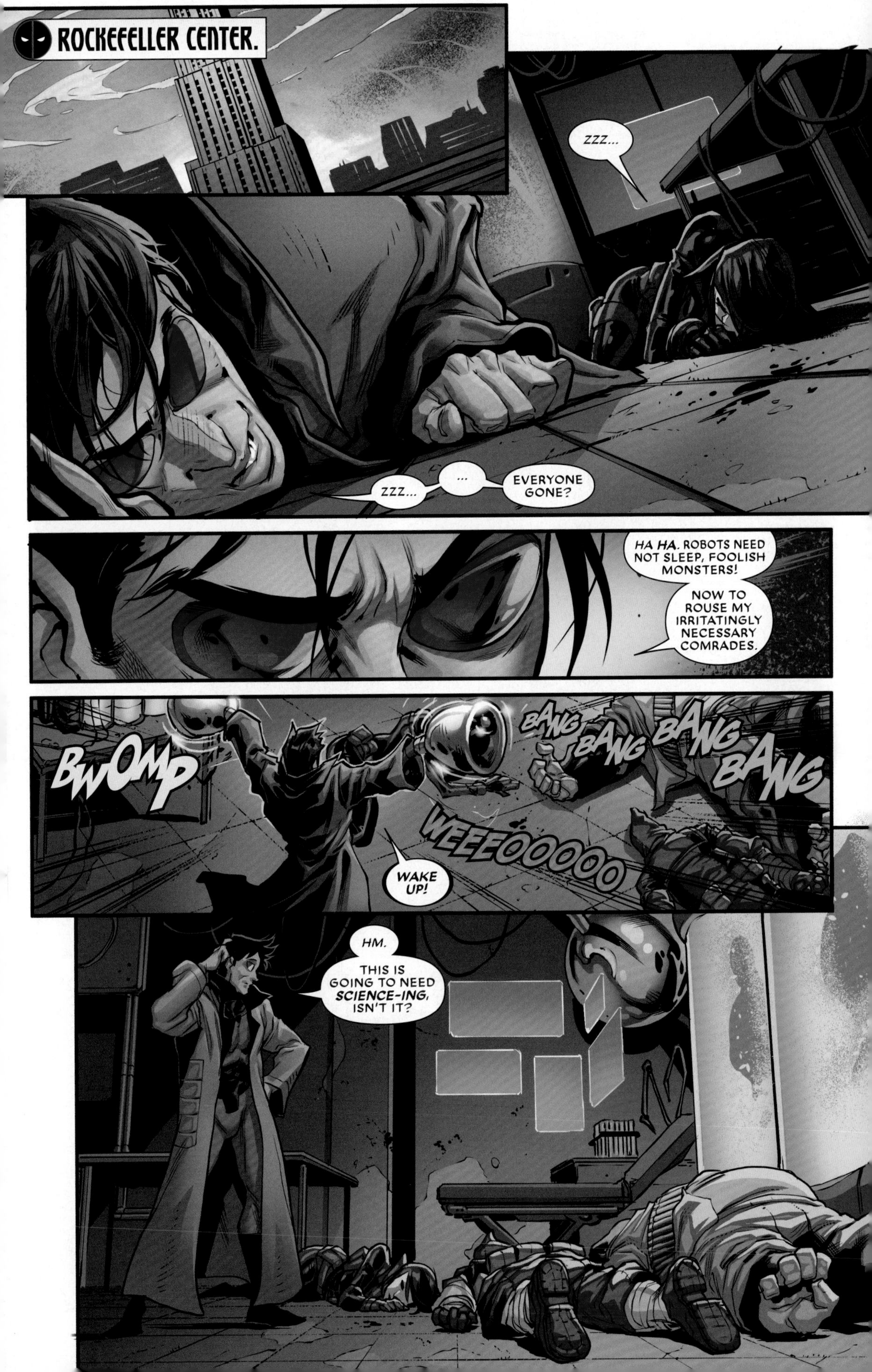
ROCKEFELLER CENTER.
ZZZ...
ZZZ...
...
EVERYONE GONE?
HA HA. ROBOTS NEED NOT SLEEP, FOOLISH MONSTERS!
NOW TO ROUSE MY IRRITATINGLY NECESSARY COMRADES.
BWOMP
BANG
BANG
BANG
BANG
WEEEOOOOO
WAKE UP!
HM.
THIS IS GOING TO NEED SCIENCE-ING, ISN'T IT?

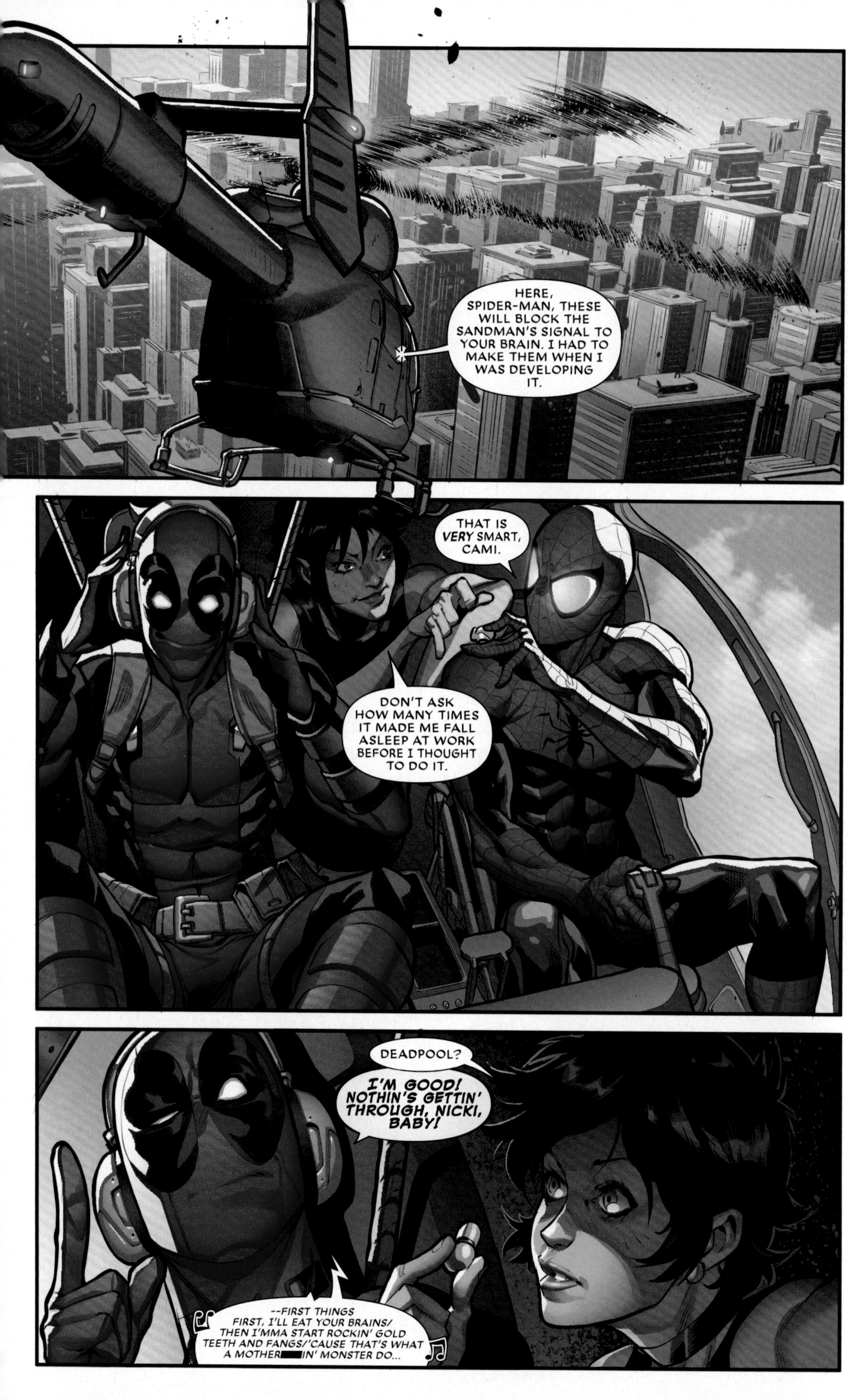
HERE, SPIDER-MAN, THESE WILL BLOCK THE SANDMAN'S SIGNAL TO YOUR BRAIN. I HAD TO MAKE THEM WHEN I WAS DEVELOPING IT.
THAT IS VERY SMART, CAMI.
DON'T ASK HOW MANY TIMES IT MADE ME FALL ASLEEP AT WORK BEFORE I THOUGHT TO DO IT.
DEADPOOL?
I'M GOOD! NOTHIN'S GETTIN' THROUGH, NICKI, BABY!
--FIRST THINGS FIRST, I'LL EAT YOUR BRAINS/ THEN I'MMA START ROCKIN' GOLD TEETH AND FANGS/'CAUSE THAT'S WHAT A MOTHER[redacted]IN' MONSTER DO...

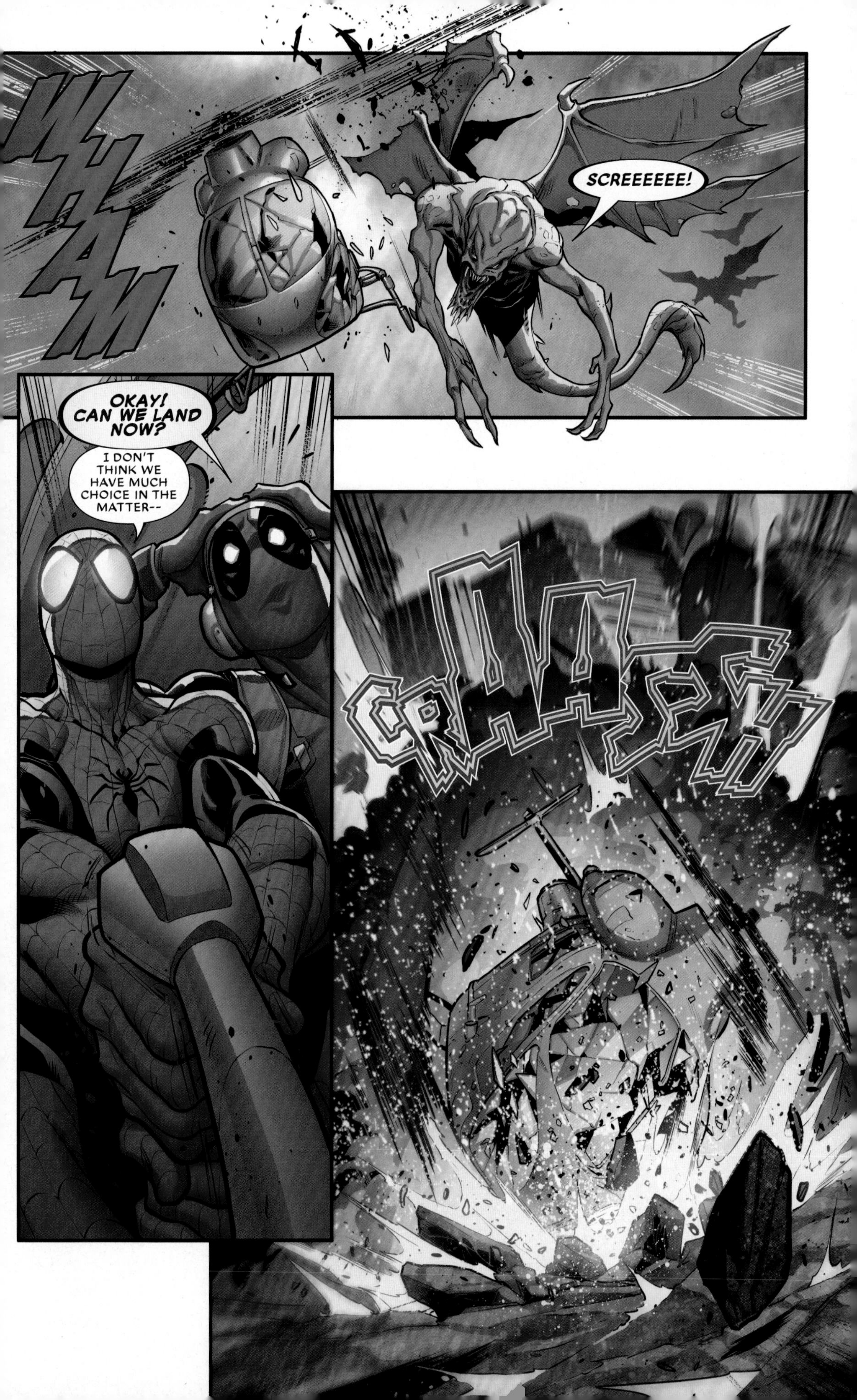
WHAM
SCREEEEEE!
OKAY! CAN WE LAND NOW?
I DON'T THINK WE HAVE MUCH CHOICE IN THE MATTER--
CRASH

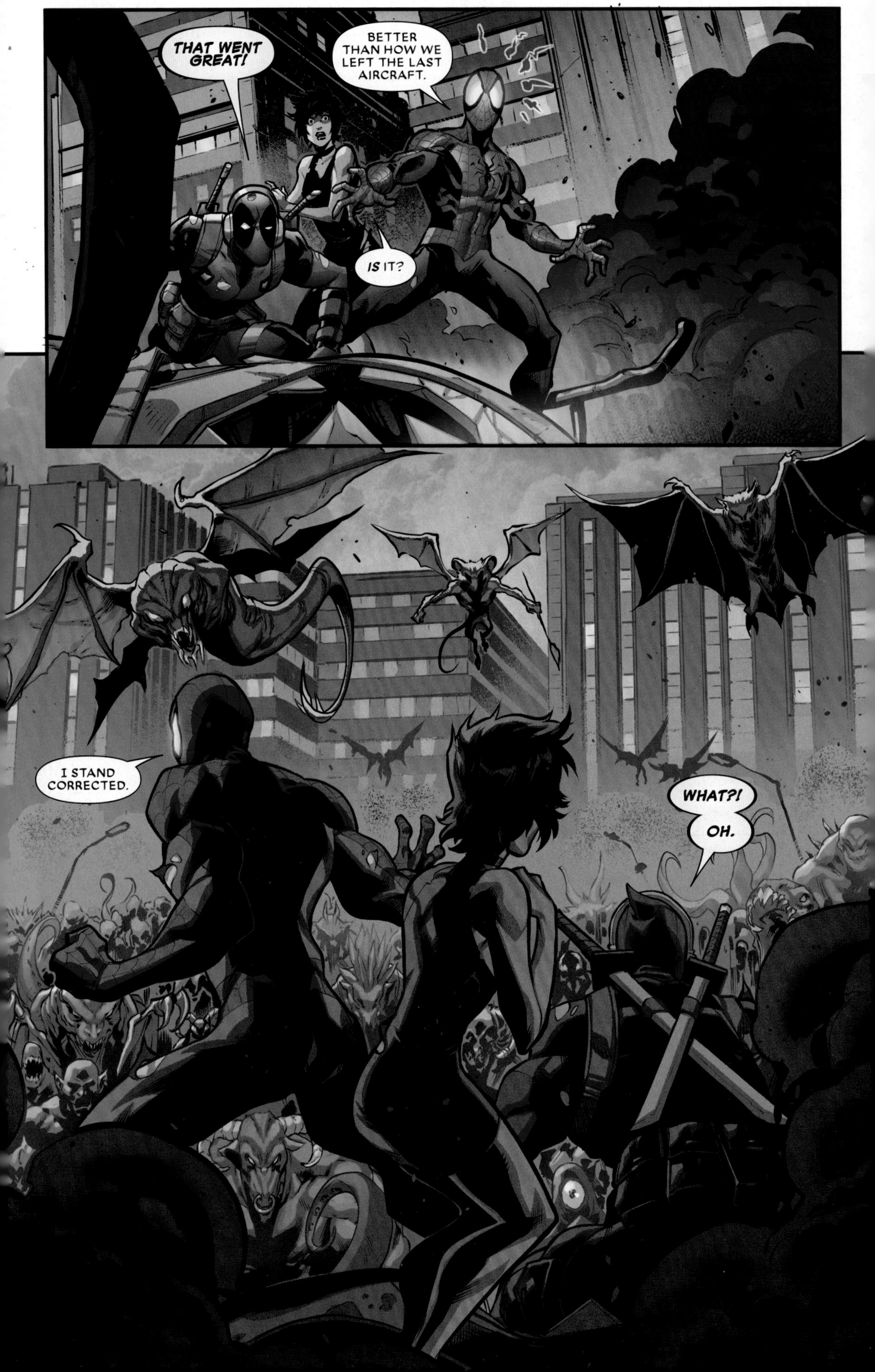
THAT WENT GREAT!
BETTER THAN HOW WE LEFT THE LAST AIRCRAFT.
IS IT?
I STAND CORRECTED.
WHAT?!
OH.

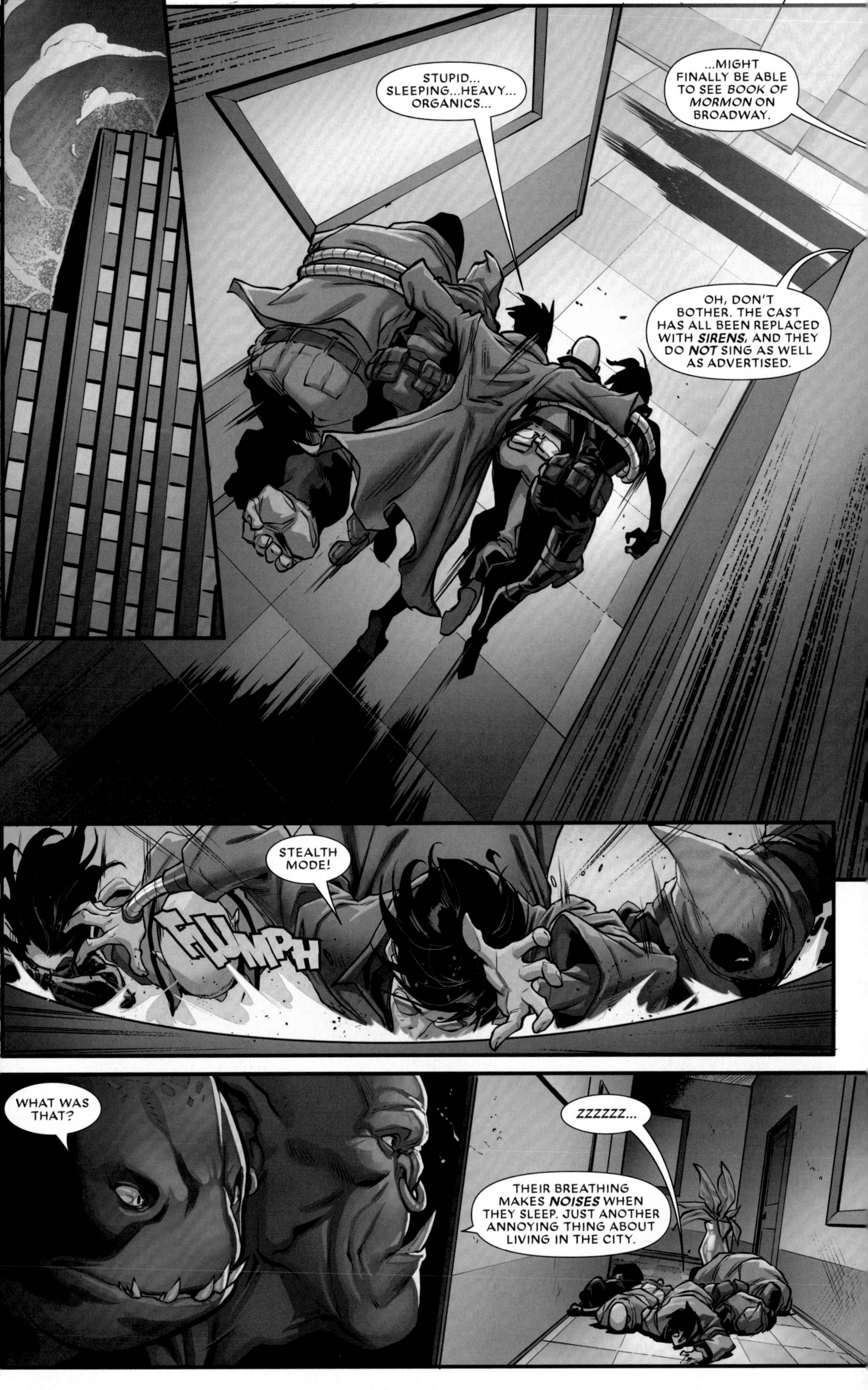
STUPID... SLEEPING...HEAVY... ORGANICS...
...MIGHT FINALLY BE ABLE TO SEE BOOK OF MORMON ON BROADWAY.
OH, DON'T BOTHER. THE CAST HAS ALL BEEN REPLACED WITH SIRENS, AND THEY DO NOT SING AS WELL AS ADVERTISED.
STEALTH MODE!
FUMPH
WHAT WAS THAT?
ZZZZZZ...
THEIR BREATHING MAKES NOISES WHEN THEY SLEEP. JUST ANOTHER ANNOYING THING ABOUT LIVING IN THE CITY.

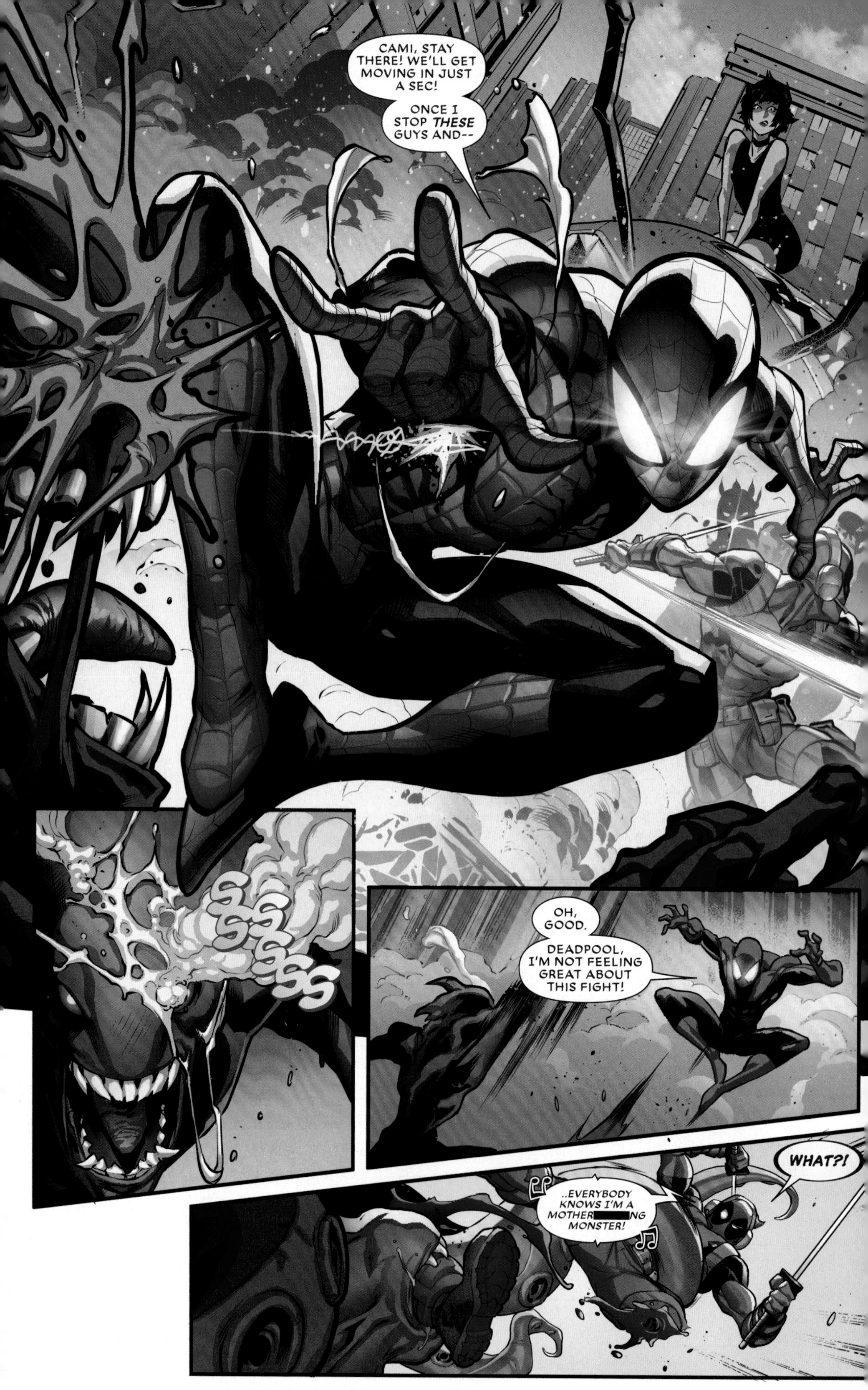
CAMI, STAY THERE! WE'LL GET MOVING IN JUST A SEC!
ONCE I STOP *THESE* GUYS AND--
SSSSSSS
OH, GOOD.
DEADPOOL, I'M NOT FEELING GREAT ABOUT THIS FIGHT!
WHAT?!
..EVERYBODY KNOWS I'M A MOTHER[redacted]NG MONSTER!

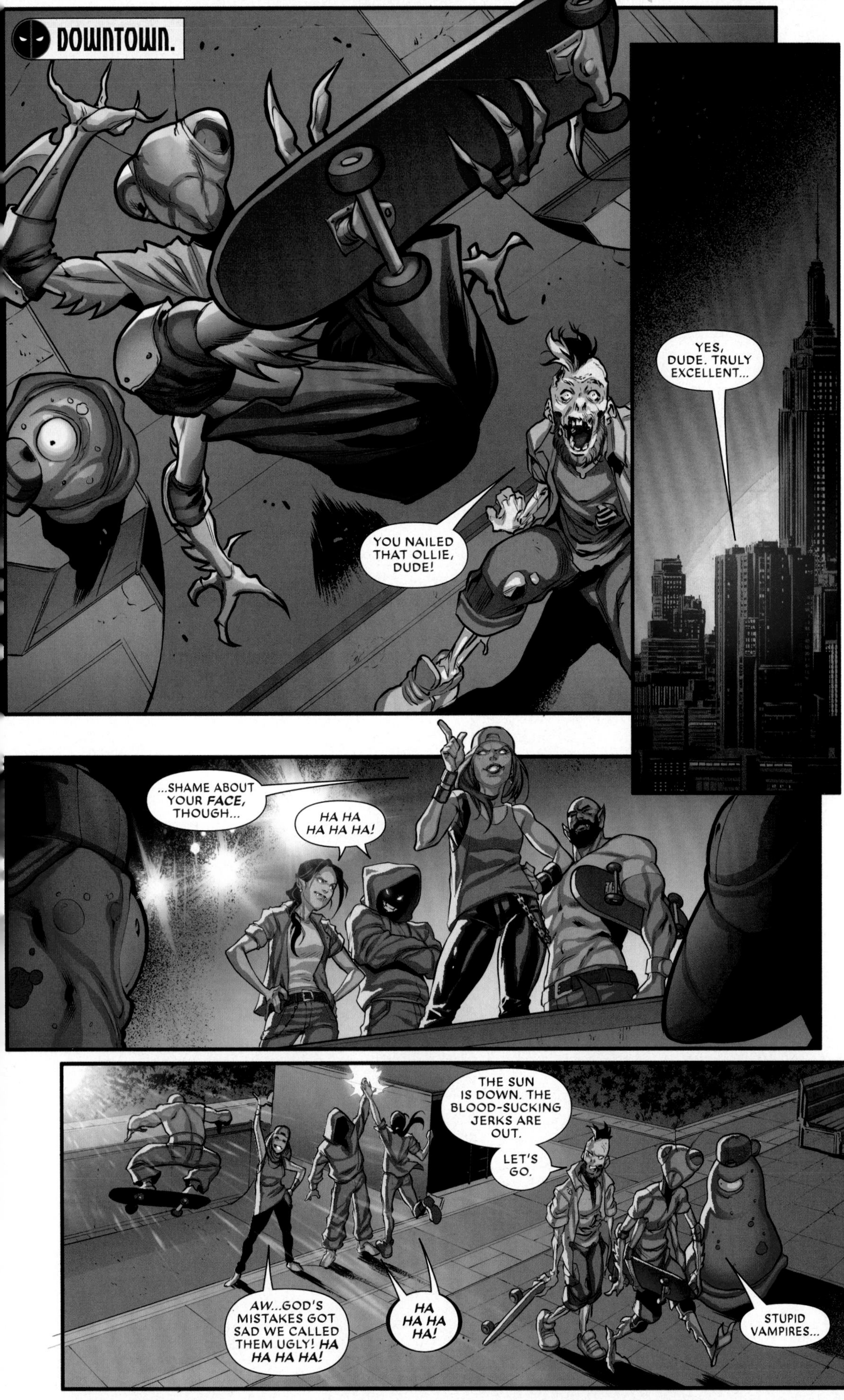
DOWNTOWN.
YOU NAILED THAT OLLIE, DUDE!
YES, DUDE. TRULY EXCELLENT...
...SHAME ABOUT YOUR FACE, THOUGH...
HA HA HA HA HA!
THE SUN IS DOWN. THE BLOOD-SUCKING JERKS ARE OUT.
LET'S GO.
AW...GOD'S MISTAKES GOT SAD WE CALLED THEM UGLY! HA HA HA HA!
HA HA HA HA!
STUPID VAMPIRES...

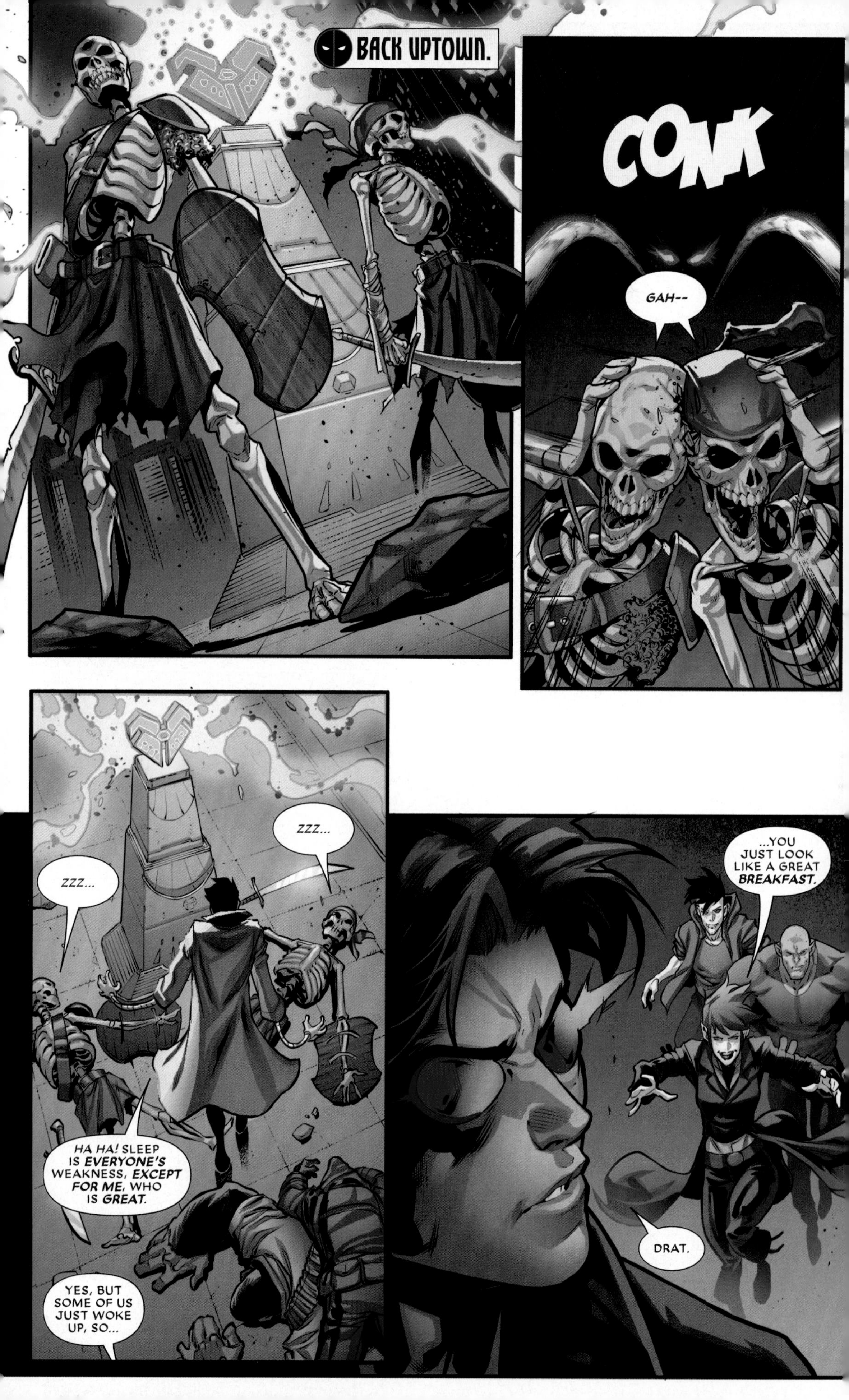
BACK UPTOWN.
CONK
GAH--
ZZZ...
ZZZ...
HA HA! SLEEP IS EVERYONE'S WEAKNESS, EXCEPT FOR ME, WHO IS GREAT.
YES, BUT SOME OF US JUST WOKE UP, SO...
...YOU JUST LOOK LIKE A GREAT BREAKFAST.
DRAT.

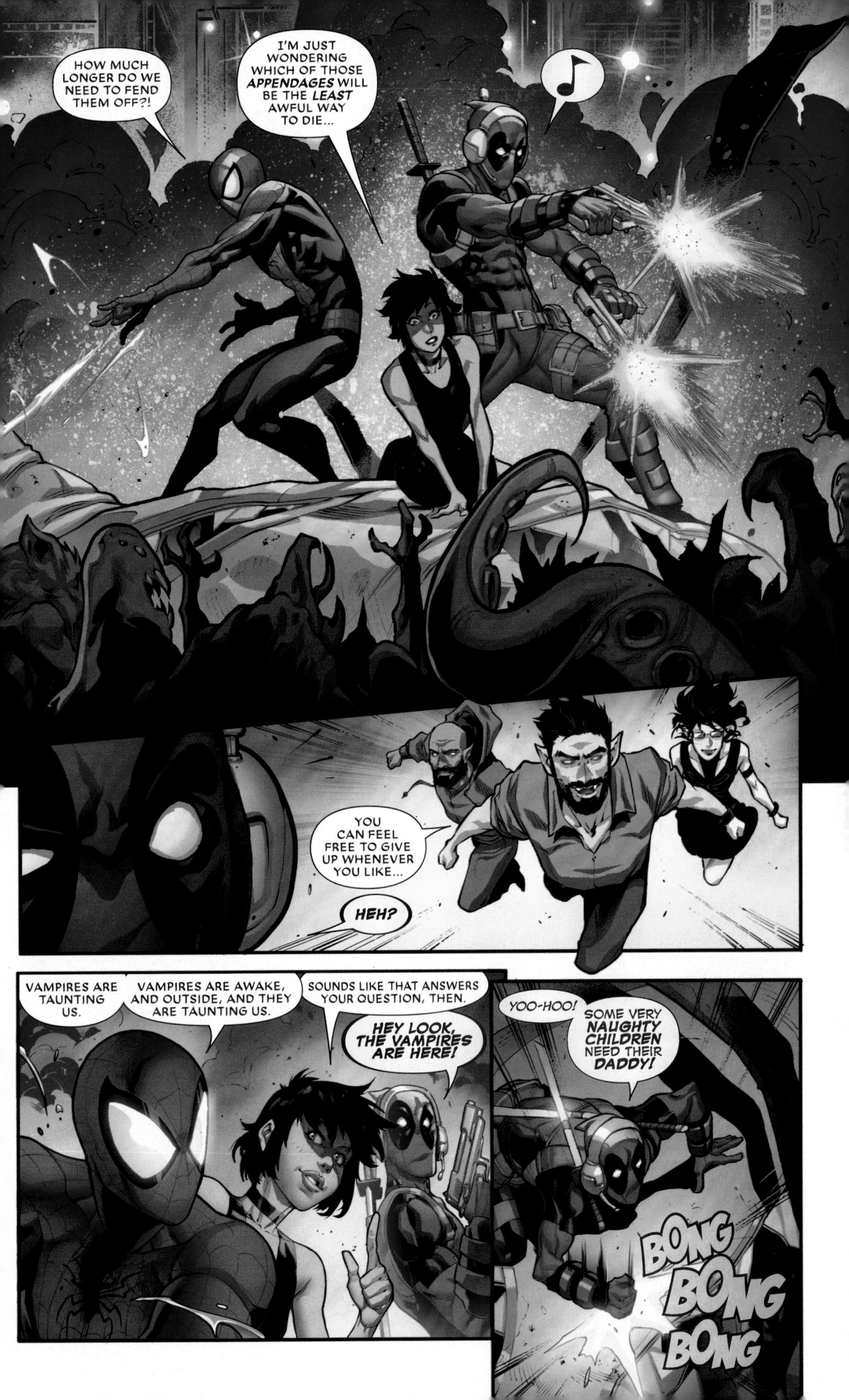
HOW MUCH LONGER DO WE NEED TO FEND THEM OFF?!
I'M JUST WONDERING WHICH OF THOSE APPENDAGES WILL BE THE LEAST AWFUL WAY TO DIE...
♪
YOU CAN FEEL FREE TO GIVE UP WHENEVER YOU LIKE...
HEH?
VAMPIRES ARE TAUNTING US.
VAMPIRES ARE AWAKE, AND OUTSIDE, AND THEY ARE TAUNTING US.
SOUNDS LIKE THAT ANSWERS YOUR QUESTION, THEN.
HEY LOOK, THE VAMPIRES ARE HERE!
YOO-HOO!
SOME VERY NAUGHTY CHILDREN NEED THEIR DADDY!
BONG
BONG
BONG

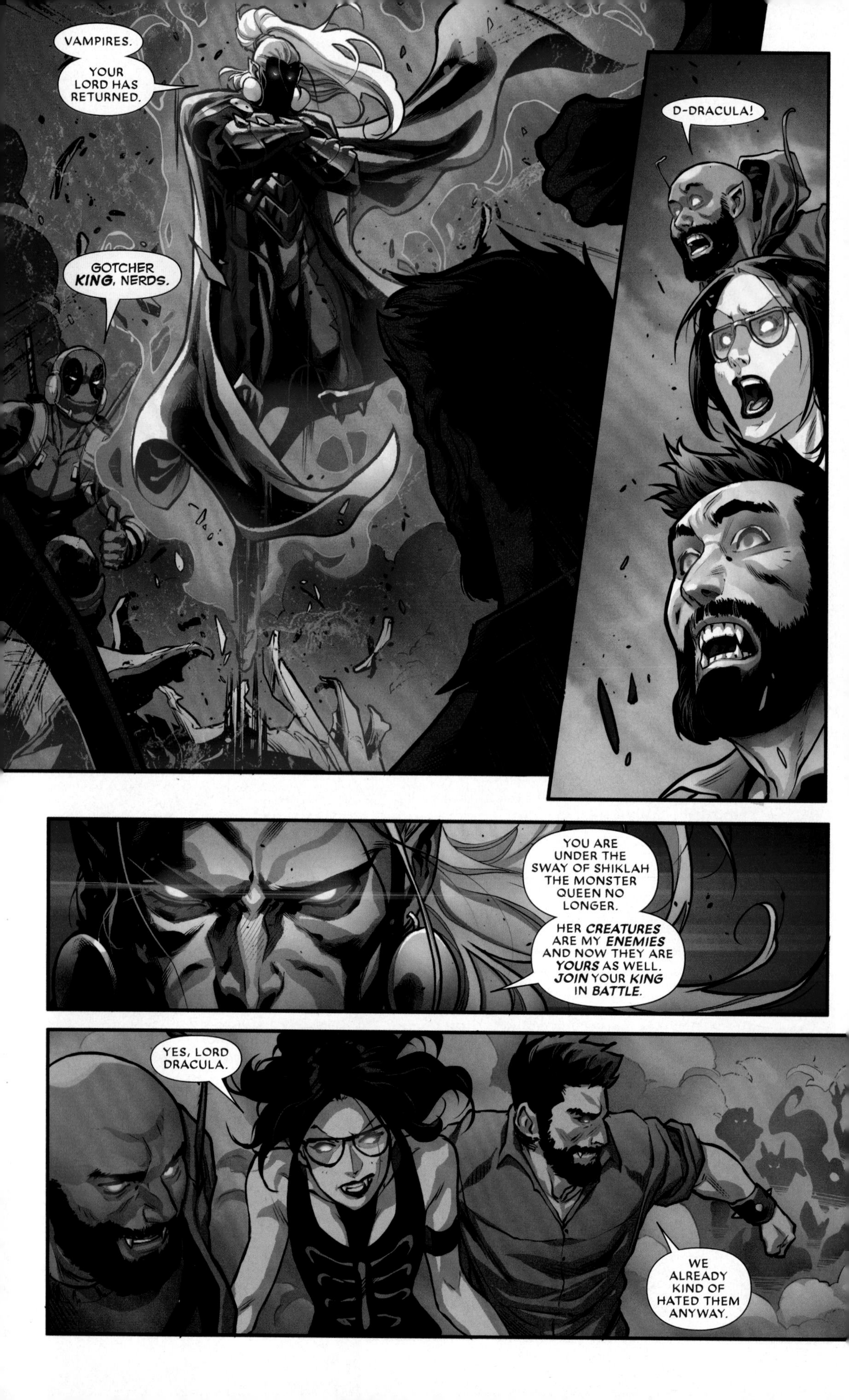
VAMPIRES.
YOUR LORD HAS RETURNED.
GOTCHER KING, NERDS.
D-DRACULA!
YOU ARE UNDER THE SWAY OF SHIKLAH THE MONSTER QUEEN NO LONGER.
HER CREATURES ARE MY ENEMIES AND NOW THEY ARE YOURS AS WELL. JOIN YOUR KING IN BATTLE.
YES, LORD DRACULA.
WE ALREADY KIND OF HATED THEM ANYWAY.

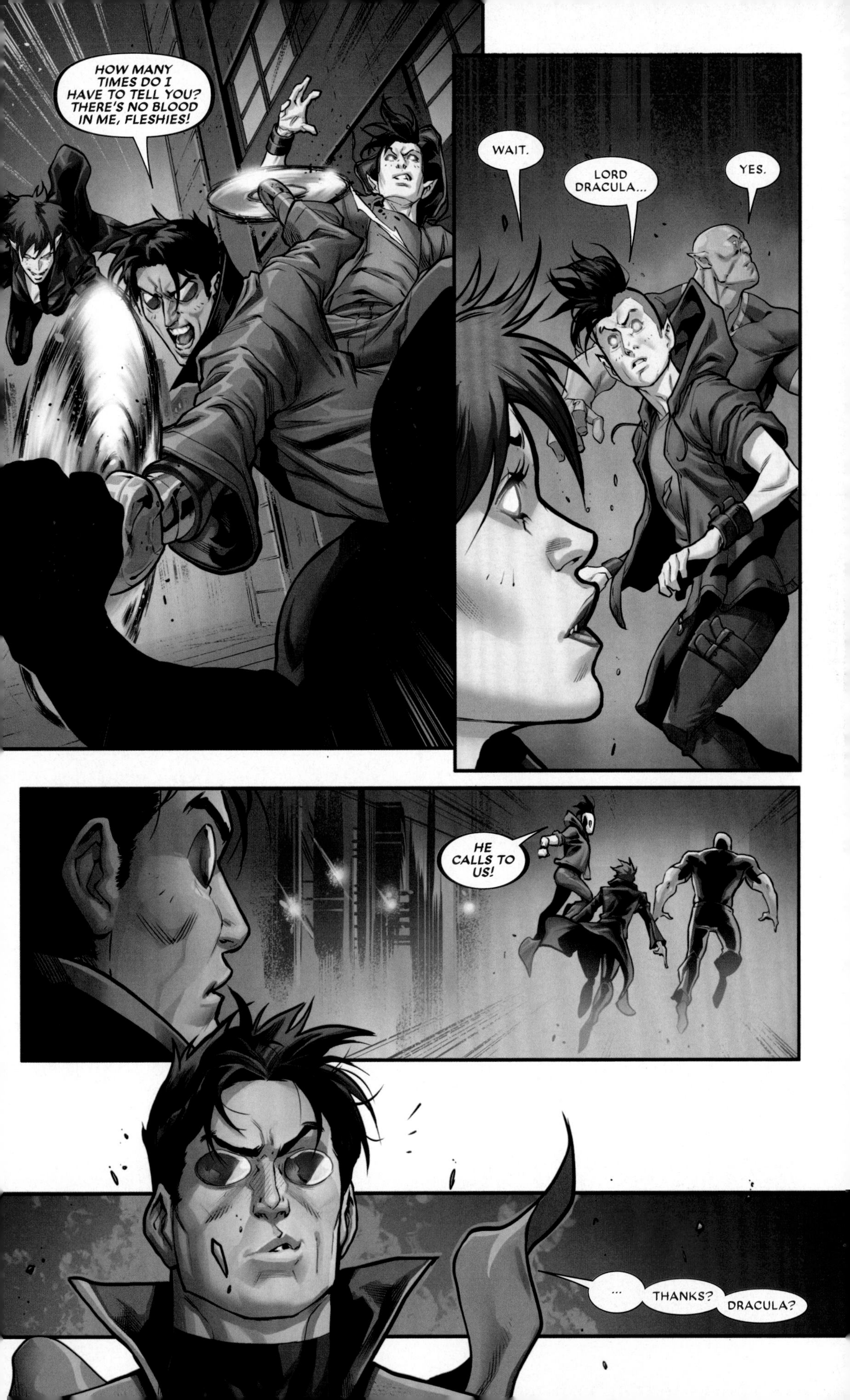
HOW MANY TIMES DO I HAVE TO TELL YOU? THERE'S NO BLOOD IN ME, FLESHIES!
WAIT.
LORD DRACULA...
YES.
HE CALLS TO US!
...
THANKS?
DRACULA?

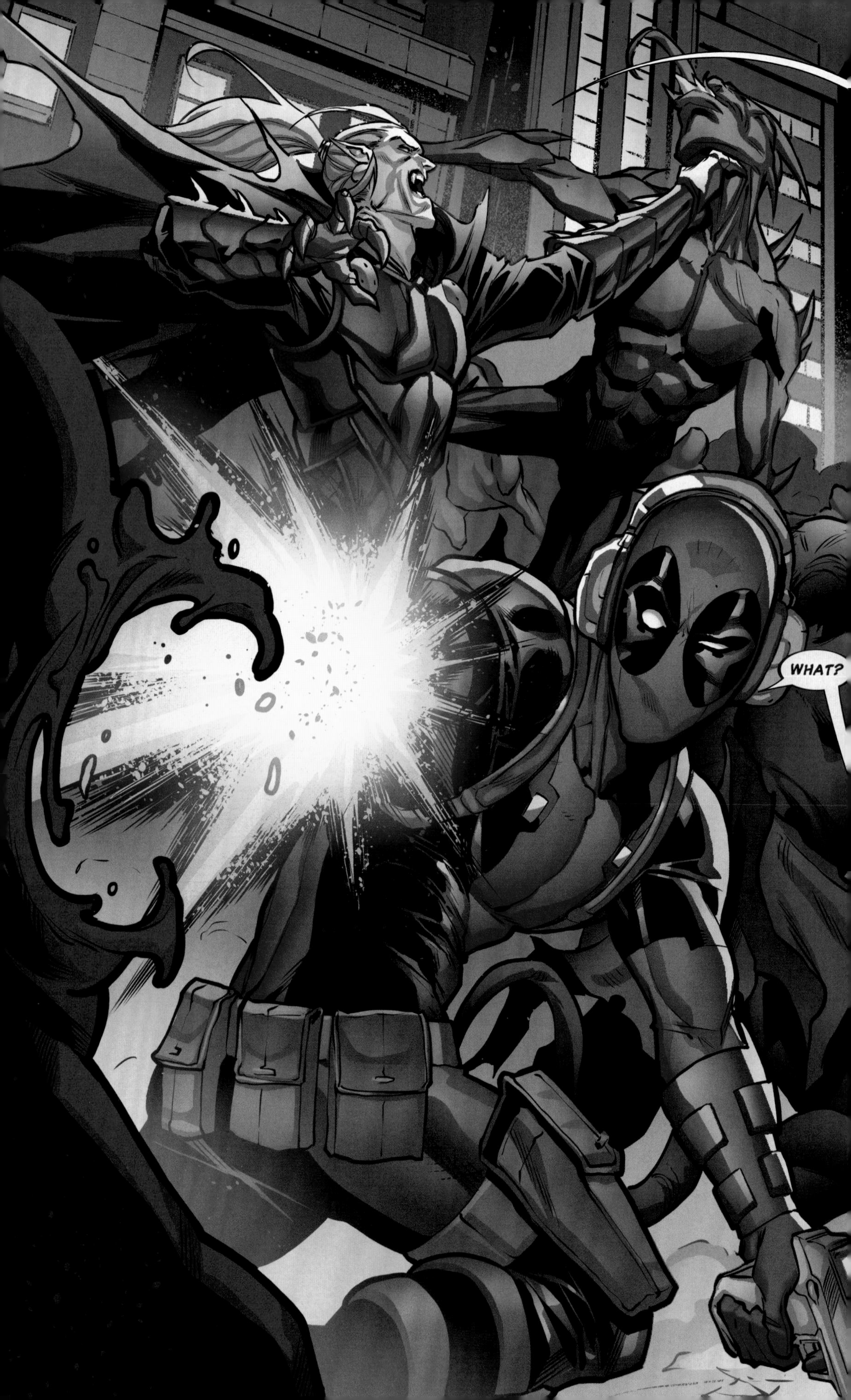
WHAT?

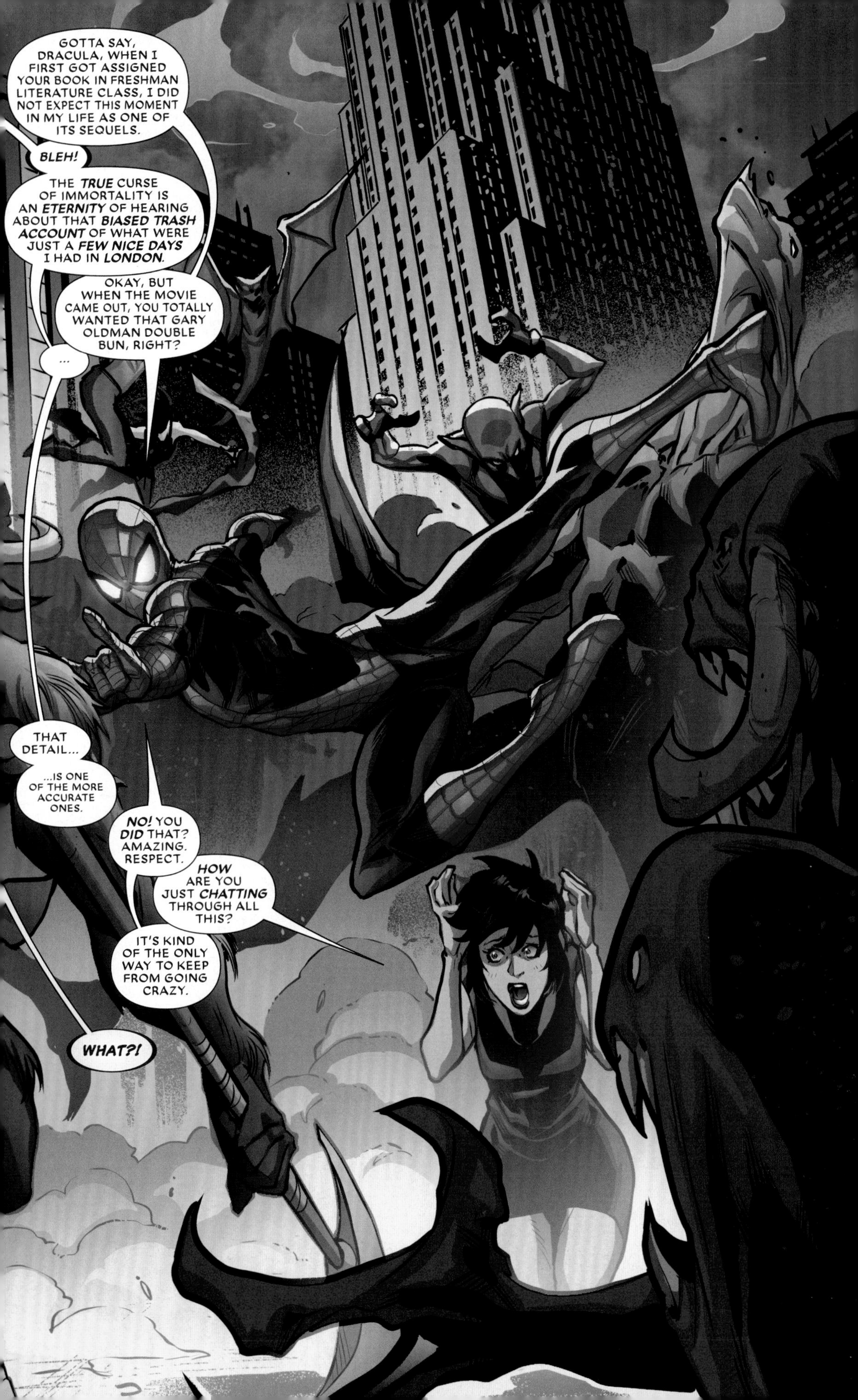
GOTTA SAY, DRACULA, WHEN I FIRST GOT ASSIGNED YOUR BOOK IN FRESHMAN LITERATURE CLASS, I DID NOT EXPECT THIS MOMENT IN MY LIFE AS ONE OF ITS SEQUELS.
BLEH!
THE TRUE CURSE OF IMMORTALITY IS AN ETERNITY OF HEARING ABOUT THAT BIASED TRASH ACCOUNT OF WHAT WERE JUST A FEW NICE DAYS I HAD IN LONDON.
OKAY, BUT WHEN THE MOVIE CAME OUT, YOU TOTALLY WANTED THAT GARY OLDMAN DOUBLE BUN, RIGHT?
...
THAT DETAIL...
...IS ONE OF THE MORE ACCURATE ONES.
NO! YOU DID THAT? AMAZING. RESPECT.
HOW ARE YOU JUST CHATTING THROUGH ALL THIS?
IT'S KIND OF THE ONLY WAY TO KEEP FROM GOING CRAZY.
WHAT?!

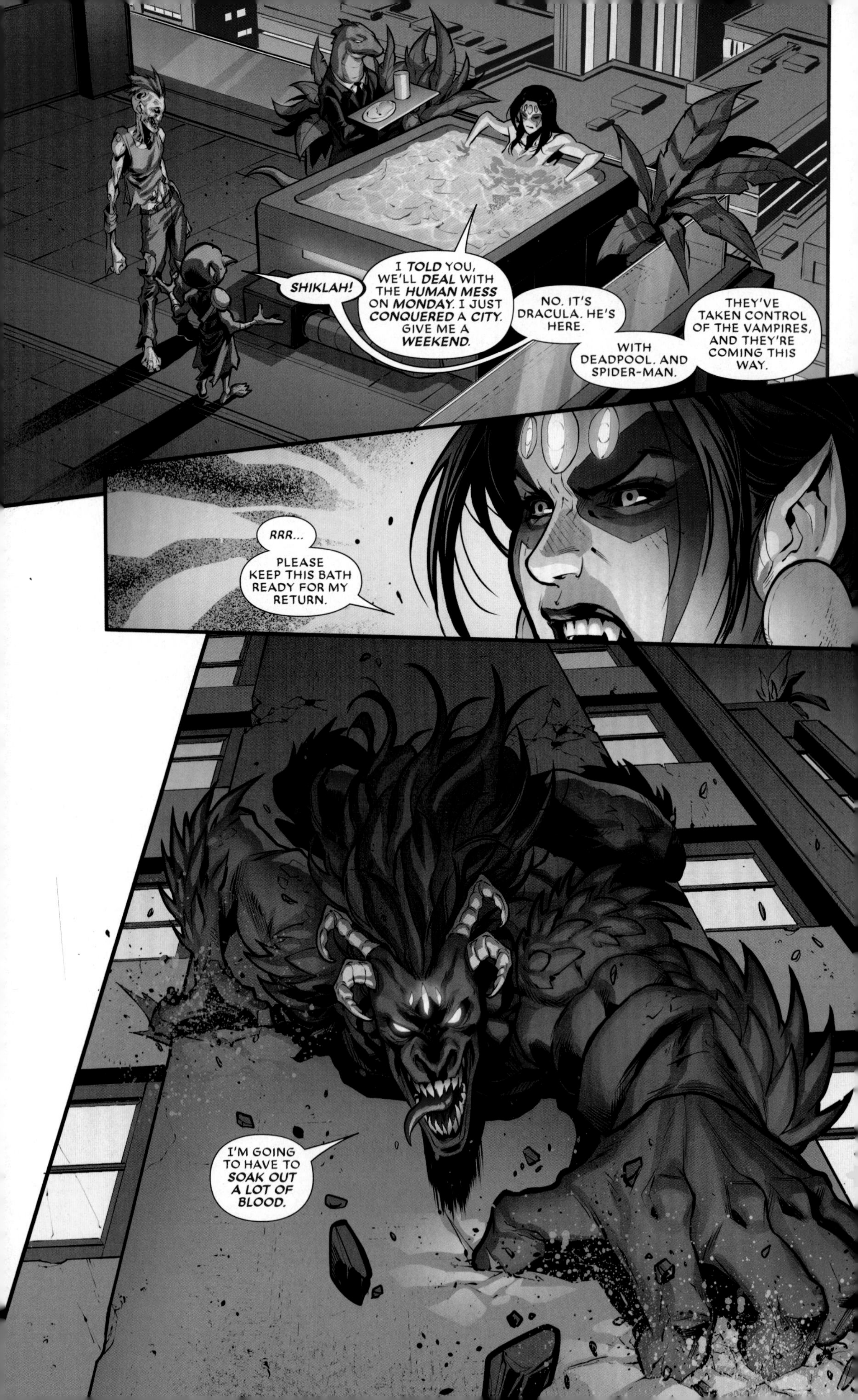
SHIKLAH!
I TOLD YOU, WE'LL DEAL WITH THE HUMAN MESS ON MONDAY. I JUST CONQUERED A CITY. GIVE ME A WEEKEND.
NO. IT'S DRACULA. HE'S HERE.
WITH DEADPOOL. AND SPIDER-MAN.
THEY'VE TAKEN CONTROL OF THE VAMPIRES, AND THEY'RE COMING THIS WAY.
RRR...
PLEASE KEEP THIS BATH READY FOR MY RETURN.
I'M GOING TO HAVE TO SOAK OUT A LOT OF BLOOD.

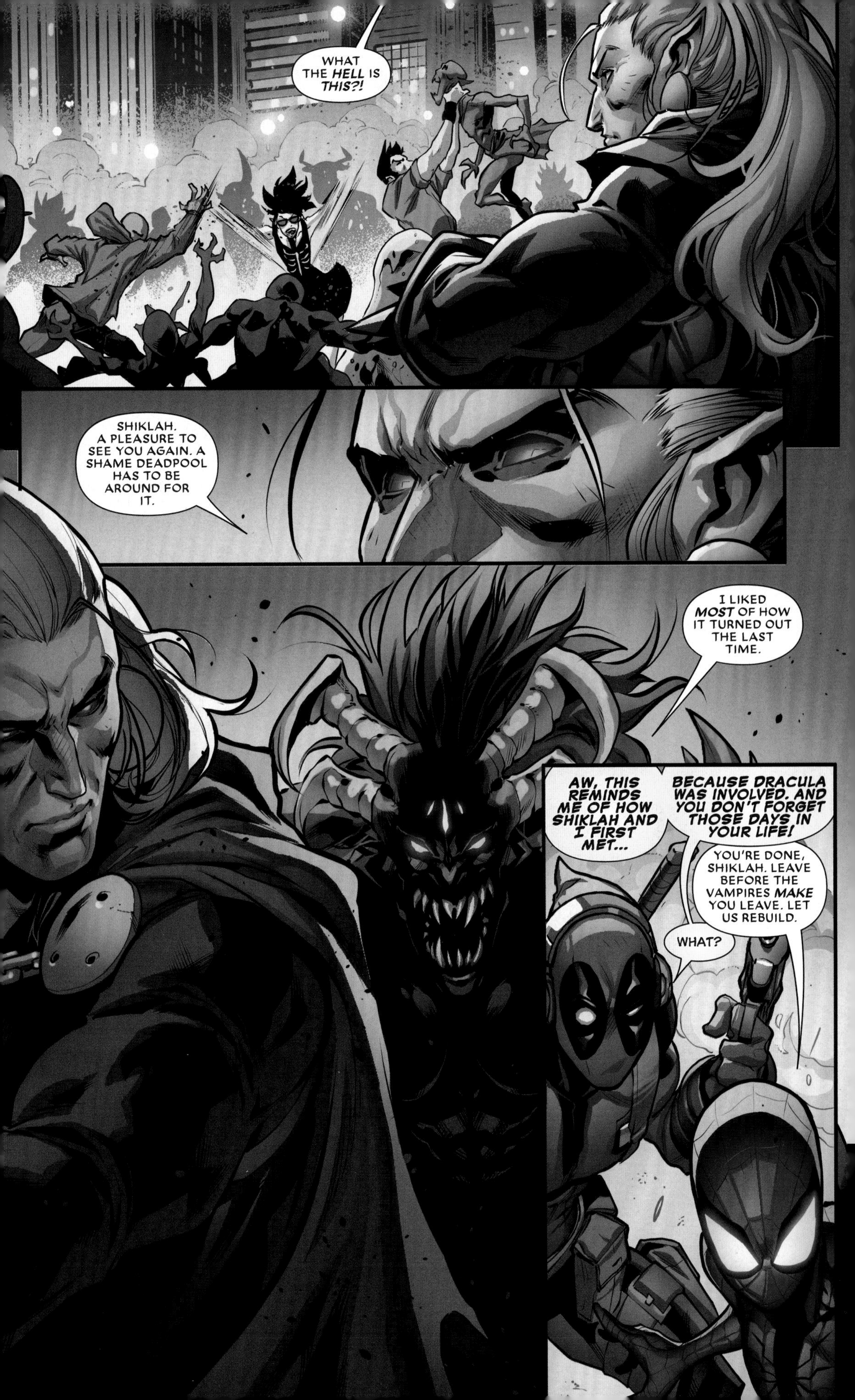
WHAT THE HELL IS THIS?!
SHIKLAH. A PLEASURE TO SEE YOU AGAIN. A SHAME DEADPOOL HAS TO BE AROUND FOR IT.
I LIKED MOST OF HOW IT TURNED OUT THE LAST TIME.
AW, THIS REMINDS ME OF HOW SHIKLAH AND I FIRST MET...
BECAUSE DRACULA WAS INVOLVED. AND YOU DON'T FORGET THOSE DAYS IN YOUR LIFE!
YOU'RE DONE, SHIKLAH. LEAVE BEFORE THE VAMPIRES MAKE YOU LEAVE. LET US REBUILD.
WHAT?

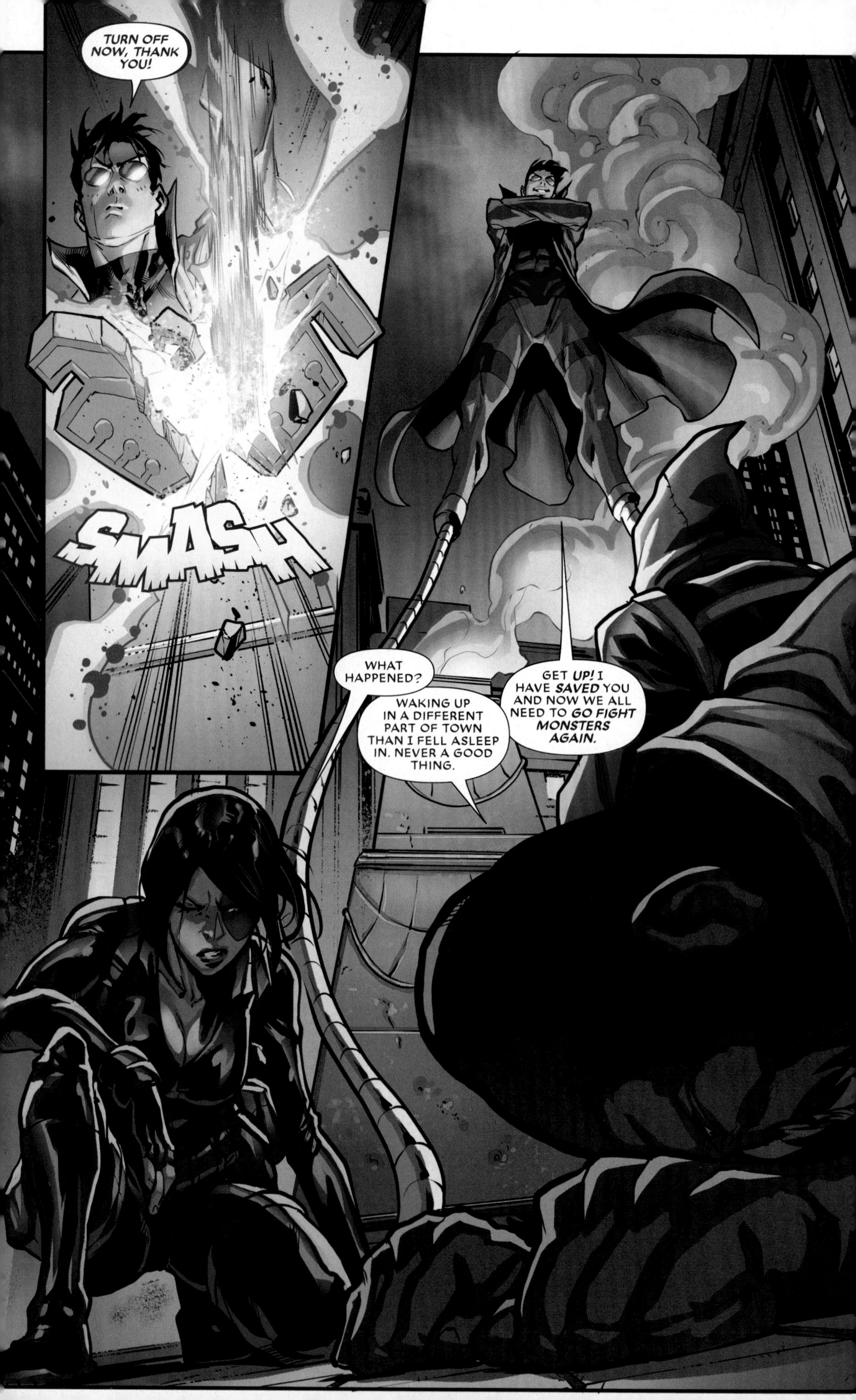
TURN OFF NOW, THANK YOU!
SMASH
WHAT HAPPENED?
WAKING UP IN A DIFFERENT PART OF TOWN THAN I FELL ASLEEP IN. NEVER A GOOD THING.
GET UP! I HAVE SAVED YOU AND NOW WE ALL NEED TO GO FIGHT MONSTERS AGAIN.

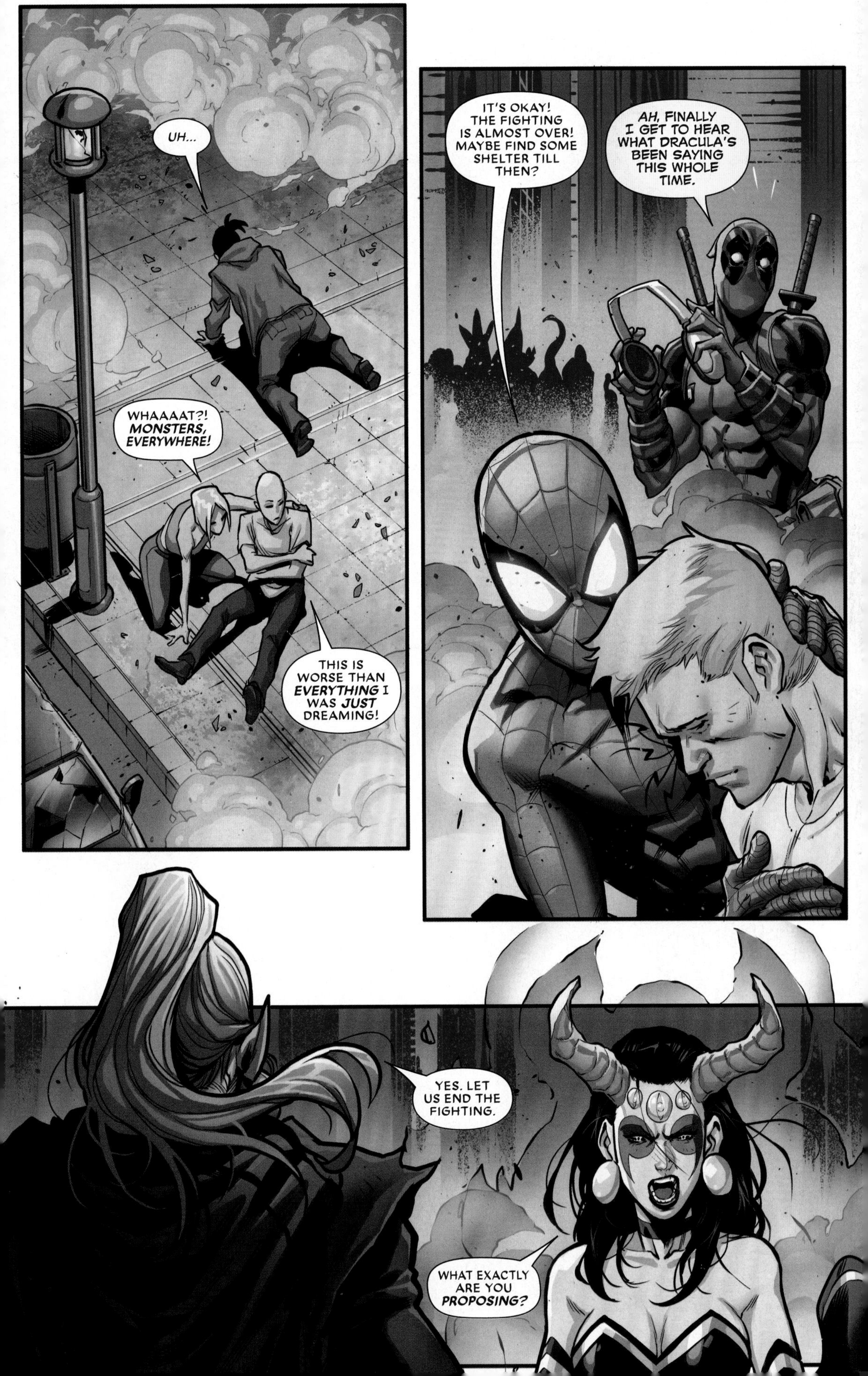
UH...
WHAAAAT?! MONSTERS, EVERYWHERE!
THIS IS WORSE THAN EVERYTHING I WAS JUST DREAMING!
IT'S OKAY! THE FIGHTING IS ALMOST OVER! MAYBE FIND SOME SHELTER TILL THEN?
AH, FINALLY I GET TO HEAR WHAT DRACULA'S BEEN SAYING THIS WHOLE TIME.
YES. LET US END THE FIGHTING.
WHAT EXACTLY ARE YOU PROPOSING?

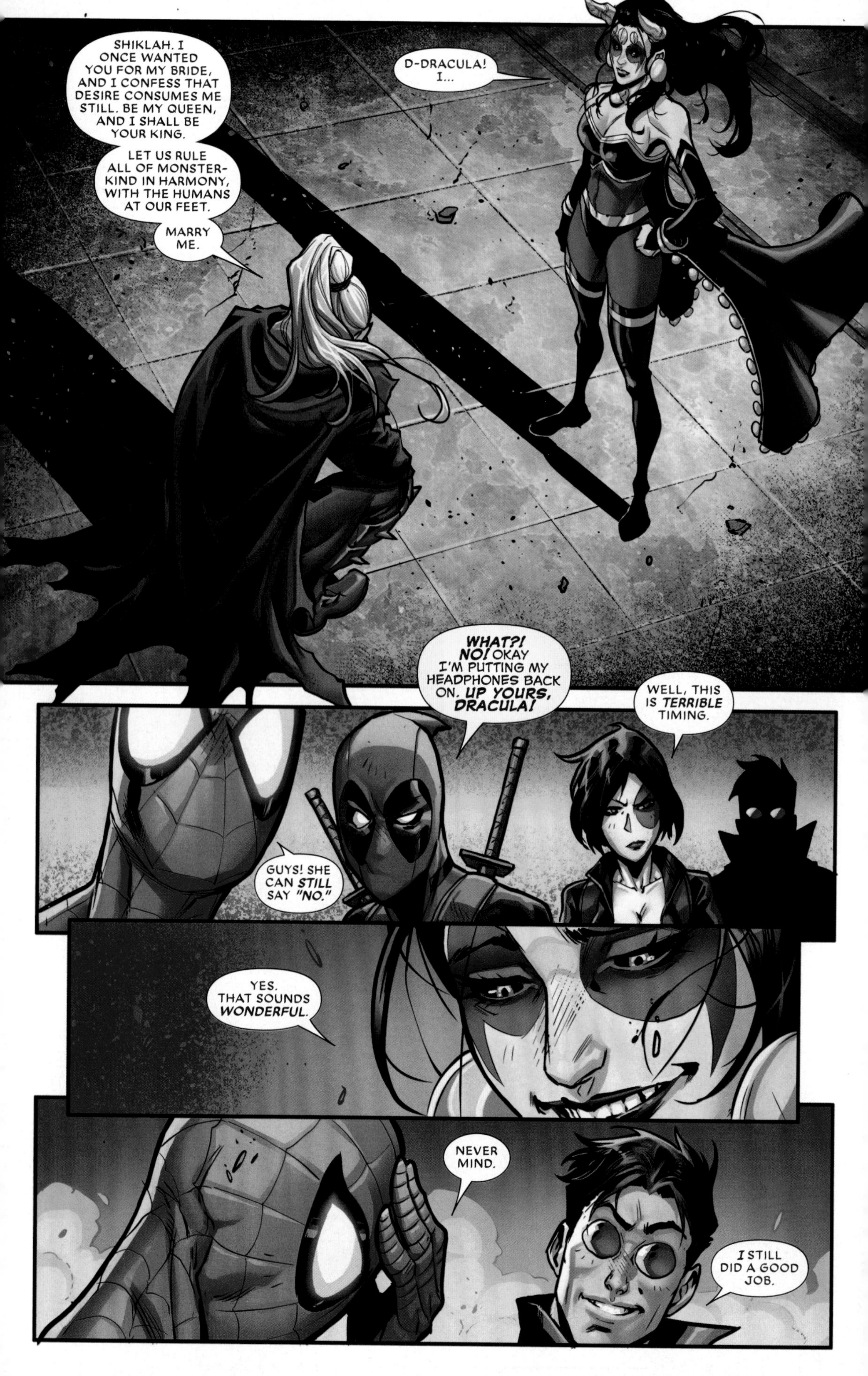
SHIKLAH. I ONCE WANTED YOU FOR MY BRIDE, AND I CONFESS THAT DESIRE CONSUMES ME STILL. BE MY QUEEN, AND I SHALL BE YOUR KING.
LET US RULE ALL OF MONSTER-KIND IN HARMONY, WITH THE HUMANS AT OUR FEET.
MARRY ME.
D-DRACULA! I...
WHAT?! NO! OKAY I'M PUTTING MY HEADPHONES BACK ON. UP YOURS, DRACULA!
WELL, THIS IS TERRIBLE TIMING.
GUYS! SHE CAN STILL SAY "NO."
YES. THAT SOUNDS WONDERFUL.
NEVER MIND.
I STILL DID A GOOD JOB.

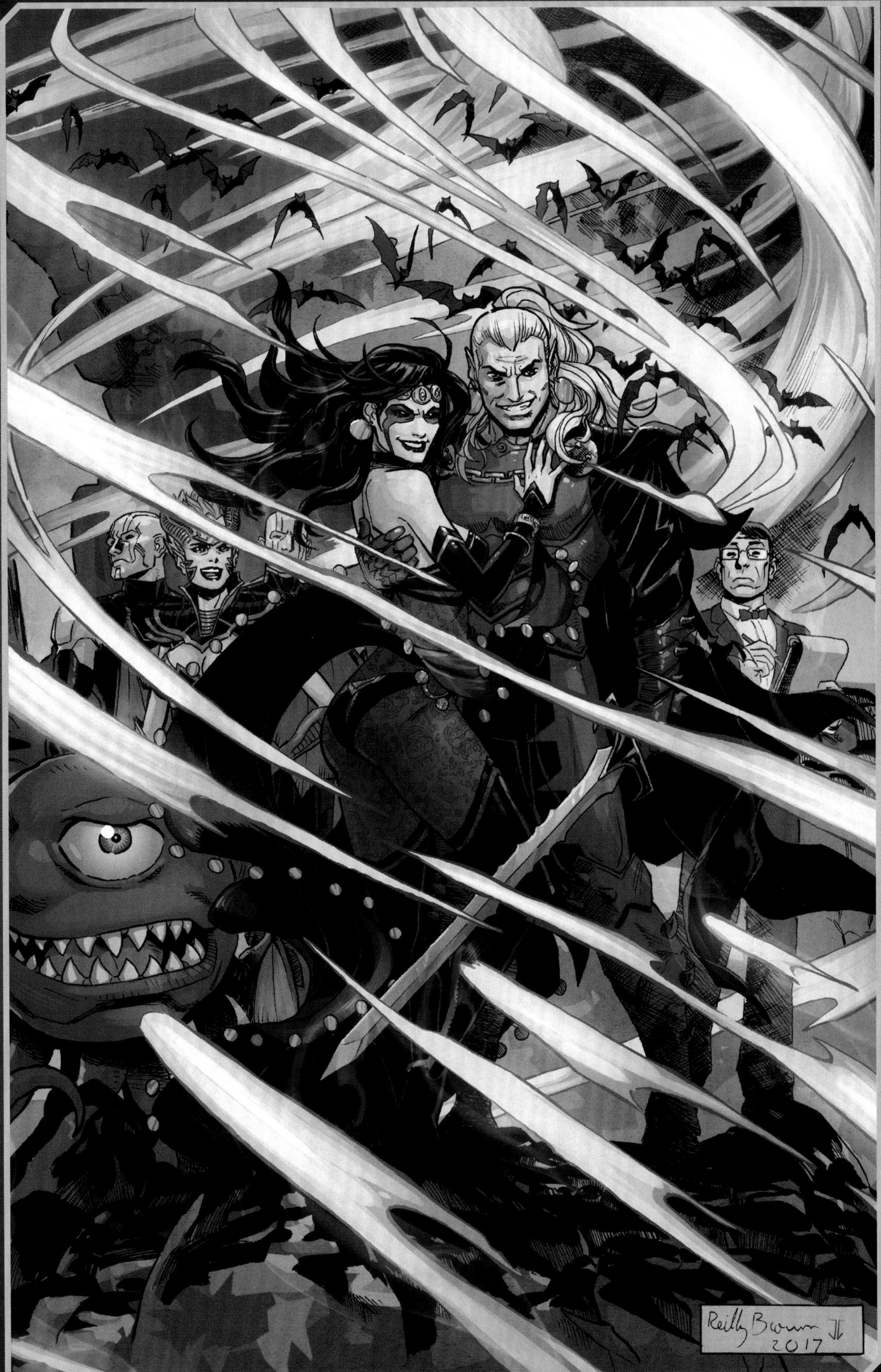
Reilly Brown JL
2017

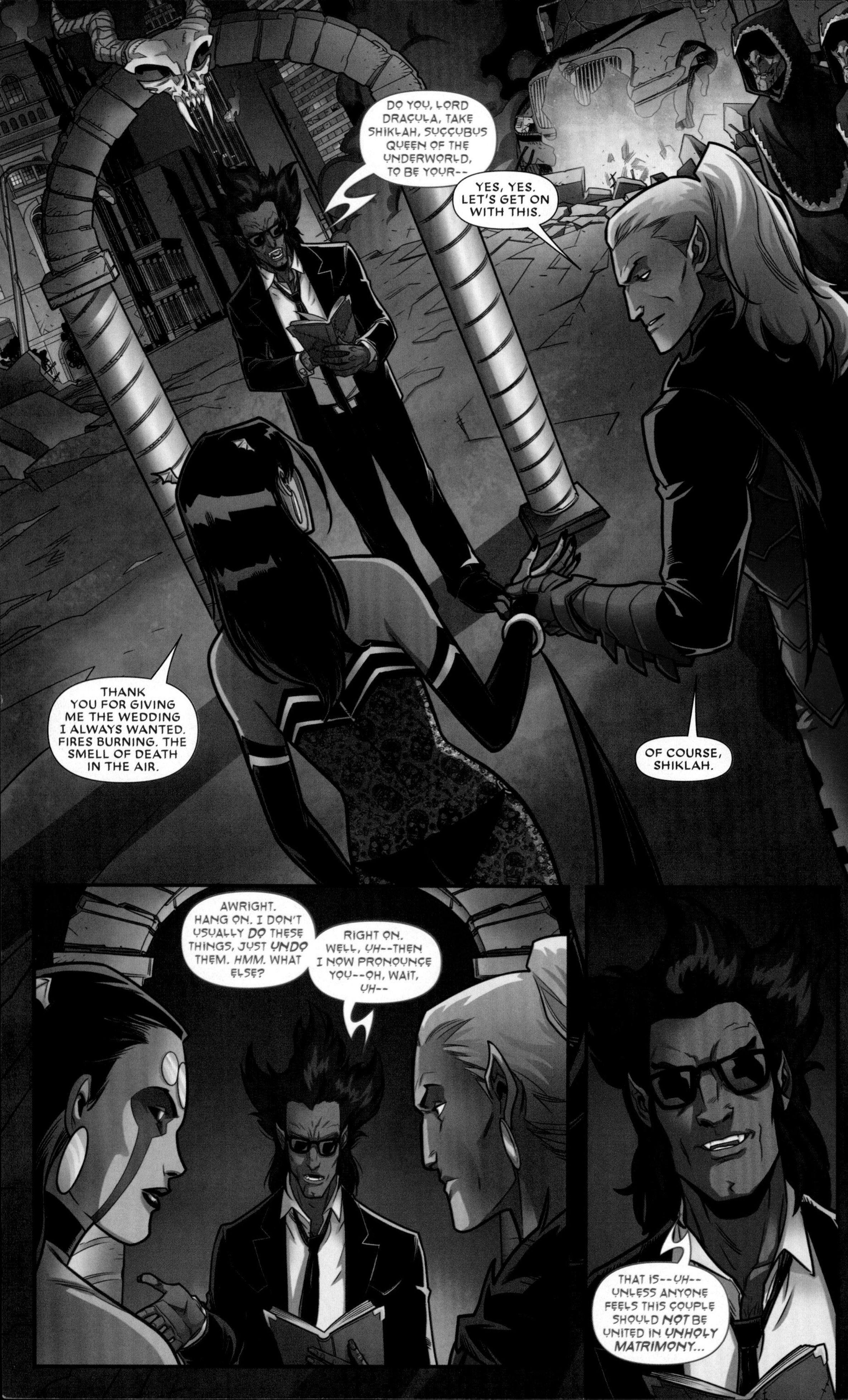
DO YOU, LORD DRACULA, TAKE SHIKLAH, SUCCUBUS QUEEN OF THE UNDERWORLD, TO BE YOUR--
YES, YES. LET'S GET ON WITH THIS.
THANK YOU FOR GIVING ME THE WEDDING I ALWAYS WANTED. FIRES BURNING. THE SMELL OF DEATH IN THE AIR.
OF COURSE, SHIKLAH.
AWRIGHT. HANG ON. I DON'T USUALLY *DO* THESE THINGS, JUST *UNDO* THEM. *HMM.* WHAT ELSE?
RIGHT ON. WELL, *UH*--THEN I NOW PRONOUNCE YOU--OH, WAIT, *UH*--
THAT IS--*UH*--UNLESS ANYONE FEELS THIS COUPLE SHOULD *NOT* BE UNITED IN *UNHOLY MATRIMONY*...

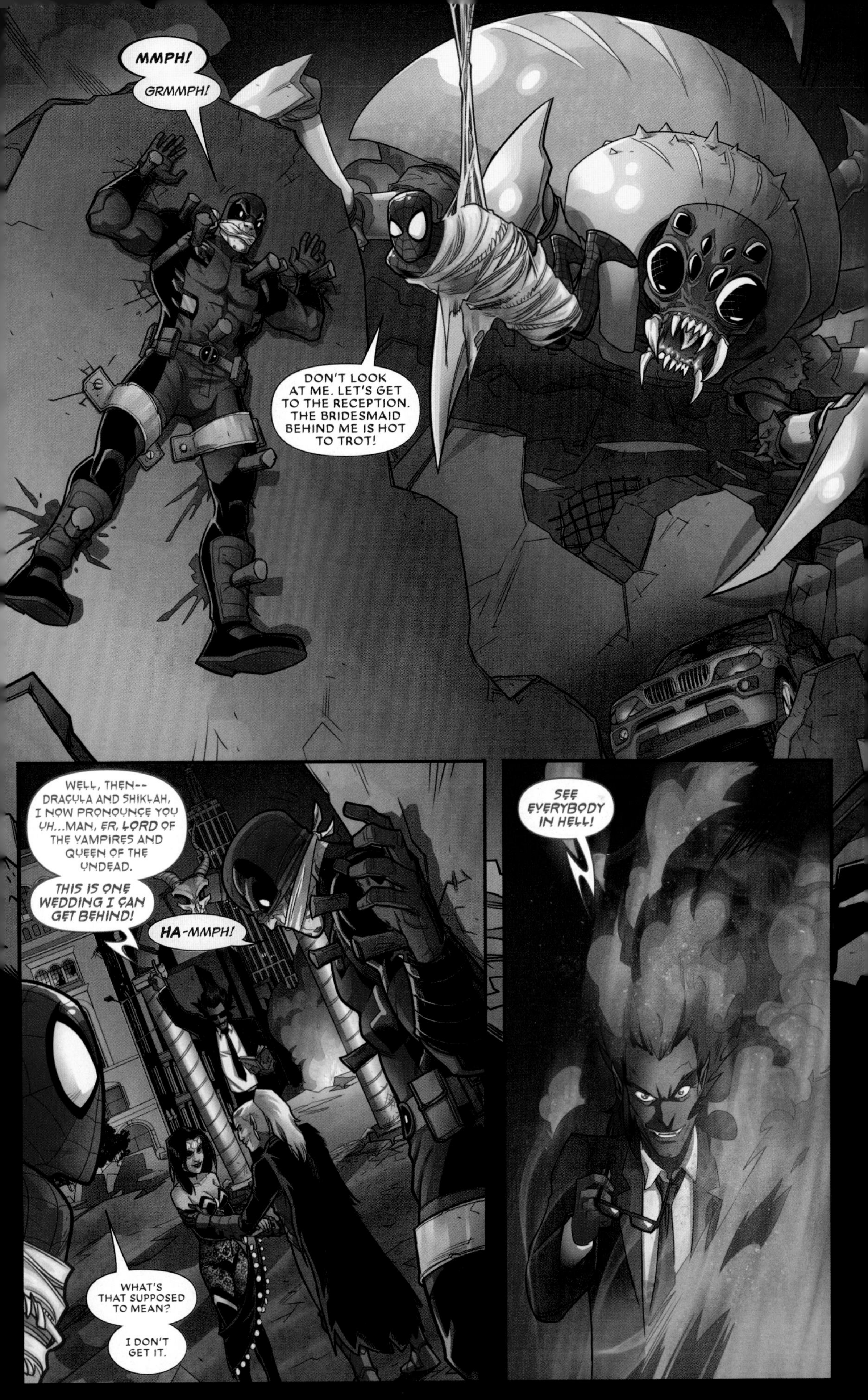
MMPH!
GRMMPH!
DON'T LOOK AT ME. LET'S GET TO THE RECEPTION. THE BRIDESMAID BEHIND ME IS HOT TO TROT!
WELL, THEN-- DRACULA AND SHIKLAH, I NOW PRONOUNCE YOU UH...MAN, ER, LORD OF THE VAMPIRES AND QUEEN OF THE UNDEAD.
THIS IS ONE WEDDING I CAN GET BEHIND!
HA-MMPH!
WHAT'S THAT SUPPOSED TO MEAN?
I DON'T GET IT.
SEE EVERYBODY IN HELL!

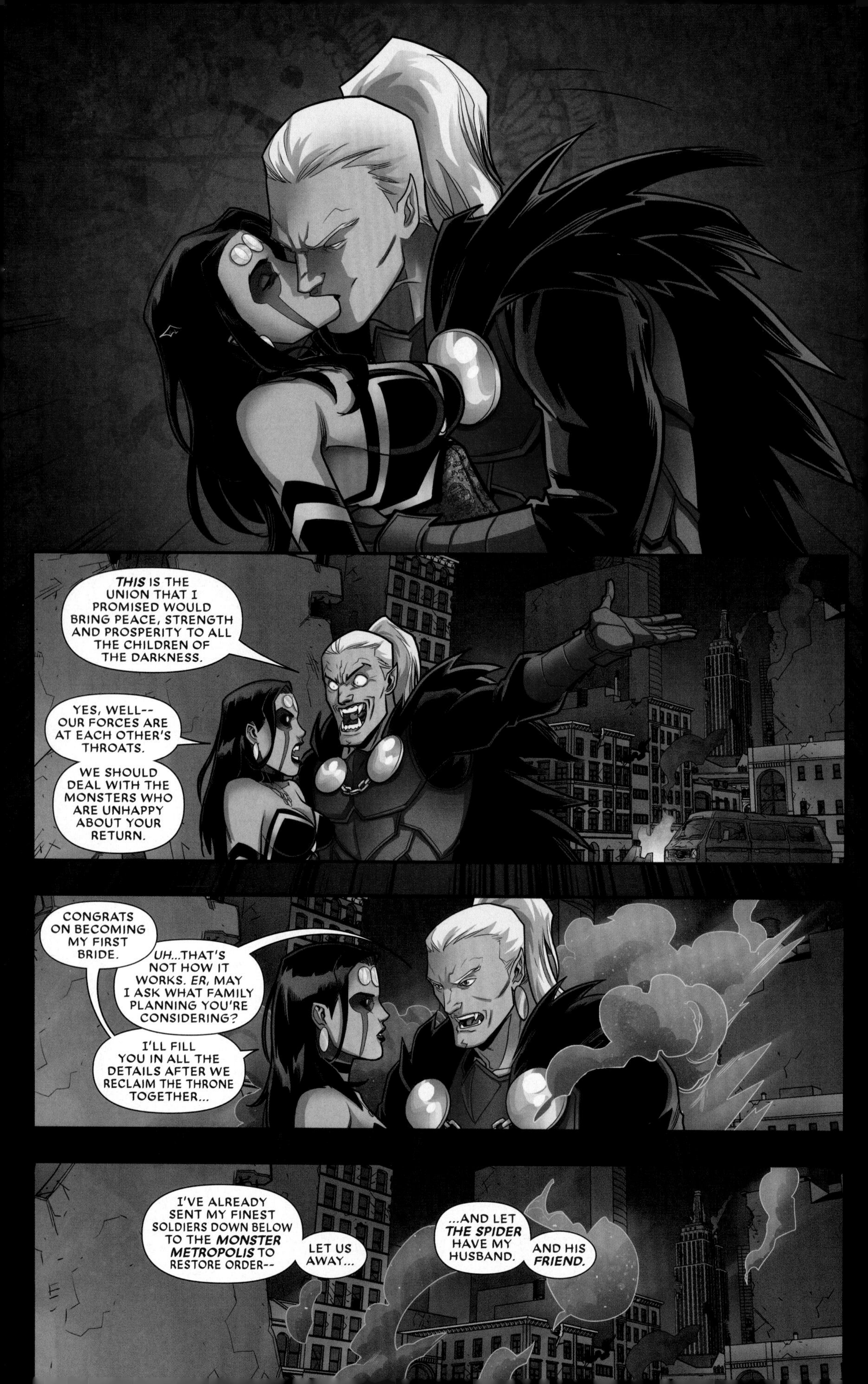
THIS IS THE UNION THAT I PROMISED WOULD BRING PEACE, STRENGTH AND PROSPERITY TO ALL THE CHILDREN OF THE DARKNESS.
YES, WELL-- OUR FORCES ARE AT EACH OTHER'S THROATS.
WE SHOULD DEAL WITH THE MONSTERS WHO ARE UNHAPPY ABOUT YOUR RETURN.
CONGRATS ON BECOMING MY FIRST BRIDE.
UH...THAT'S NOT HOW IT WORKS. ER, MAY I ASK WHAT FAMILY PLANNING YOU'RE CONSIDERING?
I'LL FILL YOU IN ALL THE DETAILS AFTER WE RECLAIM THE THRONE TOGETHER...
I'VE ALREADY SENT MY FINEST SOLDIERS DOWN BELOW TO THE MONSTER METROPOLIS TO RESTORE ORDER--
LET US AWAY...
...AND LET THE SPIDER HAVE MY HUSBAND.
AND HIS FRIEND.

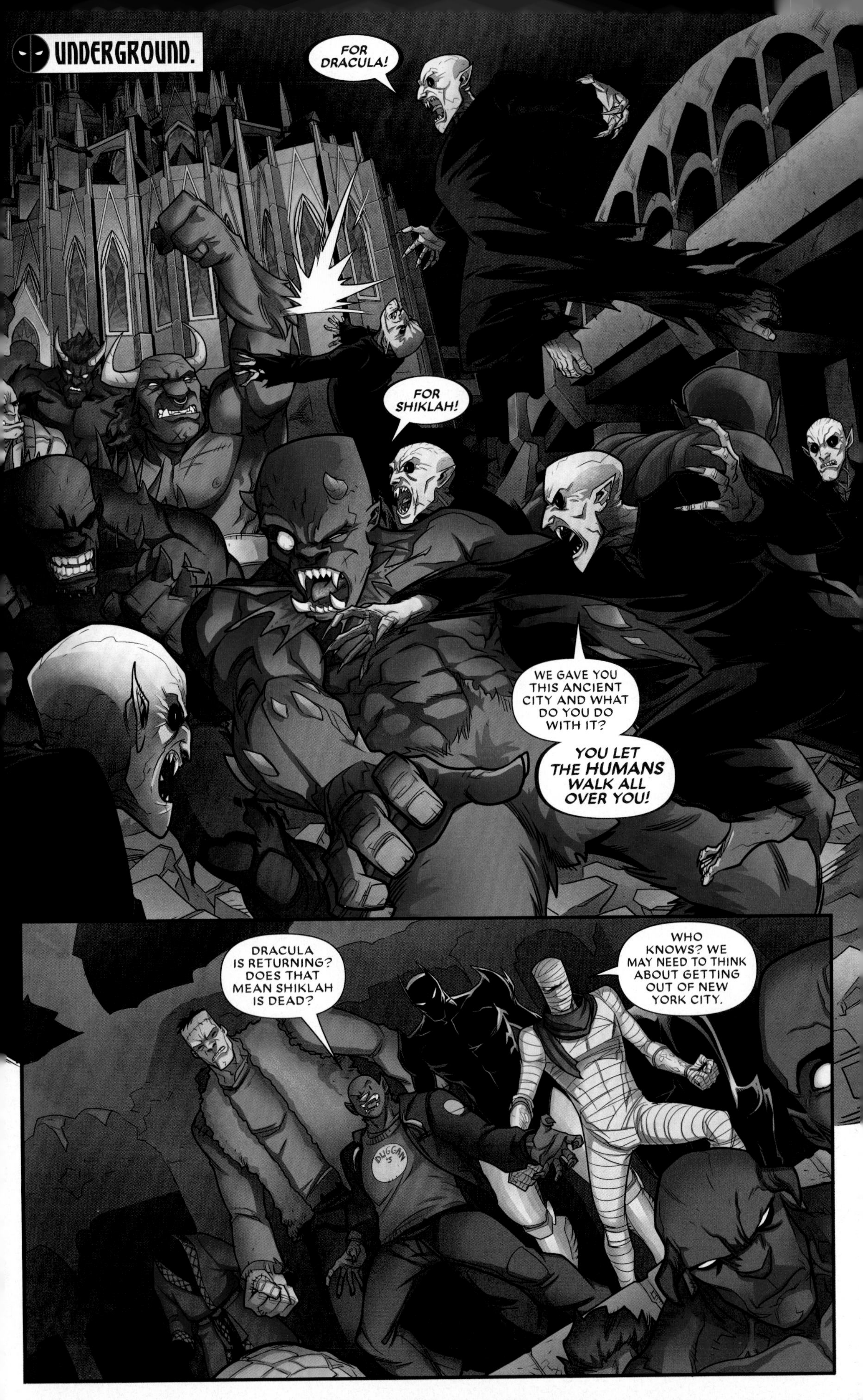
UNDERGROUND.
FOR DRACULA!
FOR SHIKLAH!
WE GAVE YOU THIS ANCIENT CITY AND WHAT DO YOU DO WITH IT?
YOU LET THE HUMANS WALK ALL OVER YOU!
DRACULA IS RETURNING? DOES THAT MEAN SHIKLAH IS DEAD?
WHO KNOWS? WE MAY NEED TO THINK ABOUT GETTING OUT OF NEW YORK CITY.
DUGGAN 5

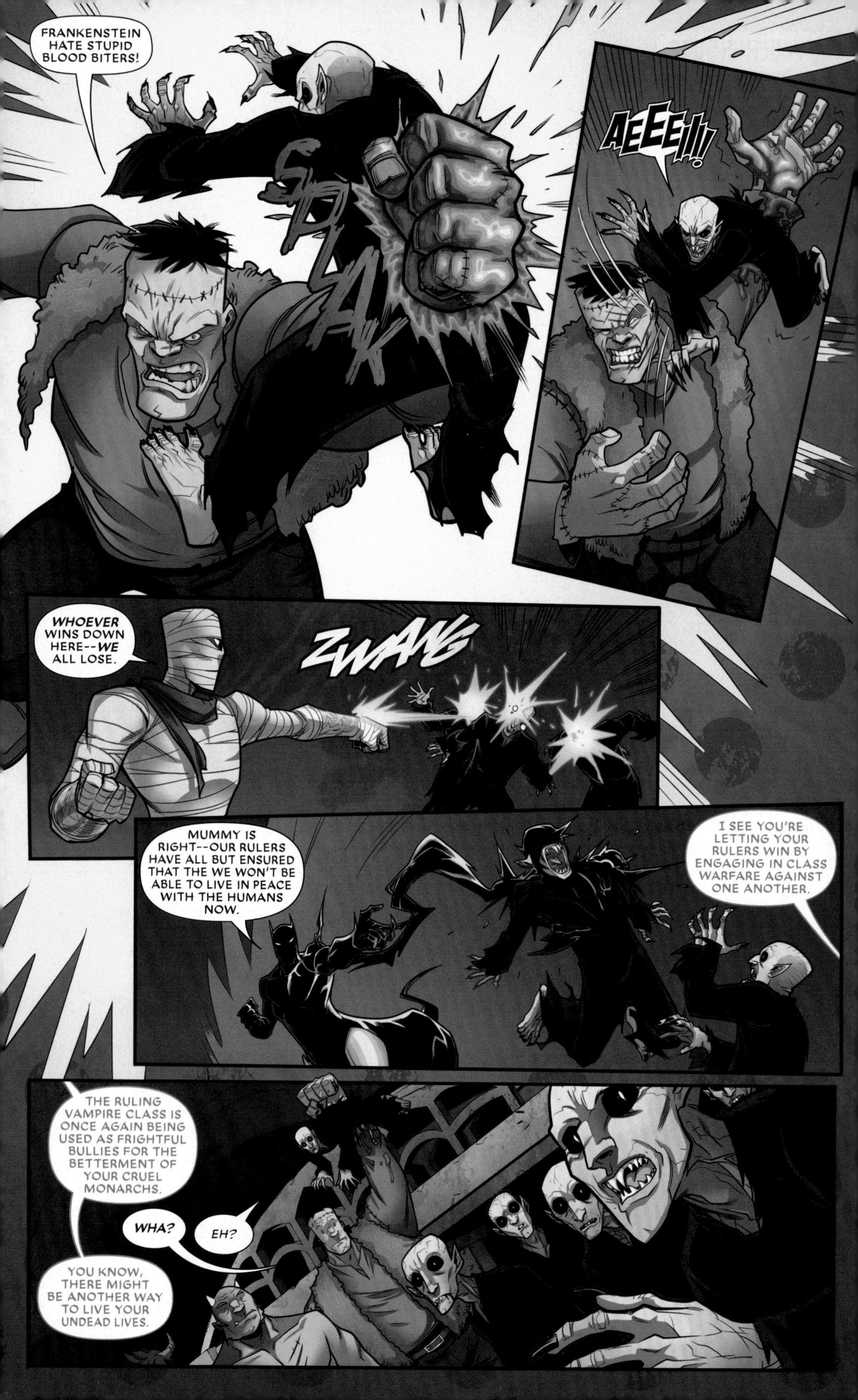
FRANKENSTEIN HATE STUPID BLOOD BITERS!
AEEE!!!!
WHOEVER WINS DOWN HERE--WE ALL LOSE.
ZWANG
MUMMY IS RIGHT--OUR RULERS HAVE ALL BUT ENSURED THAT THE WE WON'T BE ABLE TO LIVE IN PEACE WITH THE HUMANS NOW.
I SEE YOU'RE LETTING YOUR RULERS WIN BY ENGAGING IN CLASS WARFARE AGAINST ONE ANOTHER.
THE RULING VAMPIRE CLASS IS ONCE AGAIN BEING USED AS FRIGHTFUL BULLIES FOR THE BETTERMENT OF YOUR CRUEL MONARCHS.
WHA?
EH?
YOU KNOW, THERE MIGHT BE ANOTHER WAY TO LIVE YOUR UNDEAD LIVES.

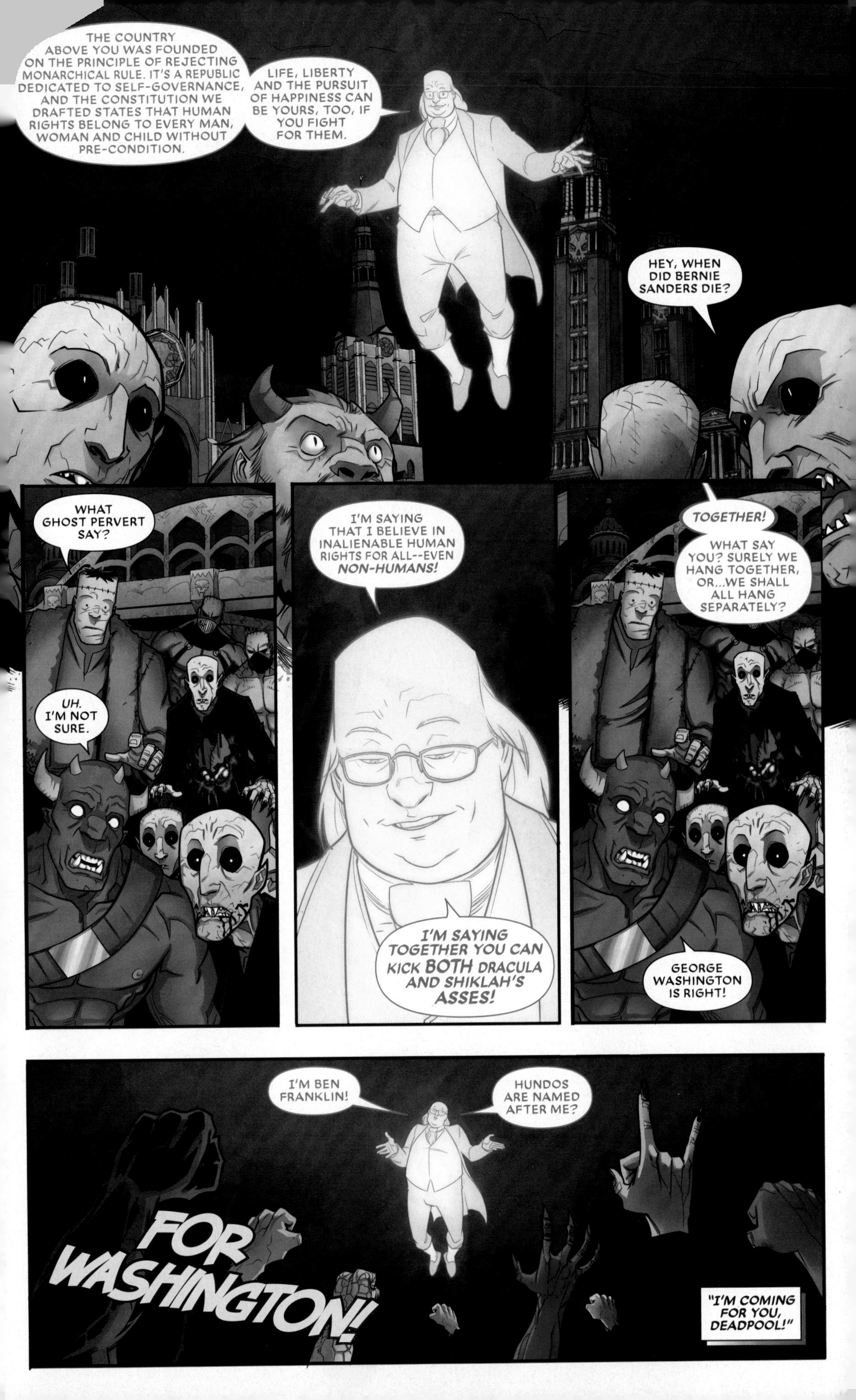
THE COUNTRY ABOVE YOU WAS FOUNDED ON THE PRINCIPLE OF REJECTING MONARCHICAL RULE. IT'S A REPUBLIC DEDICATED TO SELF-GOVERNANCE, AND THE CONSTITUTION WE DRAFTED STATES THAT HUMAN RIGHTS BELONG TO EVERY MAN, WOMAN AND CHILD WITHOUT PRE-CONDITION.
LIFE, LIBERTY AND THE PURSUIT OF HAPPINESS CAN BE YOURS, TOO, IF YOU FIGHT FOR THEM.
HEY, WHEN DID BERNIE SANDERS DIE?
WHAT GHOST PERVERT SAY?
UH. I'M NOT SURE.
I'M SAYING THAT I BELIEVE IN INALIENABLE HUMAN RIGHTS FOR ALL--EVEN NON-HUMANS!
I'M SAYING TOGETHER YOU CAN KICK BOTH DRACULA AND SHIKLAH'S ASSES!
TOGETHER!
WHAT SAY YOU? SURELY WE HANG TOGETHER, OR...WE SHALL ALL HANG SEPARATELY?
GEORGE WASHINGTON IS RIGHT!
I'M BEN FRANKLIN!
HUNDOS ARE NAMED AFTER ME?
FOR WASHINGTON!
"I'M COMING FOR YOU, DEADPOOL!"

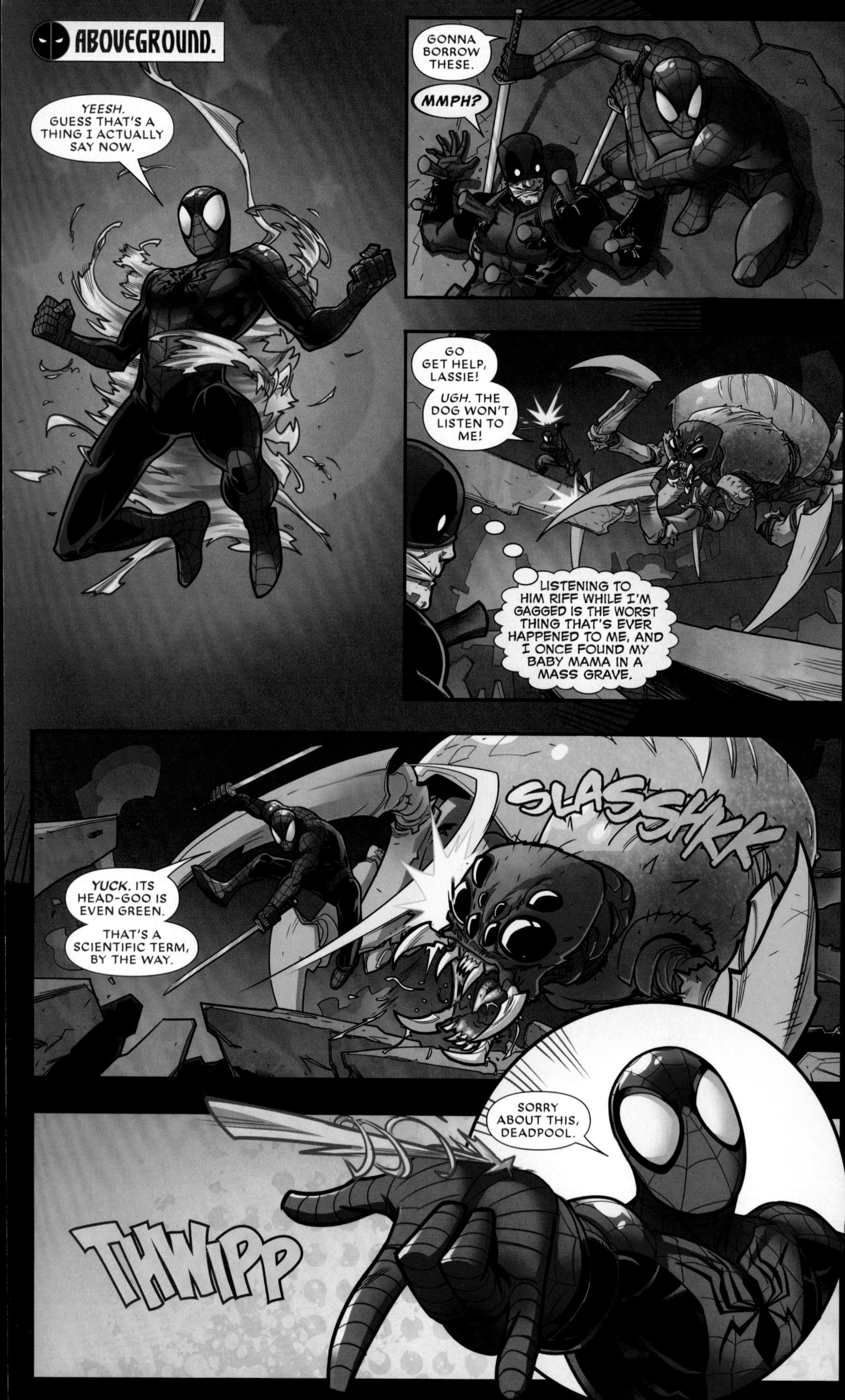
ABOVEGROUND.
YEESH. GUESS THAT'S A THING I ACTUALLY SAY NOW.
GONNA BORROW THESE.
MMPH?
GO GET HELP, LASSIE!
UGH. THE DOG WON'T LISTEN TO ME!
LISTENING TO HIM RIFF WHILE I'M GAGGED IS THE WORST THING THAT'S EVER HAPPENED TO ME, AND I ONCE FOUND MY BABY MAMA IN A MASS GRAVE.
SLASSHKK
YUCK. ITS HEAD-GOO IS EVEN GREEN.
THAT'S A SCIENTIFIC TERM, BY THE WAY.
SORRY ABOUT THIS, DEADPOOL.
THWIPP

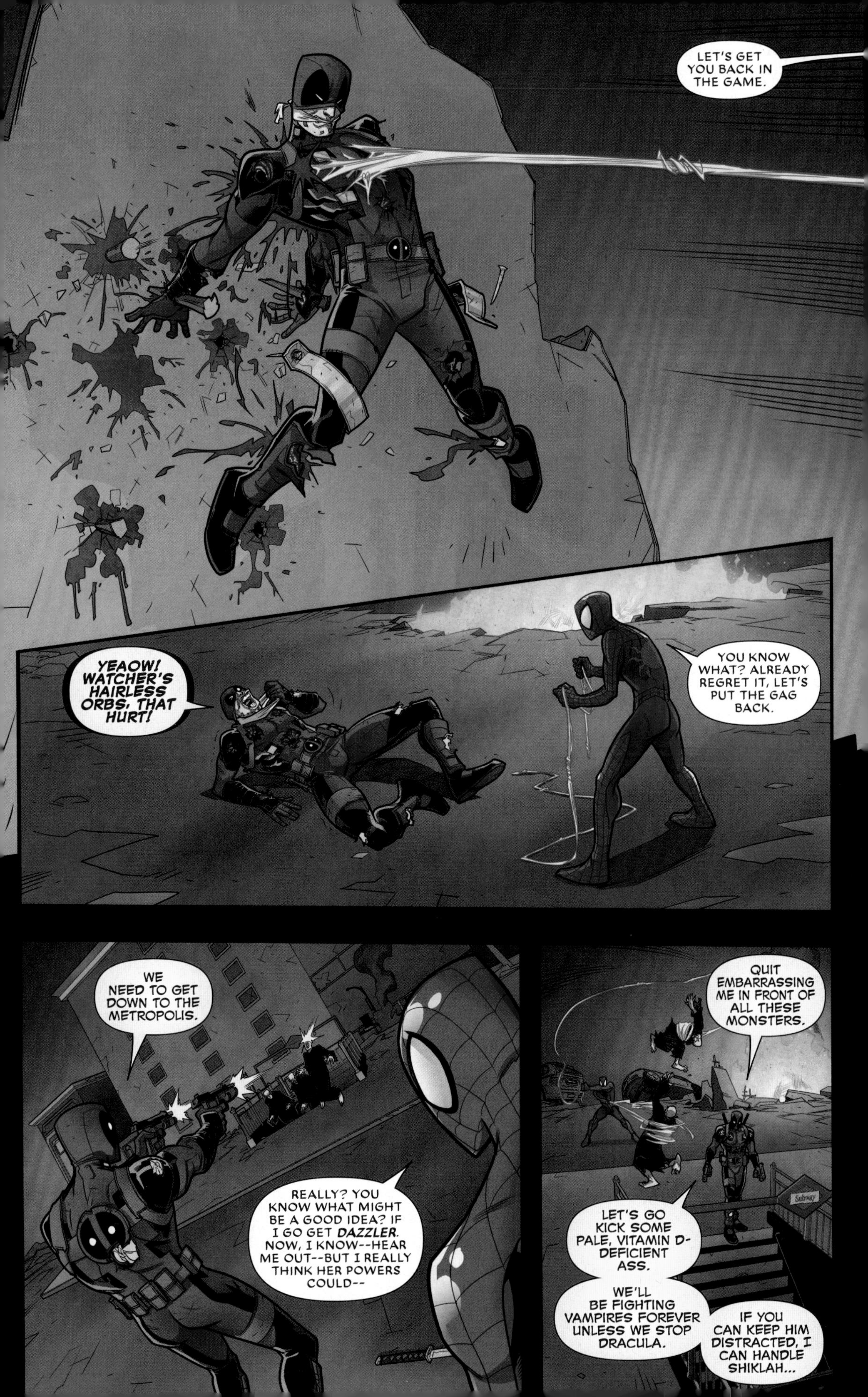
LET'S GET YOU BACK IN THE GAME.
YEAOW! WATCHER'S HAIRLESS ORBS, THAT HURT!
YOU KNOW WHAT? ALREADY REGRET IT, LET'S PUT THE GAG BACK.
WE NEED TO GET DOWN TO THE METROPOLIS.
REALLY? YOU KNOW WHAT MIGHT BE A GOOD IDEA? IF I GO GET DAZZLER. NOW, I KNOW--HEAR ME OUT--BUT I REALLY THINK HER POWERS COULD--
QUIT EMBARRASSING ME IN FRONT OF ALL THESE MONSTERS.
LET'S GO KICK SOME PALE, VITAMIN D-DEFICIENT ASS.
WE'LL BE FIGHTING VAMPIRES FOREVER UNLESS WE STOP DRACULA.
IF YOU CAN KEEP HIM DISTRACTED, I CAN HANDLE SHIKLAH...

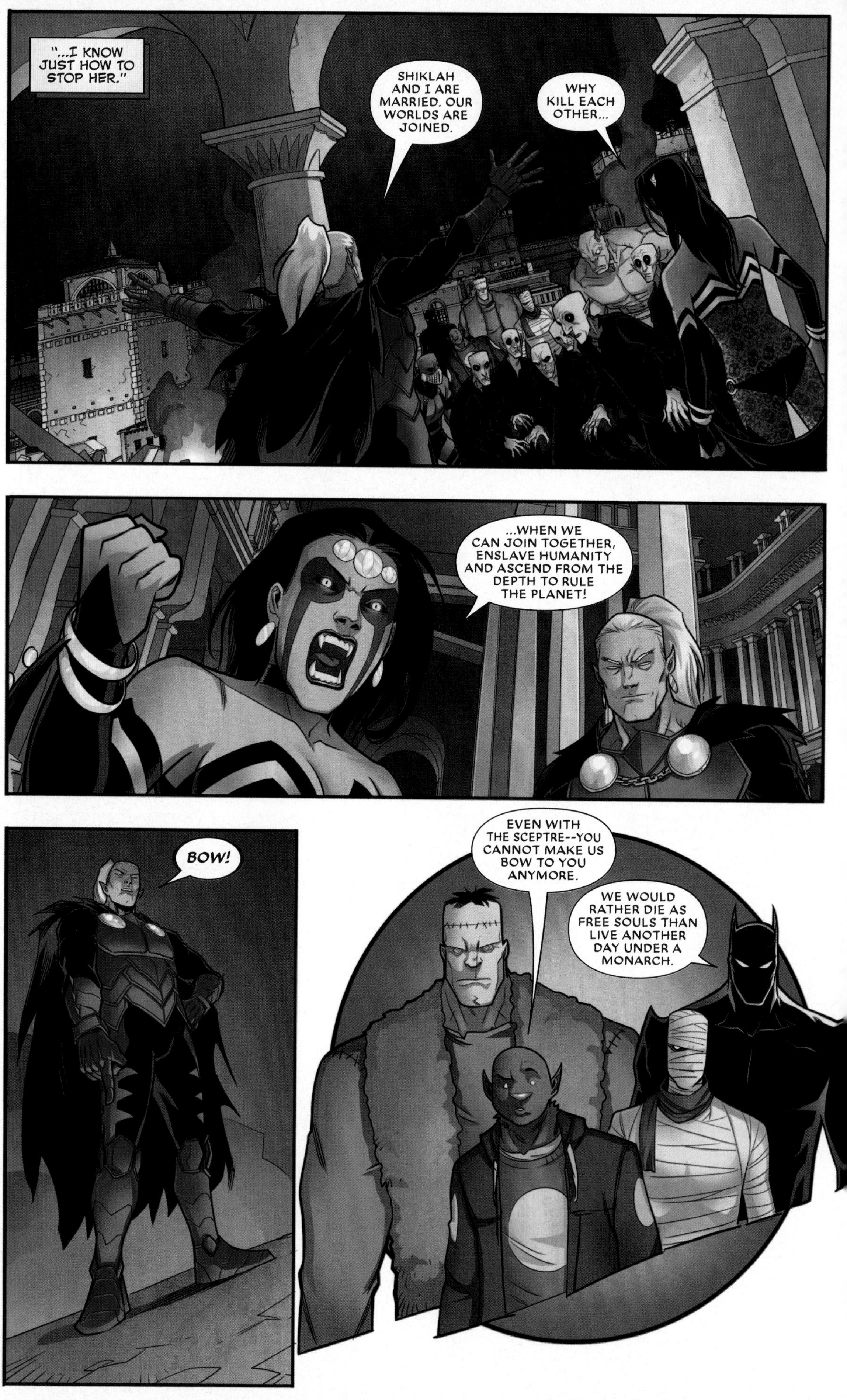
"...I KNOW JUST HOW TO STOP HER."
SHIKLAH AND I ARE MARRIED. OUR WORLDS ARE JOINED.
WHY KILL EACH OTHER...
...WHEN WE CAN JOIN TOGETHER, ENSLAVE HUMANITY AND ASCEND FROM THE DEPTH TO RULE THE PLANET!
BOW!
EVEN WITH THE SCEPTRE--YOU CANNOT MAKE US BOW TO YOU ANYMORE.
WE WOULD RATHER DIE AS FREE SOULS THAN LIVE ANOTHER DAY UNDER A MONARCH.

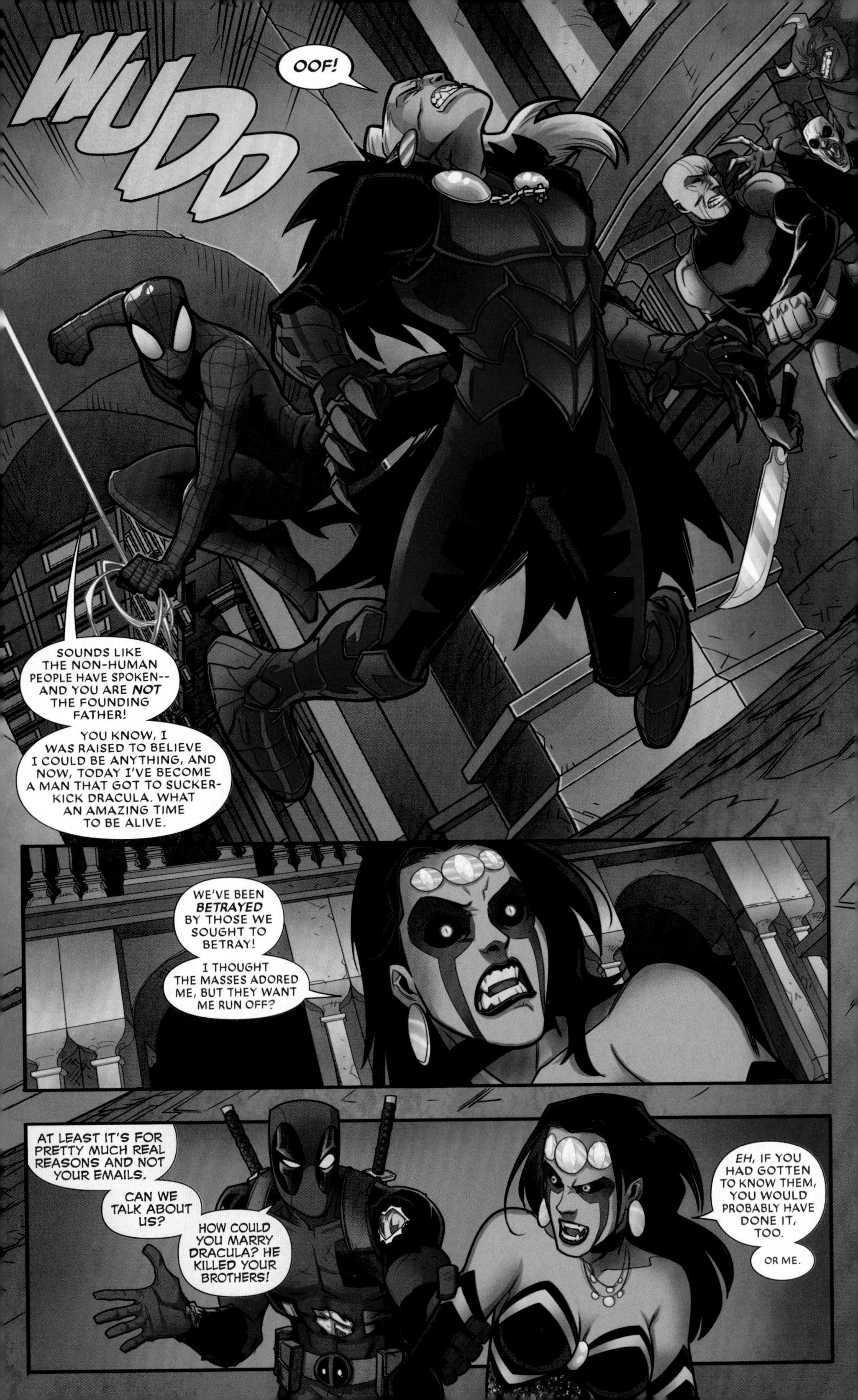
WUDD
OOF!
SOUNDS LIKE THE NON-HUMAN PEOPLE HAVE SPOKEN-- AND YOU ARE NOT THE FOUNDING FATHER!
YOU KNOW, I WAS RAISED TO BELIEVE I COULD BE ANYTHING, AND NOW, TODAY I'VE BECOME A MAN THAT GOT TO SUCKER-KICK DRACULA. WHAT AN AMAZING TIME TO BE ALIVE.
WE'VE BEEN BETRAYED BY THOSE WE SOUGHT TO BETRAY!
I THOUGHT THE MASSES ADORED ME, BUT THEY WANT ME RUN OFF?
AT LEAST IT'S FOR PRETTY MUCH REAL REASONS AND NOT YOUR EMAILS.
CAN WE TALK ABOUT US?
HOW COULD YOU MARRY DRACULA? HE KILLED YOUR BROTHERS!
EH, IF YOU HAD GOTTEN TO KNOW THEM, YOU WOULD PROBABLY HAVE DONE IT, TOO.
OR ME.

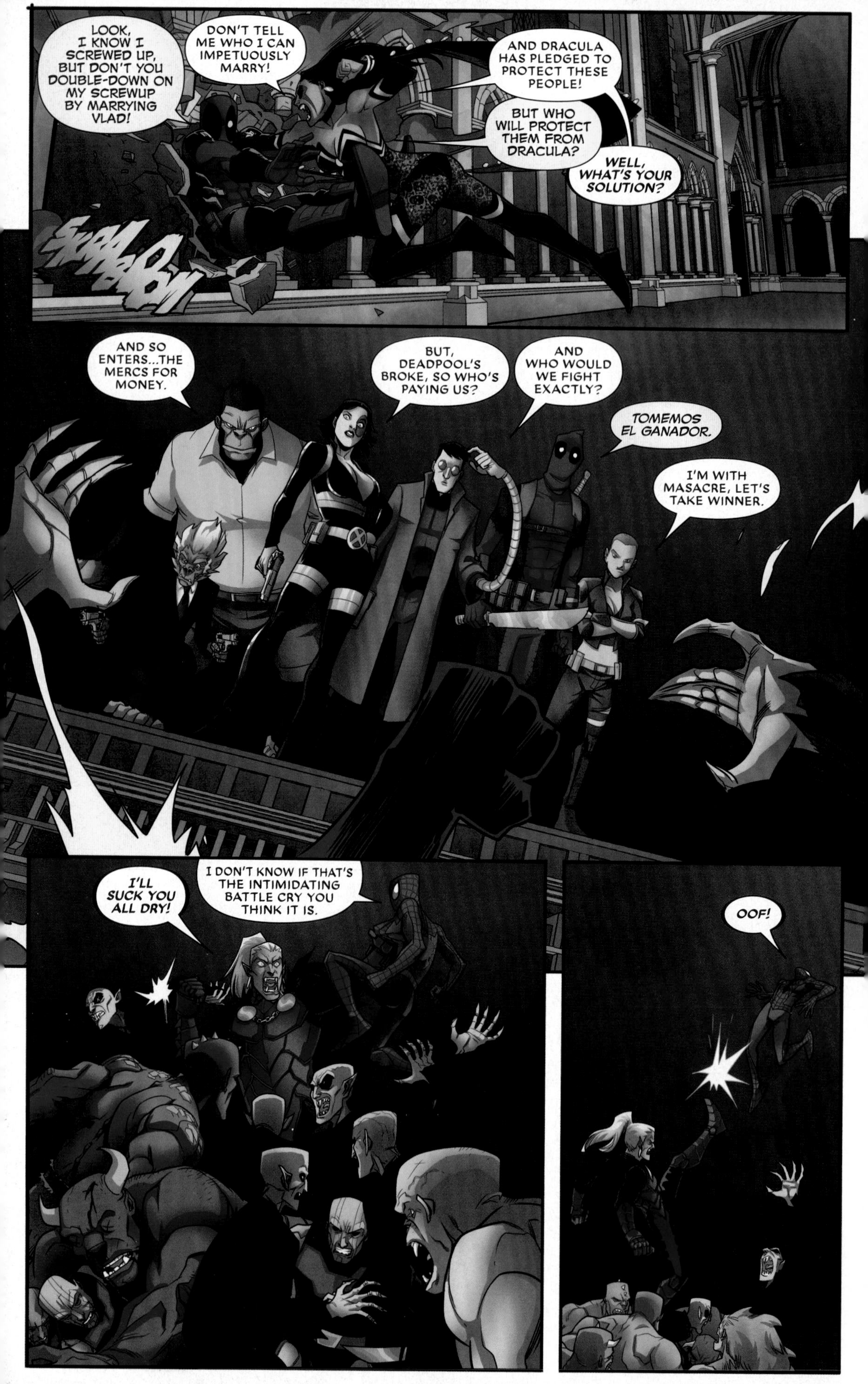

LOOK, I KNOW I SCREWED UP, BUT DON'T YOU DOUBLE-DOWN ON MY SCREWUP BY MARRYING VLAD!
DON'T TELL ME WHO I CAN IMPETUOUSLY MARRY!
AND DRACULA HAS PLEDGED TO PROTECT THESE PEOPLE!
BUT WHO WILL PROTECT THEM FROM DRACULA?
WELL, WHAT'S YOUR SOLUTION?
AND SO ENTERS...THE MERCS FOR MONEY.
BUT, DEADPOOL'S BROKE, SO WHO'S PAYING US?
AND WHO WOULD WE FIGHT EXACTLY?
TOMEMOS EL GANADOR.
I'M WITH MASACRE, LET'S TAKE WINNER.
I'LL SUCK YOU ALL DRY!
I DON'T KNOW IF THAT'S THE INTIMIDATING BATTLE CRY YOU THINK IT IS.
OOF!

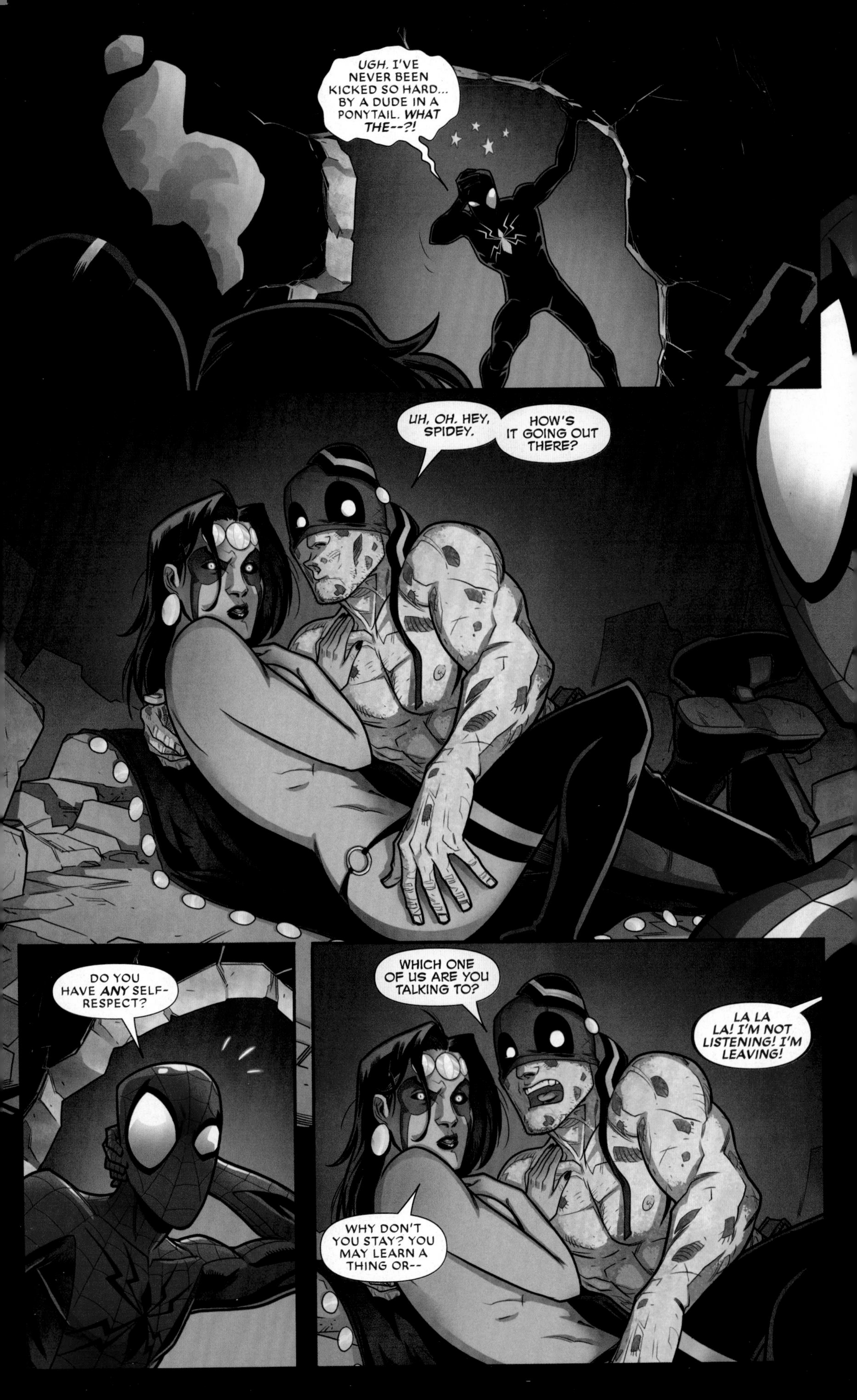
UGH. I'VE NEVER BEEN KICKED SO HARD... BY A DUDE IN A PONYTAIL. WHAT THE--?!
UH, OH. HEY, SPIDEY.
HOW'S IT GOING OUT THERE?
DO YOU HAVE ANY SELF-RESPECT?
WHICH ONE OF US ARE YOU TALKING TO?
LA LA LA! I'M NOT LISTENING! I'M LEAVING!
WHY DON'T YOU STAY? YOU MAY LEARN A THING OR--

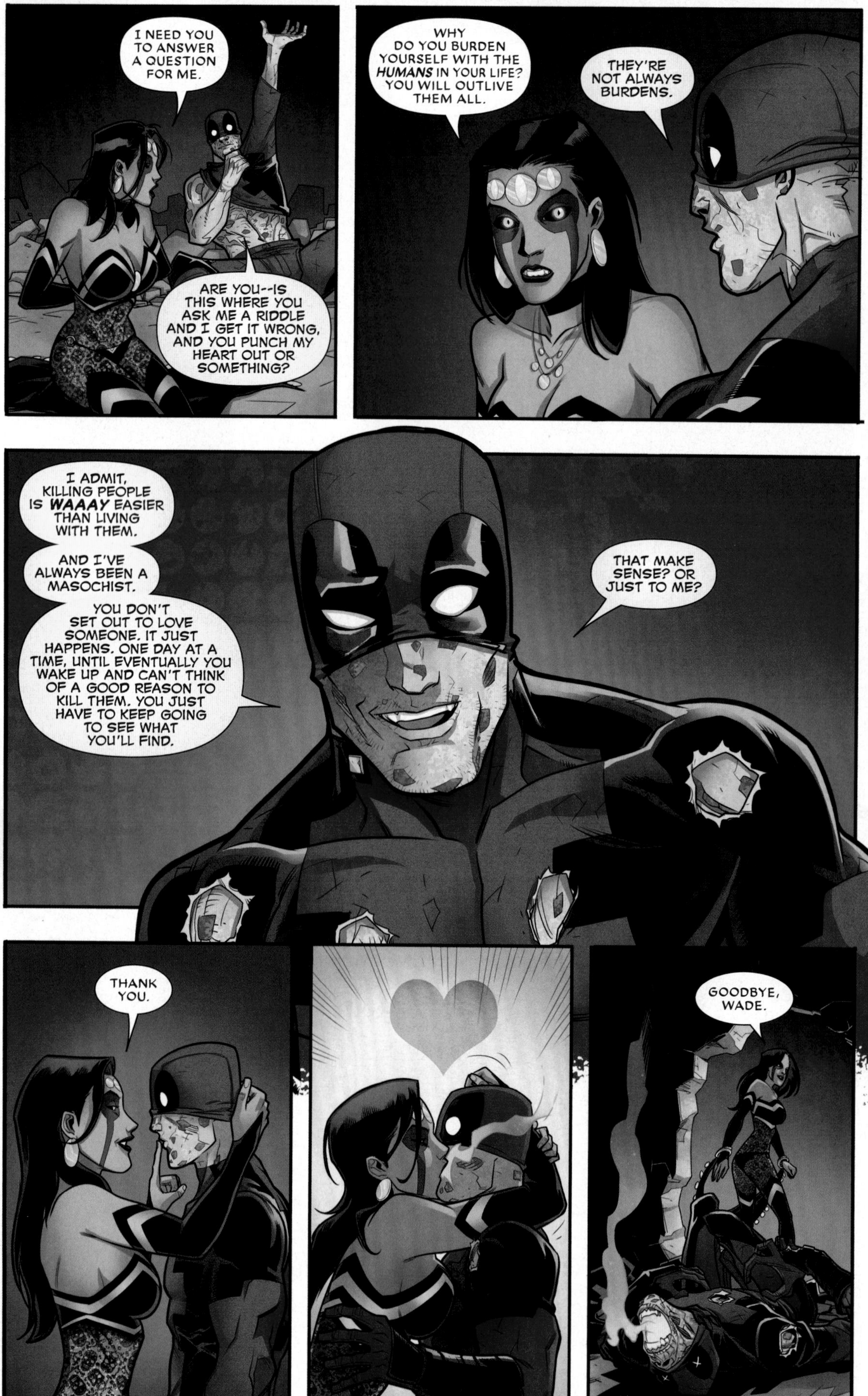
I NEED YOU TO ANSWER A QUESTION FOR ME.
ARE YOU--IS THIS WHERE YOU ASK ME A RIDDLE AND I GET IT WRONG, AND YOU PUNCH MY HEART OUT OR SOMETHING?
WHY DO YOU BURDEN YOURSELF WITH THE HUMANS IN YOUR LIFE? YOU WILL OUTLIVE THEM ALL.
THEY'RE NOT ALWAYS BURDENS.
I ADMIT, KILLING PEOPLE IS WAAAY EASIER THAN LIVING WITH THEM.
AND I'VE ALWAYS BEEN A MASOCHIST.
YOU DON'T SET OUT TO LOVE SOMEONE. IT JUST HAPPENS. ONE DAY AT A TIME, UNTIL EVENTUALLY YOU WAKE UP AND CAN'T THINK OF A GOOD REASON TO KILL THEM. YOU JUST HAVE TO KEEP GOING TO SEE WHAT YOU'LL FIND.
THAT MAKE SENSE? OR JUST TO ME?
THANK YOU.
GOODBYE, WADE.

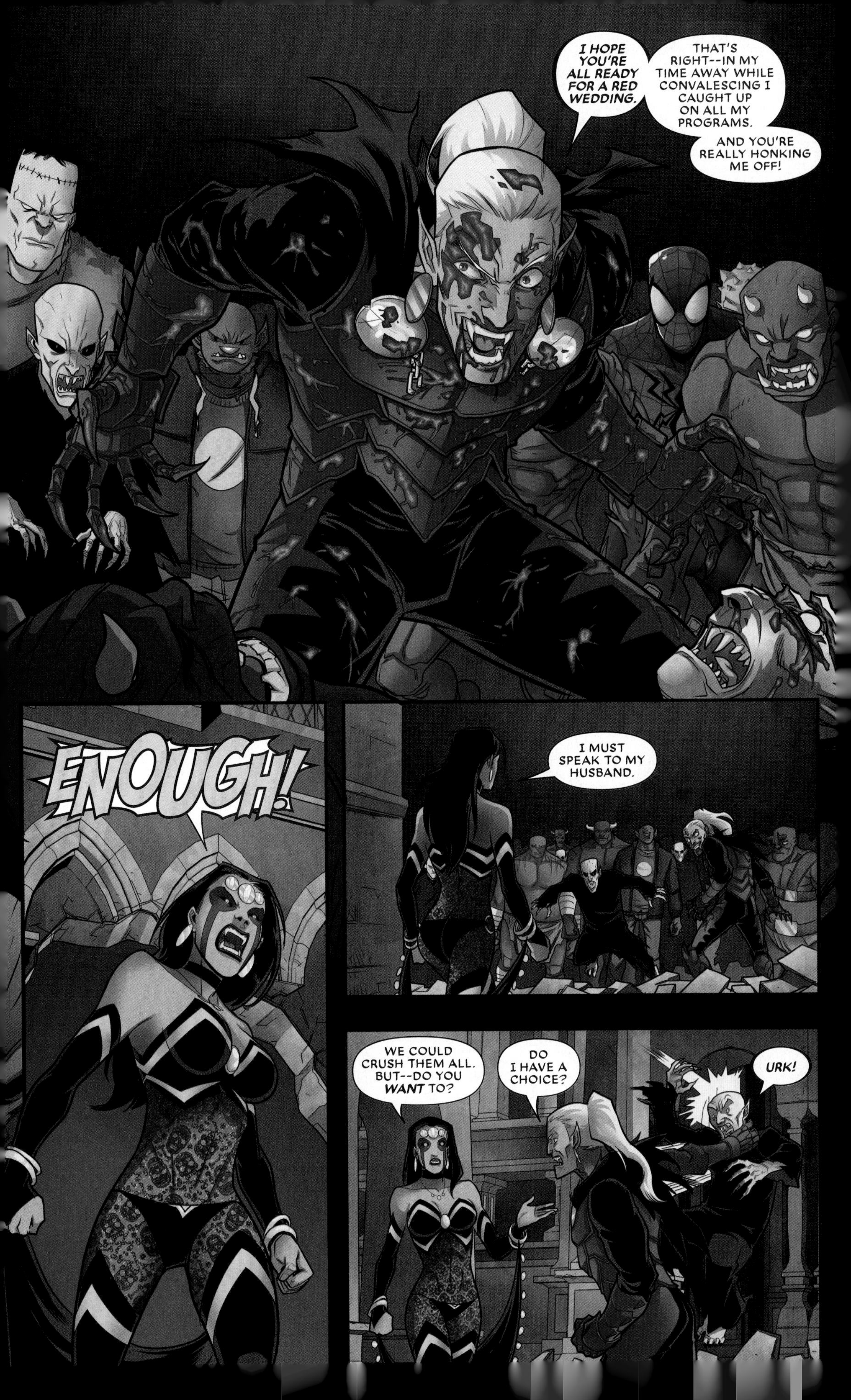
I HOPE YOU'RE ALL READY FOR A RED WEDDING.
THAT'S RIGHT--IN MY TIME AWAY WHILE CONVALESCING I CAUGHT UP ON ALL MY PROGRAMS.
AND YOU'RE REALLY HONKING ME OFF!
ENOUGH!
I MUST SPEAK TO MY HUSBAND.
WE COULD CRUSH THEM ALL. BUT--DO YOU WANT TO?
DO I HAVE A CHOICE?
URK!

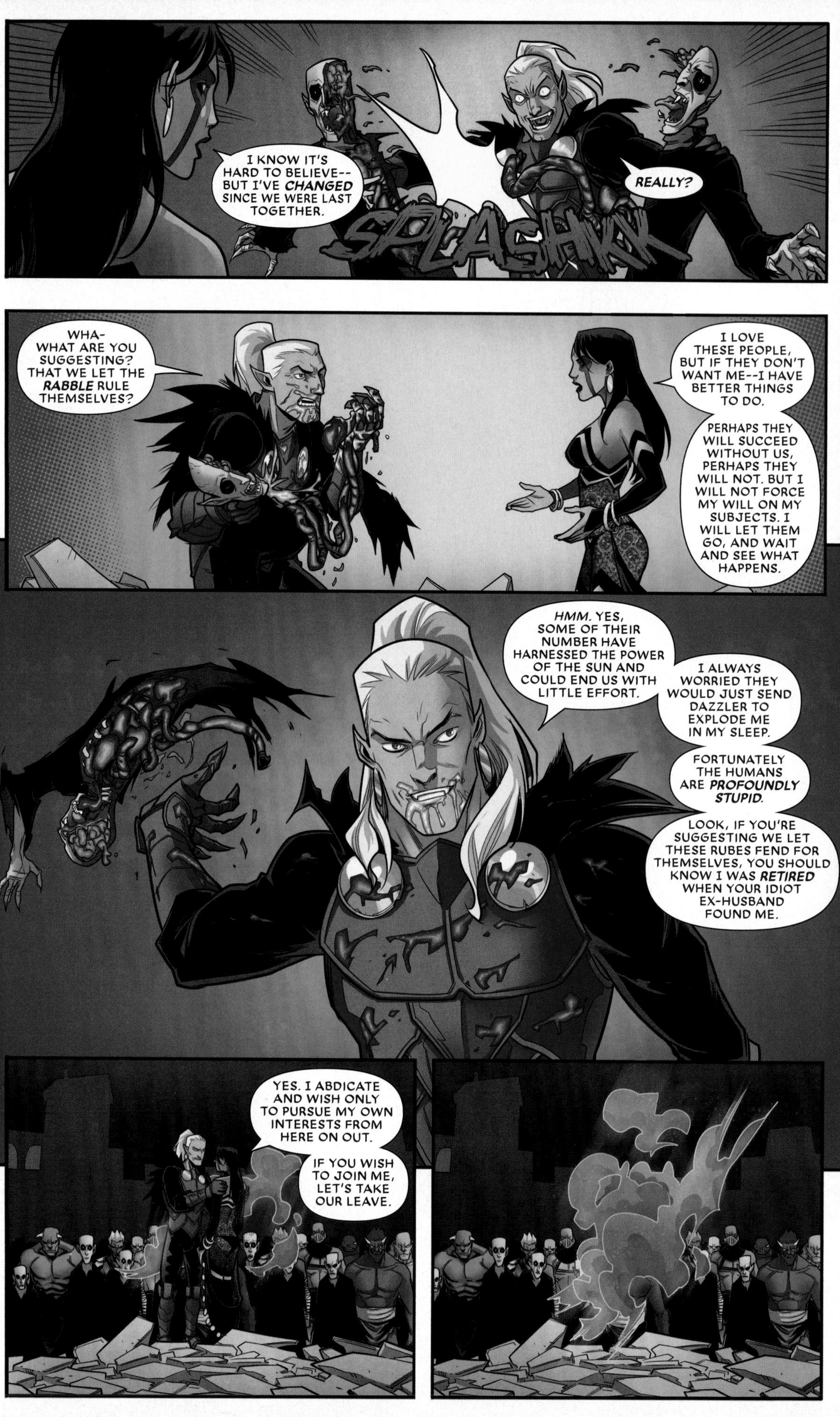
I KNOW IT'S HARD TO BELIEVE-- BUT I'VE *CHANGED* SINCE WE WERE LAST TOGETHER.
SPLASHKK
REALLY?
WHA- WHAT ARE YOU SUGGESTING? THAT WE LET THE *RABBLE* RULE THEMSELVES?
I LOVE THESE PEOPLE, BUT IF THEY DON'T WANT ME--I HAVE BETTER THINGS TO DO.
PERHAPS THEY WILL SUCCEED WITHOUT US, PERHAPS THEY WILL NOT. BUT I WILL NOT FORCE MY WILL ON MY SUBJECTS. I WILL LET THEM GO, AND WAIT AND SEE WHAT HAPPENS.
HMM. YES, SOME OF THEIR NUMBER HAVE HARNESSED THE POWER OF THE SUN AND COULD END US WITH LITTLE EFFORT.
I ALWAYS WORRIED THEY WOULD JUST SEND DAZZLER TO EXPLODE ME IN MY SLEEP.
FORTUNATELY THE HUMANS ARE ***PROFOUNDLY STUPID.***
LOOK, IF YOU'RE SUGGESTING WE LET THESE RUBES FEND FOR THEMSELVES, YOU SHOULD KNOW I WAS ***RETIRED*** WHEN YOUR IDIOT EX-HUSBAND FOUND ME.
YES. I ABDICATE AND WISH ONLY TO PURSUE MY OWN INTERESTS FROM HERE ON OUT.
IF YOU WISH TO JOIN ME, LET'S TAKE OUR LEAVE.

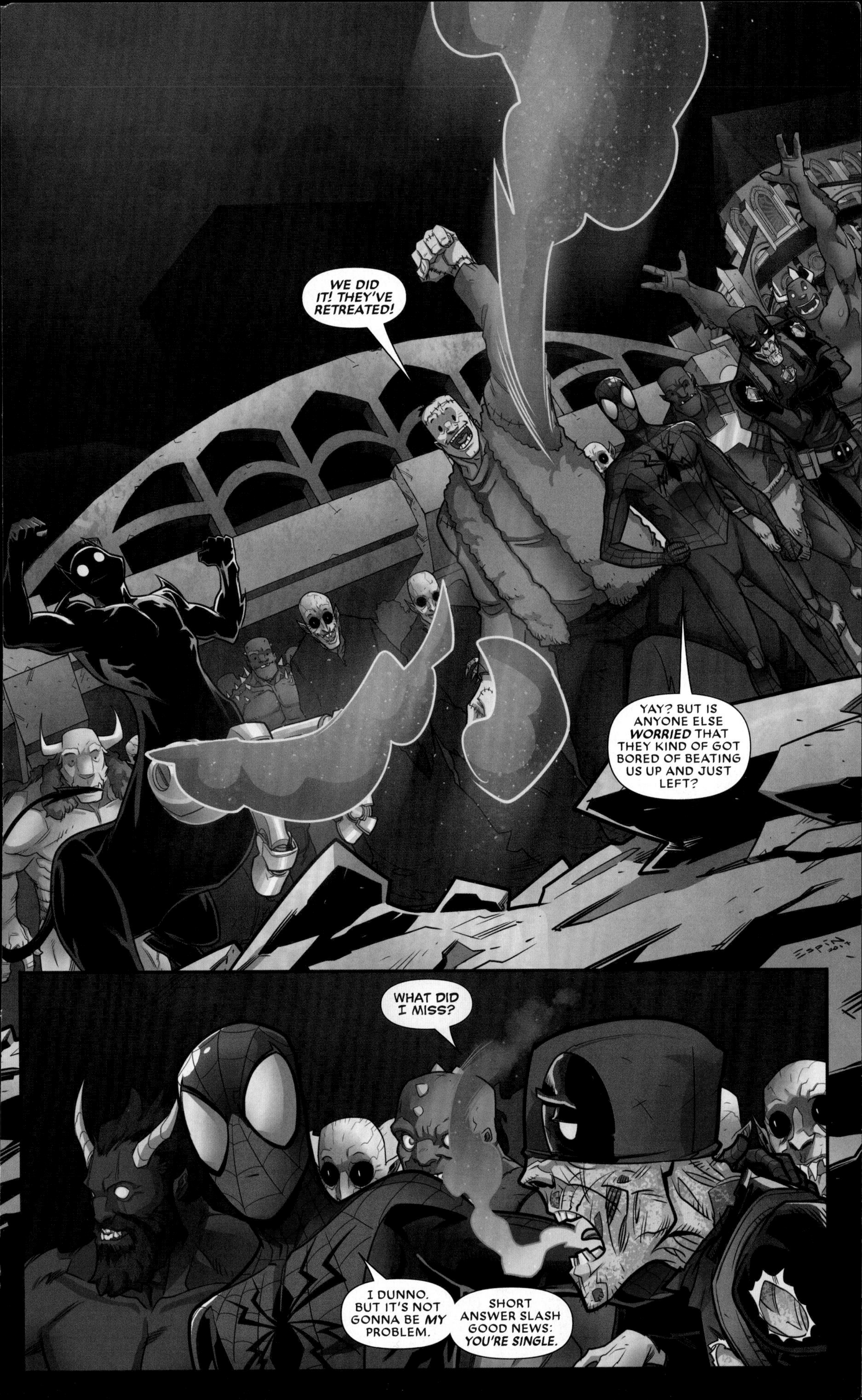
WE DID IT! THEY'VE RETREATED!
YAY? BUT IS ANYONE ELSE WORRIED THAT THEY KIND OF GOT BORED OF BEATING US UP AND JUST LEFT?
WHAT DID I MISS?
I DUNNO. BUT IT'S NOT GONNA BE MY PROBLEM.
SHORT ANSWER SLASH GOOD NEWS: YOU'RE SINGLE.

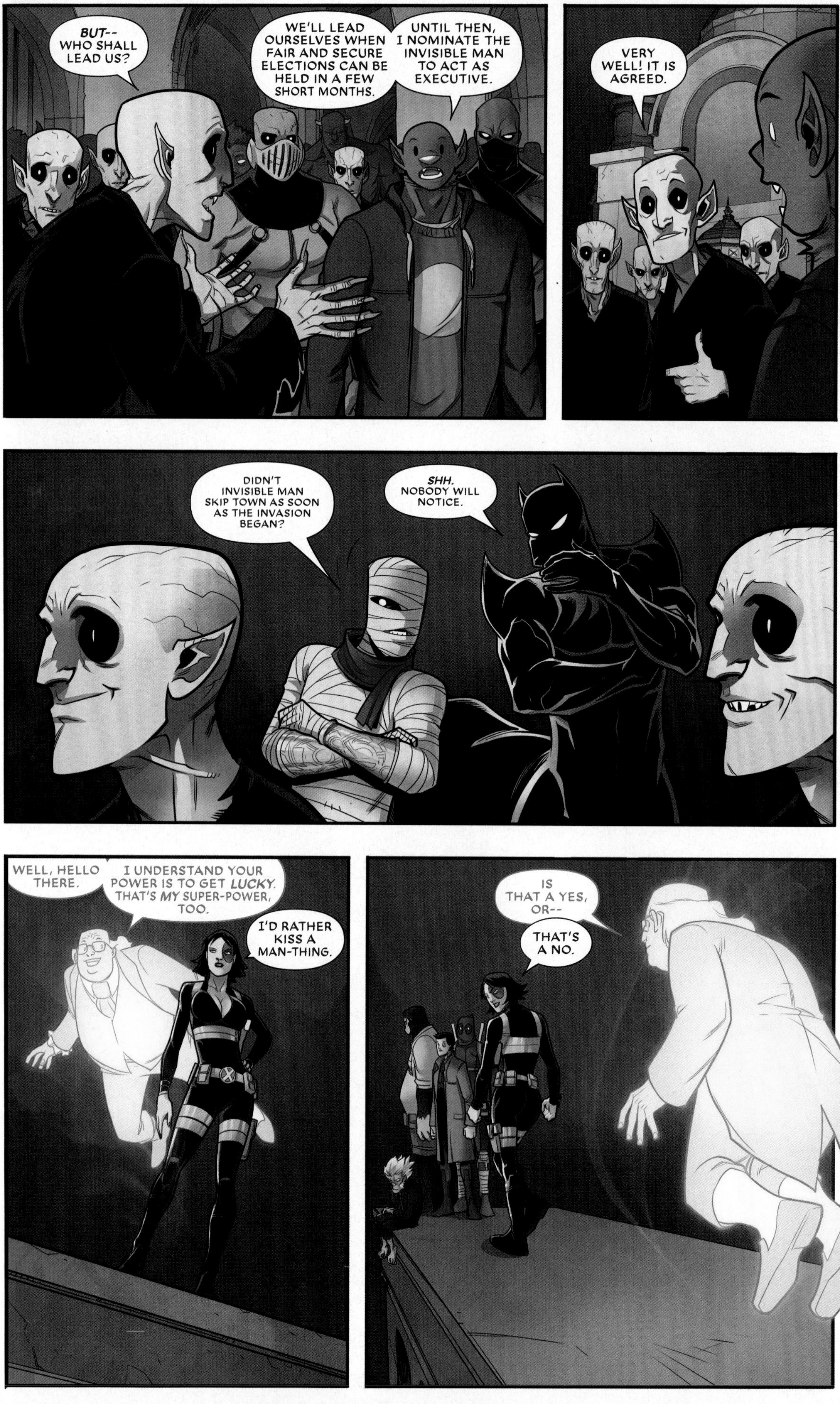
BUT-- WHO SHALL LEAD US?
WE'LL LEAD OURSELVES WHEN FAIR AND SECURE ELECTIONS CAN BE HELD IN A FEW SHORT MONTHS.
UNTIL THEN, I NOMINATE THE INVISIBLE MAN TO ACT AS EXECUTIVE.
VERY WELL! IT IS AGREED.
DIDN'T INVISIBLE MAN SKIP TOWN AS SOON AS THE INVASION BEGAN?
SHH. NOBODY WILL NOTICE.
WELL, HELLO THERE.
I UNDERSTAND YOUR POWER IS TO GET LUCKY. THAT'S MY SUPER-POWER, TOO.
I'D RATHER KISS A MAN-THING.
IS THAT A YES, OR--
THAT'S A NO.

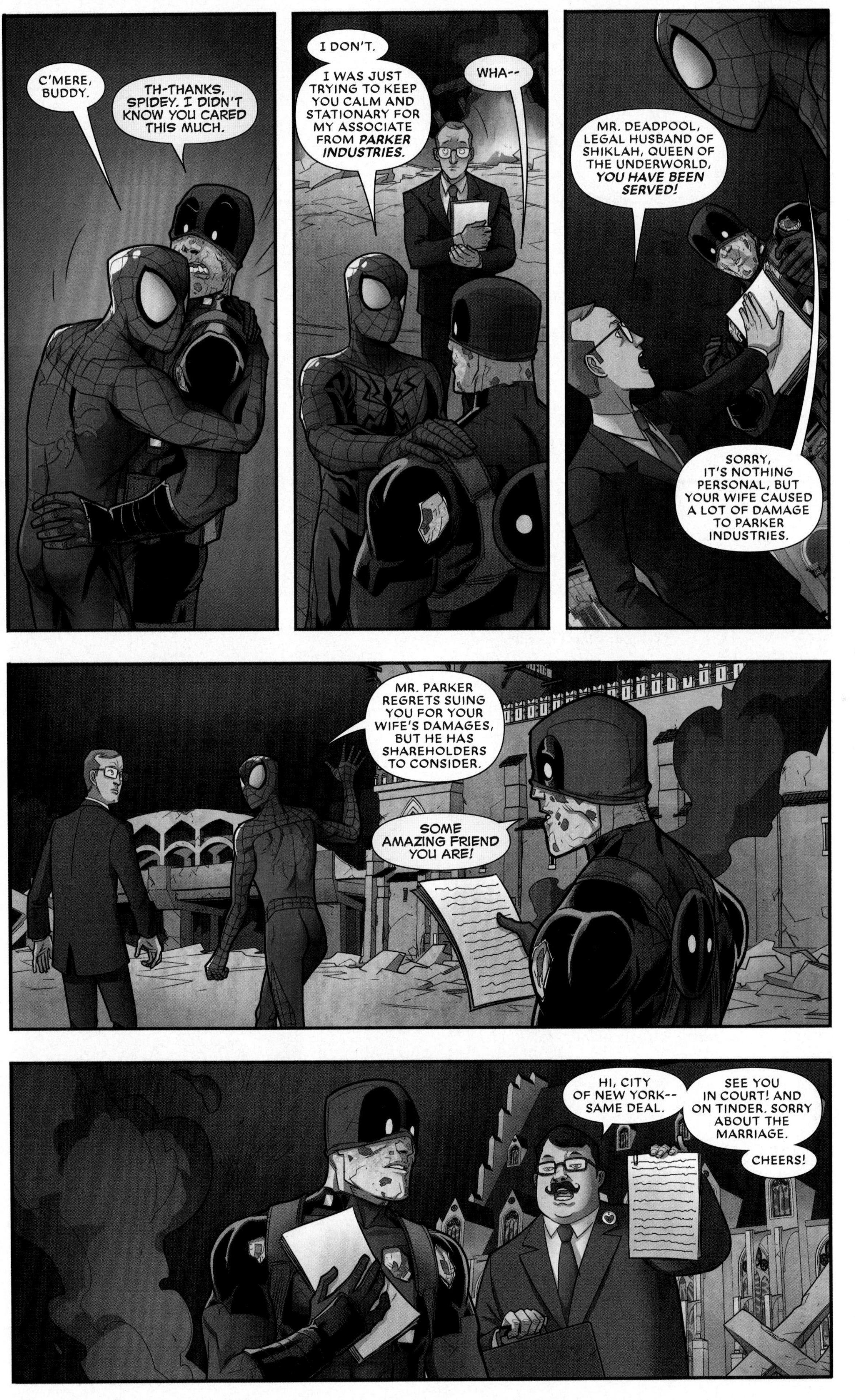
C'MERE, BUDDY.
TH-THANKS, SPIDEY. I DIDN'T KNOW YOU CARED THIS MUCH.
I DON'T.
I WAS JUST TRYING TO KEEP YOU CALM AND STATIONARY FOR MY ASSOCIATE FROM *PARKER INDUSTRIES.*
WHA--
MR. DEADPOOL, LEGAL HUSBAND OF SHIKLAH, QUEEN OF THE UNDERWORLD, *YOU HAVE BEEN SERVED!*
SORRY, IT'S NOTHING PERSONAL, BUT YOUR WIFE CAUSED A LOT OF DAMAGE TO PARKER INDUSTRIES.
MR. PARKER REGRETS SUING YOU FOR YOUR WIFE'S DAMAGES, BUT HE HAS SHAREHOLDERS TO CONSIDER.
SOME AMAZING FRIEND YOU ARE!
HI, CITY OF NEW YORK-- SAME DEAL.
SEE YOU IN COURT! AND ON TINDER. SORRY ABOUT THE MARRIAGE.
CHEERS!

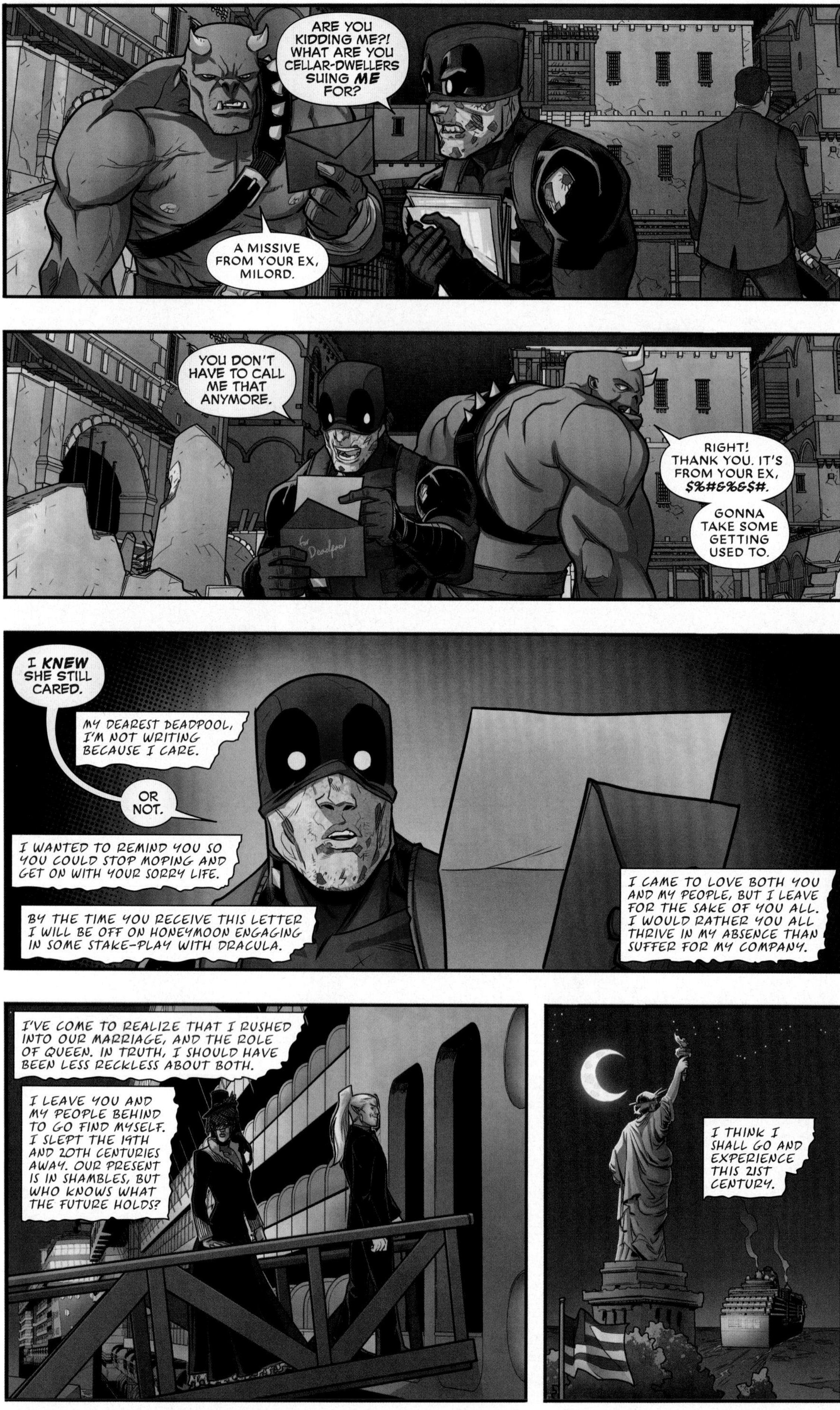

ARE YOU KIDDING ME?! WHAT ARE YOU CELLAR-DWELLERS SUING **ME** FOR?
A MISSIVE FROM YOUR EX, MILORD.
YOU DON'T HAVE TO CALL ME THAT ANYMORE.
RIGHT! THANK YOU. IT'S FROM YOUR EX, $%#&%&$#.
GONNA TAKE SOME GETTING USED TO.
I **KNEW** SHE STILL CARED.
MY DEAREST DEADPOOL, I'M NOT WRITING BECAUSE I CARE.
OR NOT.
I WANTED TO REMIND YOU SO YOU COULD STOP MOPING AND GET ON WITH YOUR SORRY LIFE.
BY THE TIME YOU RECEIVE THIS LETTER I WILL BE OFF ON HONEYMOON ENGAGING IN SOME STAKE-PLAY WITH DRACULA.
I CAME TO LOVE BOTH YOU AND MY PEOPLE, BUT I LEAVE FOR THE SAKE OF YOU ALL. I WOULD RATHER YOU ALL THRIVE IN MY ABSENCE THAN SUFFER FOR MY COMPANY.
I'VE COME TO REALIZE THAT I RUSHED INTO OUR MARRIAGE, AND THE ROLE OF QUEEN. IN TRUTH, I SHOULD HAVE BEEN LESS RECKLESS ABOUT BOTH.
I LEAVE YOU AND MY PEOPLE BEHIND TO GO FIND MYSELF. I SLEPT THE 19TH AND 20TH CENTURIES AWAY. OUR PRESENT IS IN SHAMBLES, BUT WHO KNOWS WHAT THE FUTURE HOLDS?
I THINK I SHALL GO AND EXPERIENCE THIS 21ST CENTURY.

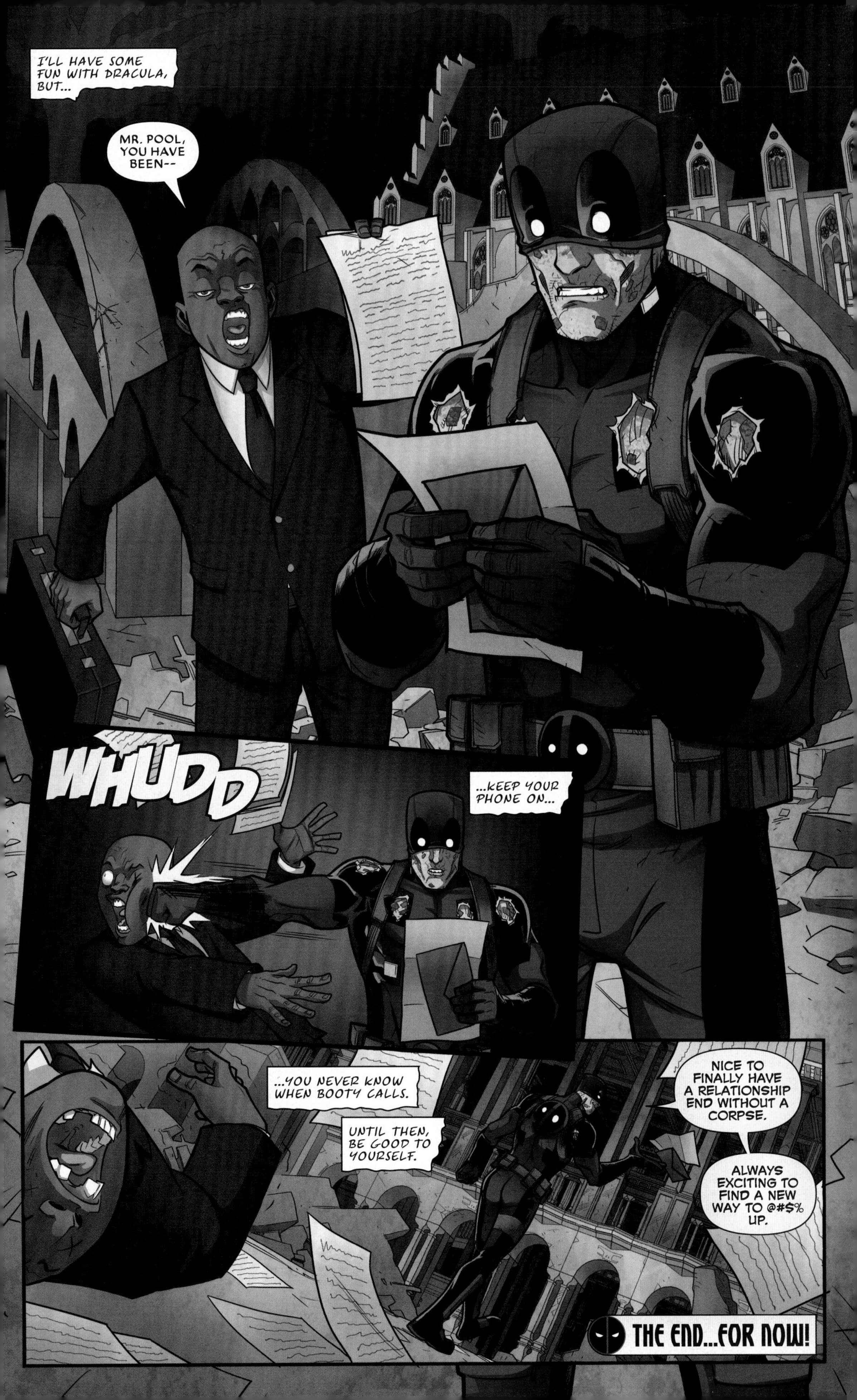
I'LL HAVE SOME FUN WITH DRACULA, BUT...
MR. POOL, YOU HAVE BEEN--
WHUDD
...KEEP YOUR PHONE ON...
...YOU NEVER KNOW WHEN BOOTY CALLS.
UNTIL THEN, BE GOOD TO YOURSELF.
NICE TO FINALLY HAVE A RELATIONSHIP END WITHOUT A CORPSE.
ALWAYS EXCITING TO FIND A NEW WAY TO @#$% UP.
THE END...FOR NOW!

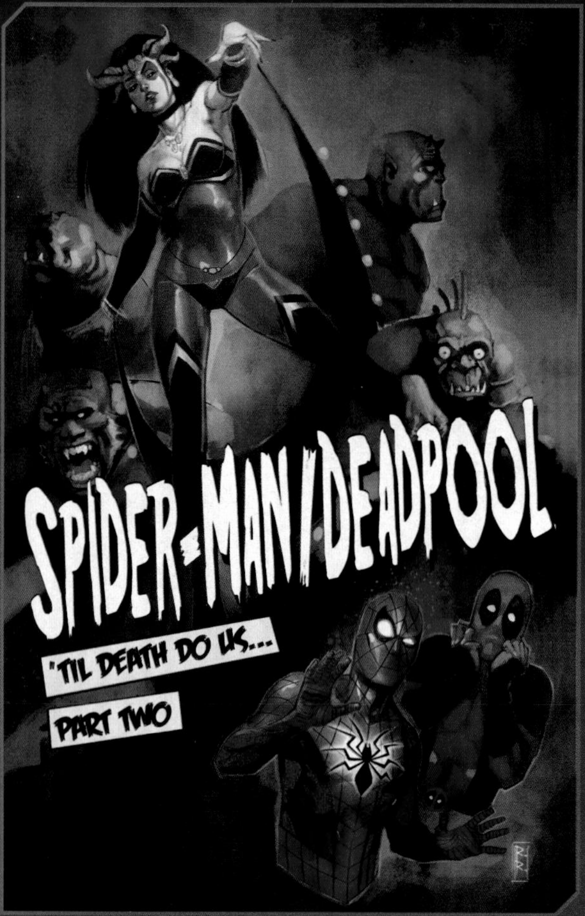
SPIDER-MAN/DEADPOOL
'TIL DEATH DO US...
PART TWO

Spider-Man/Deadpool #15
variant by
ROD REIS

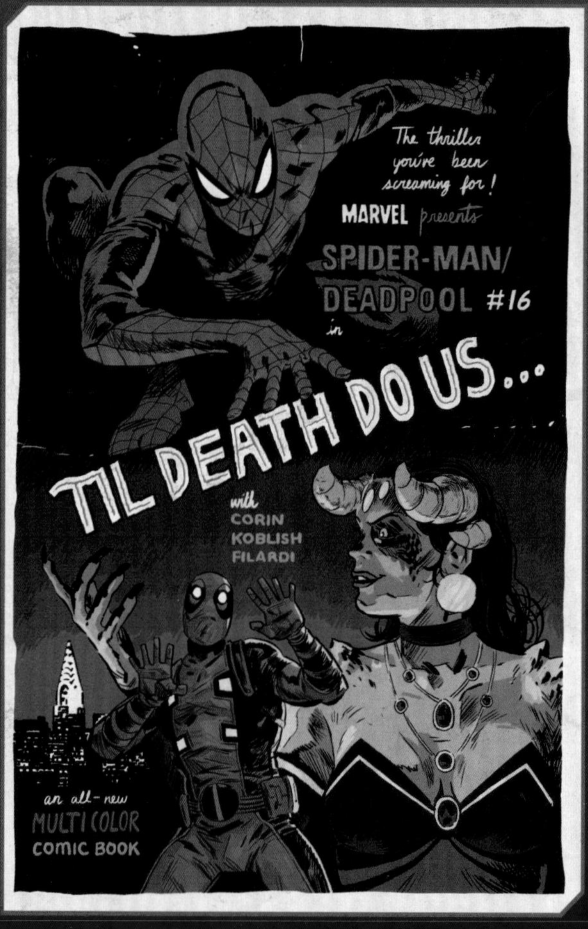
The thriller you're been screaming for!
MARVEL presents
SPIDER-MAN/
DEADPOOL #16
in
'TIL DEATH DO US...
with
CORIN
KOBLISH
FILARDI
an all-new
MULTI COLOR
COMIC BOOK

Spider-Man/Deadpool #16
variant by
MICHAEL WALSH

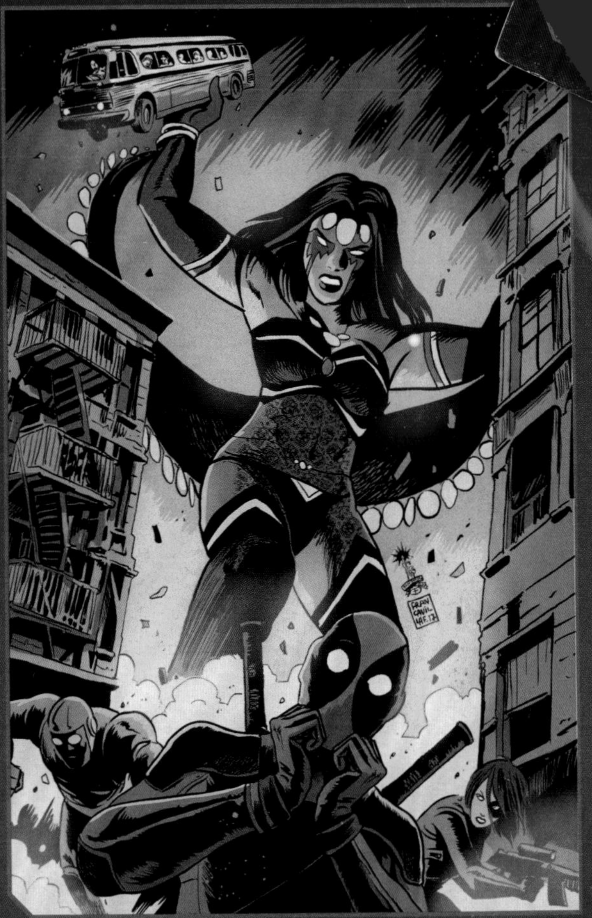

Deadpool & the Mercs for Money #9 variant by FRANCESCO FRANCAVILLA

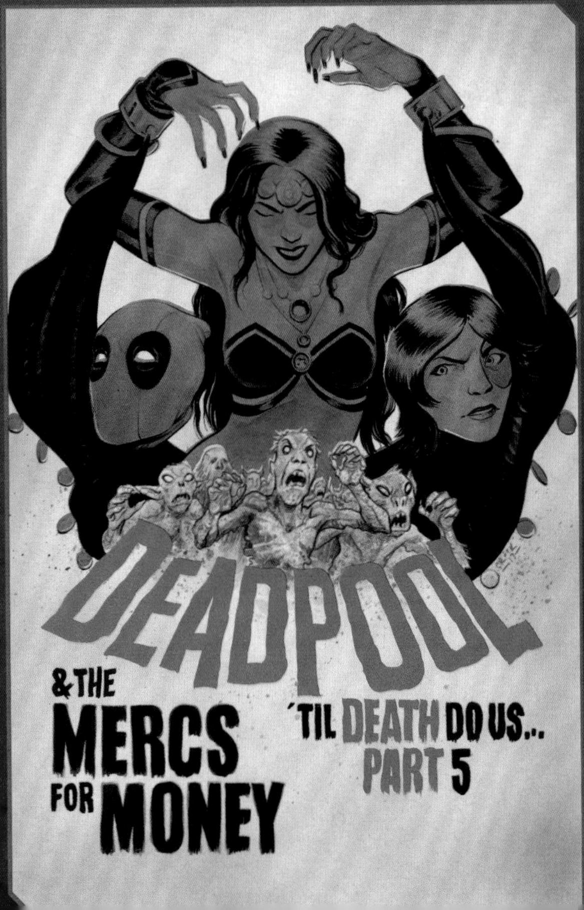

DEADPOOL
& THE MERCS FOR MONEY
´TIL DEATH DO US.. PART 5

Deadpool & the Mercs for Money #10 variant by TYLER CROOK

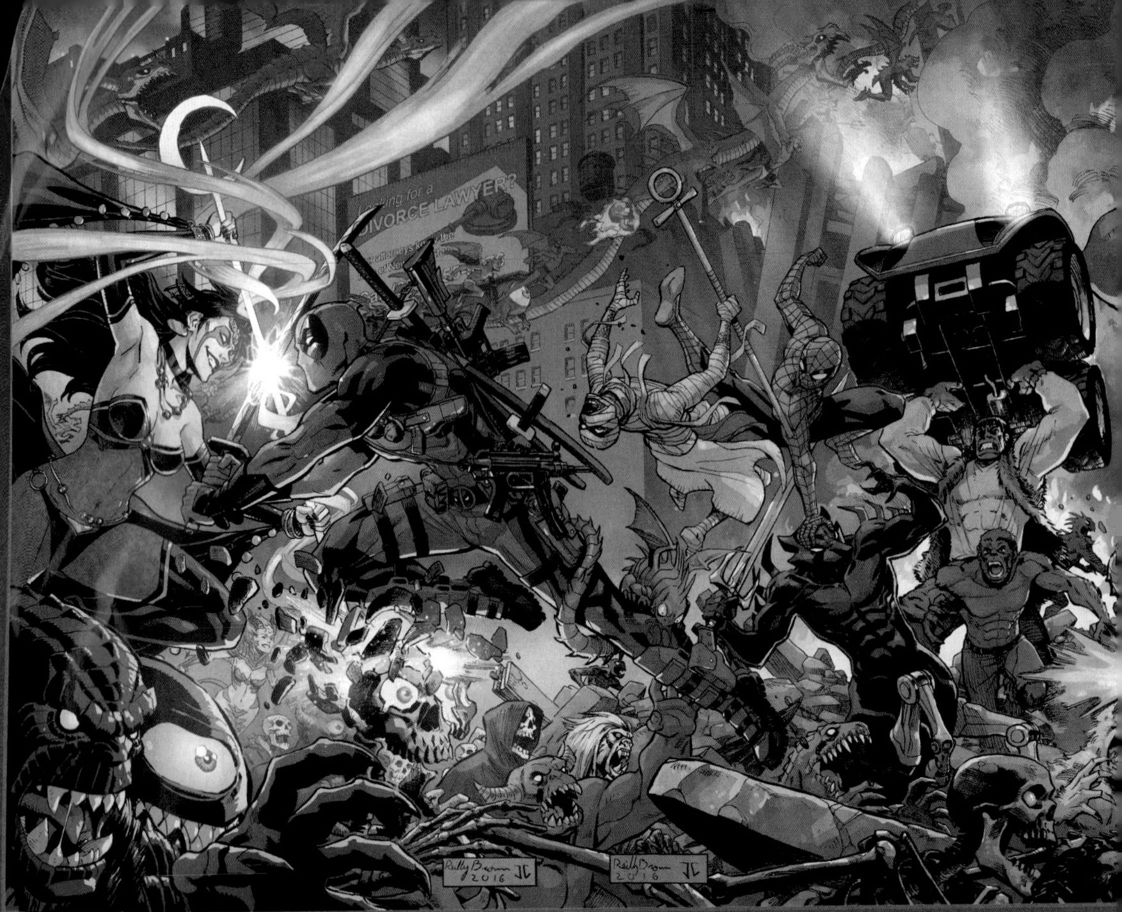
IVORCE LAWYER?

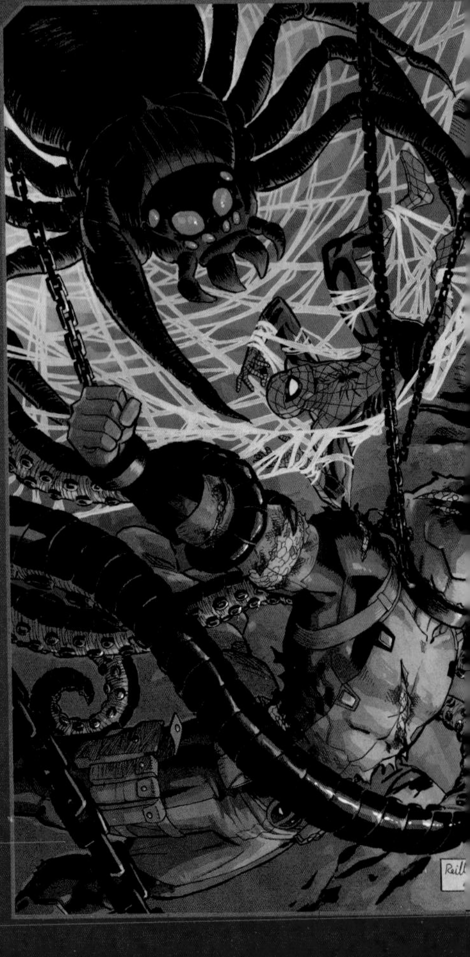

Spider-Man/Deadpool #15,
Deadpool & the Mercs for Money #10
and Deadpool #29
connecting covers